POETIC JUSTICE AND
LEGAL FICTIONS

Literature reveals the intense efforts of moral imagination required to articulate what justice is and how it might be satisfied. Examining a wide variety of texts, including Shakespeare's plays, Gilbert and Sullivan's operas, and modernist poetics, *Poetic Justice and Legal Fictions* explores how literary laws and values illuminate and challenge the jurisdiction of justice and the law. Jonathan Kertzer examines how justice is articulated by its command of, or submission to, time, nature, singularity, truth, transcendence, and sacrifice, marking the distance between the promise of justice to satisfy our moral and sociable needs and its failure to do so. *Poetic Justice and Legal Fictions* will be invaluable reading for scholars of the law within literature and among modernist and twentieth-century literature specialists.

JONATHAN KERTZER is Professor of English at the University of Calgary. His previous publications include *Poetic Argument: Studies in Modern Poetry* (1989), *"That House in Manawaka": Margaret Laurence's "A Bird in the House"* (1992), and *Worrying the Nation: Imagining a National Literature in English Canada* (1998).

POETIC JUSTICE AND LEGAL FICTIONS

JONATHAN KERTZER

CAMBRIDGE
UNIVERSITY PRESS

CAMBRIDGE UNIVERSITY PRESS
Cambridge, New York, Melbourne, Madrid, Cape Town, Singapore, São Paulo, Delhi, Dubai, Tokyo

Cambridge University Press
The Edinburgh Building, Cambridge CB2 8RU, UK

Published in the United States of America by Cambridge University Press, New York

www.cambridge.org
Information on this title: www.cambridge.org/9780521196451

© Jonathan Kertzer 2010

First published 2010

Printed in the United Kingdom at the University Press, Cambridge

A catalog record for this publication is available from the British Library

Library of Congress Cataloging in Publication Data
Kertzer, Jonathan, 1946–
Poetic justice and legal fictions : studies in literary justice / Jonathan Kertzer.
p.   cm.
Includes bibliographical references and index.
ISBN 978-0-521-19645-1 (hardback)
1. Justice in literature.   2. Law and literature.   3. Legal stories – History and criticism.
4. Justice (Philosophy)   I. Title.
PN56.J87K47   2010
809'.933553 – dc22
2009046421

ISBN 978-0-521-19645-1 Hardback

**WITHDRAWN
UTSA Libraries**

Dedicated
in loving memory of my parents
Samuel and Miriam Kertzer

* * *

And as always for Adrienne
thirty years

Contents

Acknowledgements

Earlier versions of chapters appeared in *Mosaic, English Studies in Canada, Twentieth-Century Literature*, and *Law, Culture, and the Humanities.*

My thanks to Lee Zimmerman of *Twentieth-Century Literature* for his encouragement and support.

My thanks to Nancy Chillag and Rodrigo Duran for permission to use the cover photograph of Mr. Duran's wonderful statue *Lady of Justice.*

My thanks to Cambridge University Press, especially to Sarah Roberts and to Fiona Little for her scrupulous work in editing.

CHAPTER I

Le mot juste

in justice is every virtue comprehended
(Aristotle, *Nicomachean Ethics* 108)

JUSTICE: Never worry about it
LAW (THE): Nobody knows what it is
WRITTEN: "Well written": a hall-porter's encomium, applied to the newspaper
serial he finds entertaining
(Gustave Flaubert, *The Dictionary of Accepted Ideas* 55, 58, 91)

Flaubert's mockery of bourgeois indifference to justice and legality contrasts
his own devotion to justice as the supreme literary value, the virtue in which
all others are comprehended. The just word – *le mot juste* – is a phrase
expressing his ideal of linguistic precision associated with painstaking craft
seeking exactly the right word to express exactly the right idea to convey
exactly the right impression to his readers. Writing well, he claimed, is more
than a matter of verbal felicity, although felicity is its reward. "[*T*]*o write
well* is everything," a writer's first duty, he told George Sand (Flaubert,
Letters 2.231), but it is not an end in itself. Although he once proposed
writing a book "about nothing, a book dependent on nothing external,
which would be held together by the internal strength of its style" (1.154),
his letters reveal that he was not satisfied with style for its own sake. It
should be an avenue to illumination and "exaltation" (2.80). The wrong
word is an affront not just to harmony, but to clear-sightedness and clear
thinking.

For the moment a thing is True, it is good . . . When I come upon a bad assonance
or a repetition in one of my sentences, I'm sure I'm floundering in the False. By
dint of searching, I find the proper expression, which was always the *only* one,
and which is, at the same time, harmonious. The word is never lacking when one
possesses the idea. (2.231)

The right word appears when the idea is true, but only the right word
will express its truth. *Le mot* is *juste* when it contributes to a justice of

expression, thought and judgment. It permits a fusion of aesthetic and ethical values, which is the subject of this book about the "jurisdiction" of literary language – the speaking of the law in spaces that the law defines, inhabits, protects, but also, sometimes, neglects.

Following this hint from Flaubert, let me begin by introducing some key terms concerning the justice of literature and the literariness of justice. Shoshana Felman observes that "legal meaning and literary meaning necessarily inform and displace each other" (Felman 8). An underlying assumption in this study will be that literature both informs and displaces judicial thinking by rendering it vivid yet problematic, by displaying its rhetorical and fictional structures, and by engaging the reader, judiciously or injudiciously, in its operations.

JUST WORDS

That a word can be just rather than merely harmonious suggests not only Flaubert's devotion to craft, but an underlying faith in the nature and efficacy of language. He scorned the inaccuracy of customary speech because of the shoddy thinking it conveyed. His satirical *Dictionary of Accepted Ideas* is a compendium of complacent bourgeois clichés, which are no less fatuous for occasionally stumbling into truth. They illustrate how language not only permits but also encourages stupidity. He considered adding to his final novel *Bouvard and Pécuchet*, to which the dictionary is an appendix, the subtitle *Encyclopedia of Human Stupidity* (Flaubert, *Letters* 2.193). If, when abused, language is a vehicle of self-deception, however, it can also be illuminating, provided it is used judiciously. His contempt for bourgeois smugness reflects a mistrust of human nature generally, but it is countered by a belief that language may be not only eloquent and accurate, but just. He envisioned such a style in a letter to Louise Colet:

> a style that someone will invent some day, ten years or ten centuries from now, one that would be rhythmic as verse, precise as the language of the sciences, undulant, deep-voiced as a cello, tipped with flame: a style that would pierce your idea like a dagger, and on which your thought would sail easily ahead over a smooth surface, like a skiff before a good tail wind. (1.159)

When words are beautiful in their precision and precise in their beauty, they reveal that the world, the ordering power of the mind, and the structure of language are congruent.

At its most sublime, this view asserts that the forms of reality, our perceptual and rational faculties to apprehend reality, and the power of language to articulate that apprehension all correspond. The world is intelligible to intelligent people whose command of language is supple: being, knowing, and saying are mutually supportive. In a "perfect language," Paul Ricoeur speculates, there would be "a complete homology between the sign and the thing with nothing arbitrary about it, therefore more broadly a complete homology between language and the world" (Ricoeur, *Reflections* 111). I will argue later that when justice aspires to a messianic sublimity it can become dangerous, but the danger already lurks in Flaubert's ideal. There should be a natural accord of thought, speech, and their objects; or at least, they can be brought into accord through the proper disciplining of thought and language. Words are a trustworthy medium only if used tactfully. It is tempting to oversimplify the situation by praising art for rendering justice in an unjust world, but the writers I will be examining are more cautious. As Flaubert's satire illustrates, the natural fit of mind and language to the world is not secure, because it competes with a contrary tendency, equally natural and powerful, for them to drift apart. The bourgeoisie with their "well-bred ignorance" (Barzun 8) are the latest agents of this cultural entropy; in response, artists must be vigilant. Maintaining an alignment of world, mind, and word is the function of justice understood, as Aristotle suggests in my epigraph, as the coordinating virtue of virtues, the ruling principle of balance and adequacy in human affairs. Seen in this way justice, too, appears to be "natural," that is, inherent in the very structure of things and of humanity, either because their intrinsic composition makes them so, or through divine providence. Cicero offers a famous endorsement of the latter view:

True law is right reason in agreement with nature; it summons to duty by its commands, and averts from wrongdoing by its prohibitions . . . And there will not be different laws at Rome and at Athens, or different laws now and in the future, but one eternal and unchangeable law will be valid for all nations and all times, and there will one master and ruler, that is, God, over us all, for he is the author of this law, its promulgator, and its enforcing judge.[1]

Law, he proclaims with an authority evoked by his sonorous style, is a verbal summons independent of the specific language (that of Rome or Athens) in which it is framed. It commands universally because it derives from a higher source to which the law always gestures.

Gesturing in order to invoke authority, especially when both gesture and authority strike theatrical poses, is one of the functions of art, so it is not surprising that Flaubert's cultivation of *le mot juste* reveals how a pursuit of justice pervades literary theory. Although it is a long way from the humble *mot juste* to the summons of universal law, there is a winding path between them, which I will be tracing in the following chapters. Literary justice is defined differently in different historical periods, but traditionally it is associated with the virtue of poetic thought to organize, interpret, and justify the chaotic misrule of experience. The source of that misrule also varies in different periods. For example, in *Essay on Criticism*, Alexander Pope offers "wit" as the faculty that renders justice, not only by discerning truth in a murky world, but by showing how truth pervades our thoughts, ennobles our lives, and delights us:

> *True Wit* is *Nature* to advantage dress'd,
> What oft was *Thought*, but ne'er so well *Exprest*,
> *Something*, whose Truth convinc'd at Sight we find,
> That gives us back the Image of our Mind:
> (Pope 153)

When the expression is just, knowledge seems to be grasped "at Sight" with the impact of direct sensation. The spontaneity of literary certitude, its ideas piercing like a dagger as Flaubert said, will be a recurring theme but also, as the sharp dagger suggests, a constant danger. One might also be stabbed by eloquent falsehood – *le mot injuste*. For Pope, when poetic form, content, and expression fall into perfect alignment, the mind and nature reflect each other through a reciprocal animation by which each enhances the other:

> Those RULES of old *discover'd*, not *devis'd*,
> Are *Nature* still, but *Nature Methodiz'd*;
> *Nature*, like *Liberty*, is but restrain'd
> By the same Laws which first *herself* ordain'd.
> (Pope 146)

Pope might have been recalling Shakespeare's lines in *The Winter's Tale*:

> Yet nature is made better by no mean
> But nature makes that mean: so, over that art
> Which you say adds to nature, is an art
> That nature makes.
> . . . This is an art
> Which does mend nature – change it rather – but
> The art itself is nature.   (4.4.89–92, 95–7)

Nature is governed by its own rules, which must be articulated through art, especially language, which, unfortunately, can also be deceitful. For this reason, inept criticism – which, Pope warns, abounds "in these Flagitious Times" (Pope 160) – is all the more hazardous. When thought is not guided by "right reason," when language is not scrupulous, they lead the mind away from nature into an illusory world of their own devising. Samuel Johnson raised the same concern when he scorned those writers who "being able to add nothing to truth, hope for eminence from the heresies of paradox" (Johnson 239). The enticement of heresy will also be a recurring theme in this study. Literature not only permits but encourages stupidity, and like Flaubert, Pope delighted in the foolishness of the duns around him.

One of our greatest linguistic talents is lying; indeed, it is hard to imagine many non-verbal means of deception or of self-delusion. The fear that thought and language may perversely conspire to become heretical agents of injustice intensified in romantic theory, when the times were even more flagitious (criminal, scandalous) and the alienation of thought from reality seemed more intense. All the stronger, therefore, was the demand to reconcile them through perfected speech. Literary schools often begin with a call to reform language as the first step in a larger program of cultural renewal. We hear this call in Wordsworth's rejection of poetic diction in his "Preface" to the *Lyrical Ballads*, leading to his assurance: "[The Poet] considers man and nature as essentially adapted to each other, and the mind of man as naturally the mirror of the fairest and most interesting properties of nature" (Wordsworth 17). We hear it enthusiastically in Emerson's essay "The Poet," which declares: "The world being thus put under the mind for verb and noun, the poet is he who can articulate it . . . so the poet turns the world to glass, and shows us all things in their right series and procession" (Emerson 230). And of course, we hear it in Flaubert's defense of *le mot juste*:

In the precise fitting of its [a well-written book's] parts, the rarity of its elements, the polish of its surface, the harmony of the whole, is there not an intrinsic Virtue, a kind of divine force, something eternal, like a principle? (I speak as a Platonist.) If this were not so, why should there be a relation between the right word and the musical word? (Flaubert, *Letters* 2.233)

In modernist writing, *le mot juste* is not regarded as an agent of transcendental or platonic insight, but as one of realism. It is "just" in its ability to do justice to its subject, that is, to touch the world and render the intensity of its physical presence. The sense of touch is often adduced to explain the heft of the right word. For example, one spokesman of the English imagist poets, T.E. Hulme, extolled "the luxurious torture of the finger" (Hulme, *Speculations* 237) as it grates against reality. He advocated a "concrete" style that is "a compromise for a language of intuition which would hand over sensations bodily. It always endeavours to arrest you, and to make you continuously see a physical thing, to prevent you gliding through an abstract process" (134). Here, "touch" does the metaphorical job previously assigned to "taste," but in an earthier way. Poetry becomes tactile rather than tasteful. By making the experience of reading feel tangible, it offers what Pope praised: the conviction that knowledge can be grasped with the immediacy of sensation, or that knowledge and the experience that gives rise to it occur simultaneously. Similarly Ford Madox Ford recalled that he and Joseph Conrad spent hours assessing the relative weights of different French and English words. What was "the desirability of the word *bleu-foncé* as an adjective to apply to cabbages in a field" (Ford Madox Ford, *Joseph* 53)? What were the merits of "blue" as opposed to "azure" (171), of "penniless" as opposed to "without a penny" (87)? By distinguishing between "penniless" and "without a penny," Ford wanted to show not only that he was as scrupulous as Flaubert, but that words are the small currency of literary justice, which is due even to cabbages. Paradoxically, he said, the more physical a word feels, the more it operates invisibly as if to present reality directly rather than represent it verbally: "We wanted the Reader to forget the Writer – to forget that he was reading. We wished him to be hypnotized into thinking that he was living what he read" (Ford Madox Ford, *Thus* 53).

When realism becomes hypnotic, it becomes something more than real, if not quite Platonic or Ciceronian. Ford was content to be called an impressionist rather than a realist, and Flaubert denied that he was a realist writer, but both indicate that a preoccupation with literary justice, even when firmly rooted in physical sensation, aspires to some kind of transcendence. This survey shows that the justice of *le mot juste* may be formulated differently, but in each case it relates consciousness to the world by seeking higher forms of accommodation and satisfaction, both of which are implied in the notion of jurisdiction.

GENRE AS JURISDICTION

If Flaubert's aim was to cure French writers of inane speech and thought, then to do so would deprive him of his wicked delight in mocking their inanities. The spectacle of failure was precious to him not only in order to correct it, but for its own sake, as a revelation of our absurdly flawed humanity. We are never more human than when we exhibit our failings, especially when we lie to ourselves. To relish the spectacle, however, one must be keenly aware of how and why we are flawed. When Flaubert insists that a writer must find the just word, he implies that all other words are wrong, and his own scrupulous revisions, word by word, page by page, show how composition proceeds by excluding the false in order to arrive at the true. Once found, *le mot juste* stabs like a dagger, but until it is found, it must be sought. This exclusionary task illustrates a process of limitation inherent in any judicial judgment, which succeeds only by setting and policing limits, that is, by establishing a jurisdiction.

To be effective, justice must suspend proceedings at key moments signaled, for instance, by the banging of a judge's gavel signifying that an authoritative judgment has been pronounced and must now prevail. It is necessary to impose a halt ceremonially in order to restrain a contrary judicial impulse to be comprehensive, to seek "the whole truth" from an ever greater frame of reference. In a courtroom, exclusionary acts are continually enforced, for instance when evidence or testimony is ruled inadmissible. Corresponding ceremonies appear in literature, both to frame a work as a whole and to define its jurisdiction – its area of command – as it proceeds. The final words "The End," once routinely placed at the end of a novel or film, are a clumsy example. More elegant is the formal Epilogue with which *A Midsummer Night's Dream* declares its limit by bidding farewell to the audience and soliciting its applause. Earlier in the play, when the audience enters fairyland, the fairies sing to drive away the vicious, natural forces that threaten their Queen. By singing, they draw a protective circle around their festive comedy:

> You spotted snakes, with double tongue,
> Thorny hedgehogs, be not seen;
> Newts and blind-worms do no wrong;
> Come not near our Fairy Queen.
>
> (2.2.9–12)

Note for future reference that the dangerous forces are natural; the protective force is supernatural. The latter chants a magic spell to define a comic jurisdiction, a space in which the voice of comedy can speak and rule.

The resemblance of genre to jurisdiction begins as a useful analogy, but as this book progresses, it should become something more. By "jurisdiction" I understand not just the political, social, and conceptual area within which a set of laws wields authority, but as the terms "juris-diction" suggest, the speaking of the law – the many ways in which language articulates judiciousness. In *A Power to Do Justice*, Bradin Cormack studies jurisdictions as intersecting literary and legal categories in sixteenth- and seventeenth-century English writing. Even as they proclaim the scope of their authority and the validity of their norms, he argues, jurisdictions cannot avoid revealing their limits, not only when they confront rival authorities or unforeseen circumstances, but also when they encounter unruly kinds of experience that stubbornly defy any administrative control. Even as a jurisdiction claims sovereignty, it "allows a nonjuridical regime to issue from the juridical" (Cormack 9).[2] This regime is not criminal, since criminality is defined and policed by law. Rather, it baffles the definitional power of any authority, in which case even the word "regime" (the province of a ruler) is paradoxical, since no ruler and no rule could be adequate to the task. At such moments, literature is especially valuable for exposing "a governing and productive instability in the law" (5). How can instability be said to "govern" in any intelligible manner, and what can it "produce" of value other than more instability? I, too, am interested in challenges posed by this unruly rule, but my focus will be on genres as literary jurisdictions insofar as they satisfy, or fail to satisfy, a vision of justice.

I will begin with comedy because, as a form in which traditional laws apply yet can be contested, it expresses so many of the ideals, aims, and disappointments of judicial discourse. It will serve as a touchstone to which I will return periodically. Like justice, comedy is a vehicle of hope sustained by confidence in human intellectual, verbal, and moral powers (*le mot juste*); but it is suspicious of how easily those faculties grow unruly; and intolerant, even cruel, when those same faculties lead us astray, as – comedy ruefully implies – they usually will. Northrop Frye observes that the rhetoric of comedy is similar to the rhetoric of jurisprudence (Frye, *Anatomy* 166) with the advantage of being funny. Comedy offers itself as a rectifying, rewarding genre, which assures us that the earth is our home. Nature offers all the conditions necessary for human flourishing provided that we ward off its dangers, using reason when appropriate, magic when necessary, and provided that we do not abuse our intellectual and verbal powers. Comedy shows that, of course, we will abuse these powers, but only in foolish or ridiculous ways that can be remedied by act 5, when human rationality is realigned with natural abundance.

One might say that, viewed in this way, John Rawls's *A Theory of Justice* aspires to be a philosophical comedy by defining what is fair and then clarifying procedures to make it attainable. His hypothetical starting point, "the original position of equality [which] corresponds to the state of nature in the traditional theory of the social contract" (Rawls 12), establishes a perspective to survey the requisite logical and social conditions, a discursive space rather like the comic jurisdiction. And as in comedy, its prospect of natural bounty, fair distribution, and reasonable reward requires a calculated limitation, a setting of limits. Accurate judgments are possible only if we do not know too much; a "veil of ignorance" ensures that justice will begin by being impartial and end by being satisfactory (136 ff). The veil of ignorance that makes justice clear-sighted is like the magic circle keeping natural perils at bay.

The veil also reveals a puzzle in defining a jurisdiction, which must be both self-limiting (the circle) and self-exceeding (the magic). This dilemma is usually analyzed as a tension between justice as an ethical ideal, the virtue of virtues, and law as a series of practical accommodations. Walter Benjamin depicts their tension as a confrontation between two violent, social urges: law-preserving (restrictive, repressive) and law-making (expansive, revolutionary) (Benjamin 284). Their rivalry appears even in Shakespeare's lovely song, which illustrates how comedies must ceremonially acknowledge deadly forces in order to keep them away. Literature is always about making and breaking rules, establishing new rules to be challenged in turn, working within genres whose borders are permeable. This, too, is a violent process, because violence is inherent in all literary forms: in their twists of plot and obsessive characters, in the *agon* (struggle) they depict, in their power to evoke sympathy ("feeling, suffering with"). The impulses to make and break rules are staged in accordance with the presiding genre of a work, whose conventions define what I am calling its jurisdiction. In *A Midsummer Night's Dream* the protective, law-preserving force is expressed as benevolent magic and music; the contrary, liberating, law-disrupting force is represented by Puck, the mischievous agent of misrule who lets affairs get wildly out of control until he, too, is restrained by Oberon and, in the Epilogue, domesticated by carrying a broom.

Malvolio in *Twelfth Night* is a more ambiguous figure in this contest, because his role shifts as the play proceeds until he threatens its comic rule. At first he is a puritannical agent of repressive law as he squabbles with Sir Toby, who obeys only the commands of delight and appetite: "Dost thou think, because thou art virtuous, there shall be no more cakes and ale?" (2.3.114–15). Later, however, Malvolio, yields to his own wild desires, first ridiculously by displaying his legs to Olivia, and later, when he is tormented, in baffled frustration. At the end of the play, when the conservative forces of comedy reassert their authority, he becomes a malcontent who refuses to join the festivities and stomps off swearing revenge. Depending on how the performance is staged, he can embody a bitterness so disruptive that he unsettles the comic fabric of the play. Like the snakes and hedgehogs he must be banned from the stage, but he stills lurks outside. Every instance of literary justice has its Malvolio, and must devise a way of coping with his "ill will."

As a puritan Malvolio imposes the law in a spirit of nasty self-satisfaction, but as an innocent if foolish victim he demands justice in a way that the rules of comedy cannot satisfy. Although he is not heroic, only absurd, he reveals – if only briefly before the festivities continue – how a thirst for justice can upset the law, and because it is a thirst or appetite, it is not entirely reasonable. On the one hand, as Cicero proclaims, justice is transcendent, a "messianic" hope beyond "calculated proportion" (Cornell 113); a "social fullness" continually expanding its scope (Laclau 184); a "structural urgency" yearning for some future event that "exceeds calculation, rules, programs, anticipations and so forth" (Derrida, "Force" 27). The messianic impulse can be highly disruptive, and I will study its appetite in the next chapter under the heading of "Life plus ninety-nine years," a judicial sentence that pushes punishment into fantasy. For this very reason, on the other hand, justice must call a halt by declaring, "this case is closed." It is also enclosed. In one of its meanings, "jurisdiction" refers to the political arena (city, state, nation) or conceptual space (criminal, civil, family law) within which laws have authority, and authorities impose laws. We glimpse its limiting force in English expressions forbidding further activity, doubt, or hesitation: "that's just the way things are," "just do it," "just because I say so," "just because you must." The word "just" both announces that a limit has been reached and claims the authority to impose such a limitation. Later chapters will explore how these colloquial phrases define a jurisdiction by invoking authorities of several kinds. They may appeal to a supreme power (God, parent, king, tradition) which issues a verdict that cannot be questioned. They may appeal to a moral limit – seen most boldly in the Kantian categorical imperative – by marking duties that oblige us to choose between right and wrong, but forbid us from evaluating those choices any further. They may appeal to nature (just the way things are) by marking primary causes or sources. Rudyard Kipling's *Just So Stories*, which tell how the tiger got its stripes and the camel its hump, are literary expressions of this mode of justification. Or they may appeal to a controlling design by marking ends or inevitable effects that conclude a story. Literary designs are always fatal, whether the verdict is marriage in comedy or death in tragedy. Death is a poetically just ending in tragedy, not because it is what the hero deserves, but because it fulfills a pattern imposed internally by the plot, and externally by the generic laws governing tragedy. Tragic heroes like Hamlet rarely deserve their catastrophic fates, which is why tragedy is a transgressive genre that looks for something beyond justice, something that justice cannot satisfy.

POETIC JUSTICE AND INJUSTICE

When fairy tales end with the refrain "and they lived happily ever after," they predict an enduring satisfaction unavailable in ordinary life. Its impossibility makes it more, not less, attractive.

> Jack shall have Jill;
> Nought shall go ill;
> The man shall have his mare again, and all shall be well.
> (*Midsummer* 3.2.461–3)

"Poetic justice" is a phrase coined by Thomas Rymer in *The Tragedies of the Last Age* (1692) to explain why poetry must offer something "better than the truth" if it is to improve on "historical justice," which is notoriously unreliable. Only "poetical decency" can ensure an exact apportioning of reward and punishment so that "the satisfaction be compleat and full" (Rymer). Understood in this specific sense, poetic justice intensifies the confidence implicit in *le mot juste* by insisting on its adequacy. That is, it assures readers that we can know exactly what characters deserve, because secure knowledge of motives, actions, and responsibilities, as well as faith in the moral standards by which to assess them, are readily available to us. This is a comforting belief, but Rymer's own examples show that literary affairs are rarely so simple, because their judgments are solicited and enforced inconsistently. When he declares, "a Poet must of *necessity* see justice *exactly* administred [*sic*; my emphasis]," the necessity he invokes is a moral demand that will be satisfied with aesthetic exactitude. His easy fusion of moral and aesthetic qualities is captured nicely by his phrase "poetical decency." Readers are invited into a work's field of influence in the sense that, through a willing suspension of disbelief, they accept its standards of judgment and respond favorably. They agree about what characters deserve and feel satisfied when they are treated appropriately. Even more basically they agree, at least temporarily, about what *is* appropriate so that artistic and moral propriety can sustain each other. Such calculations seem no longer arbitrary, biased, or historically relative, but poetical and just.

Reading "with the grain" in this manner requires first that the grain – the vector of judgment and response – be discerned, and then that it be approved. The first decision involves recognizing a work's genre; the second involves accepting those terms. The role of the reader is crucial in assessing a literary jurisdiction. Sometimes our reactions are instinctive, for instance when we explode in laughter at a painful mishap in slapstick comedy, but usually they require more vigilance. As to the first decision regarding the textual grain, a work may deliberately (or accidentally) give mixed signals so that its genre is not clearly defined. As to the second, readers may choose to read "against the grain," which means that they hear a work's invitation but resist its appeal. Any literary performance will require shifting negotiations of this sort, and may even make their interaction explicit. For example, when the Duke of Albany announces at the end of *King Lear*, "All friends shall taste / The wages of their virtue, and all foes / The cup of their deservings" (5.3.308–10), he seems to be offering the solace of poetic justice after all the suffering that has occurred, but his lordly verdict is immediately disproved by the deaths of Cordelia and Lear. Neither deserves to die. Like Malvolio, but in a very different tone, Albany claims an authority that he cannot exercise. In this case poetic justice is unavailing, because it is exposed within the play as a feeble etiquette – a mere poetical decency – overwhelmed by a fiercer, tragic law. Rymer would not approve, of course, but in that case he would be reading against the grain. *King Lear* openly displays its refusal to produce the justice that Rymer demands, but in so doing it defines its own tragic jurisdiction, providing its own kind of satisfaction or, as Aristotle called it, *catharsis*.

It is ironic that Rymer should devote his study to tragedy, the most gloriously indecent of genres. In *The Tragedies of the Last Age* he condemns plays that fail to meet his exacting standard, even offering to revise their worst scenes. (Thomas Bowdler would take up this thankless task, and in Nahum Tate's infamous revision of *King Lear*, Cordelia survives to marry Edgar.) This was a losing battle, however, because literature loves outlaws, heretics, and over-reachers. It loves to be outrageous and to outrage its readers, where the prefix "out" signifies transgressing proper limits. "In His strength I will dare, and dare, and dare, until I die," proclaims Bernard Shaw's Saint Joan (Shaw 864), defying church and state as she defends the noble cause of "protestantism" and "nationalism," which, through a deft display of wit, incongruity, and pathos, Shaw encourages the audience to accept as both just and historically inevitable. The heresy proclaimed at her trial asserts a more authentic justice, at least according to Shaw. Other heroes and anti-heroes do not claim the moral high ground or seek the audience's approval for their transgressions, although they may elicit admiration for their nerve. They may claim to reject the hypocrisy of conventional morality, or they may aspire to go beyond good and evil entirely. In either case, there must be some value that makes the transgression, however despicable, seem worthwhile, even if it is only the daring act of transgressing that is itself the goal. The law to break the law can be compelling.

As Michel Foucault often shows, it is impossible to break the law unless there are laws to break, so the more repressive a society, the greater the sense of daring and liberation that comes from their trespass. The law defines what is forbidden, reins it in, punishes it, and so endows it with a heretical power that literature enhances through its own rhetorical seductions. For Foucault, transgression is not an act with specific content so much as a ritual of approaching and breaching a moral or conceptual limit, then obstinately circling back to make a new breach between the thinkable and the unthinkable (Foucault, *Language* 34). Through this restless cycle, justice as law-preserving is periodically reasserted so that justice as law-making can be enhanced. This is the in-between territory that Malvolio enters when he storms offstage. I grant that he and Rymer make strange bedfellows, but both are puritannical revisionists. Earlier in the play Malvolio has ridiculously tried to rewrite *Twelfth Night* by casting himself as romantic lead ("having come from a day-bed, where I have left Olivia sleeping" [2.5.47–8]), but at the end he is far too noxious a presence to remain in view, and so must be banished. However, if members of the audience choose to imaginatively follow him offstage – to commit their own transgression – they might sense another play as Malvolio would rewrite it.

My point is not that he is the play's hidden hero, but that at key moments *Twelfth Night* seems dissatisfied with its own comic regulation. The same dissatisfaction is even more provocative when Shylock is banished at the end of *The Merchant of Venice*, another comedy ill at ease in its own jurisdiction and all the more fascinating as a result. Shylock does not rush offstage, but after being outwitted, humiliated, and deprived of his property and family, he never returns. Northrop Frye notes that comedy "tends to include as many people as possible in its final society" (Frye, *Anatomy* 165), but the most troublesome characters must be repudiated through ridicule. We are told that Shylock has been redeemed through enforced conversion to Christianity, but even this happy poetic (in)justice is not sufficient to make his reappearance tolerable, since his mere presence would poison the celebratory scene. Presenting him without his Jewish clothes or wearing a cross would be beyond outrageous.

SATISFACTION

Comedy promises something "better than the truth" (Rymer's phrase), but it grows wary when the truth is unpalatable and must be expelled. Some truths are intolerable. However, when justice is assessed only according to its limiting function, when it is both done and seen to be done, then it is "satisfied." As my glance at Shakespearean comedy illustrates, the satisfaction or dissatisfaction of literary justice operates not only as theme, but as form and audience response. Satisfaction is therefore a function of genre, which offers an imaginative sanctuary, a privileged space where rules can be legislated, enforced, relaxed, or even dispelled. Genres are characterized by the kind of satisfaction they define and provide, where satisfaction involves a vision of what is just and proper. To govern in this way, their satisfaction must be understood not only subjectively as gratification or complacency, but also structurally as suggested by the word's Latin root, *satis*, "enough." Satisfaction is a matter of fulfillment, sufficiency, completion to exactly the right degree. There is nothing more to be done, because enough has been done, and done properly – the end. We feel satisfied when justice is satisfied, and it is satisfactory when it fulfills its own principles and formal procedures. This ideal may seldom be realized in everyday experience, but one of the joys of literature is that it convinces us, at least for as long as we are reading, that we can know exactly what is sufficient, and be content when it is achieved.

For many years contemporary literary critics have waged a campaign against closure, which is judged a pernicious effect that stifles a text's more liberating possibilities. In even the most self-satisfied works they detect open or ambiguous endings, heterogeneity or undecidability. Before proceeding along this line, I would stress that the satisfaction afforded by literary forms may be an illusion, but like the magic circle in *A Midsummer Night's Dream* and the "baseless fabric of this vision" in *The Tempest* (4.1.151), it is a wonderful illusion worthy of respect. It distinguishes art from life, if only precariously. Nevertheless, literature can indeed have the reverse effect. It can unsettle certainty about all its satisfying conditions: certainty about what actions mean, what characters deserve, what is fair or unfair. As *The Merchant of Venice* illustrates, it can breed a fertile, critical discontent which is, in its own provocative way, satisfying. Wai Chee Dimock argues that justice speaks "a language of structural *guarantee*" that "demands from the world a grammatical uniformity" (Dimock 110). This is her version of *le mot juste's* coordinating mind and world, but unlike Flaubert, she mistrusts its Platonic, integrating power. Instead, she calls it an "adequating rationality" that establishes correspondences to "[image] forth the world as a commensurate order, so that problem and solution [are] not only reflexively generated but also instrumentally corresponding" (166). The world makes sense, but only for as long as the "compensatory equilibrium" (166) of justice enforces an economy whereby effects are always seen to arise from and match causes, punishments always arise from and match crimes. By contrast, Dimock admires literature when it is profligate. It depicts a world of accidents and irresolution, entangling readers in all the messy particulars of life ignored by justice, which insists on general rules impartially imposed. The novel especially presents "something like a constitutive ground for incommensurability" (168), because it is alert to the odd exceptions to the rule, and to the oddity of rules. Martha Minow defends the value of storytelling in law in similar terms: "Storytelling can disrupt the illusion that social sciences create in the service of rational administration, the illusion that the world is a smoothly managed household. Storytelling invites both teller and listener to confront messy and complex realities – and to do so in a way that promotes communication and thinking about how to connect the past and the future by thinking about what to do" (Minow 33).

Here is another version of poetic justice. It is just, not because it honors an exact system of moral accountability, but because it is true to what is irregular in human experience and unaccountable in the convolutions of thought. Rymer asks literature to supply something "better than the truth"; Dimock worries that justice, if it is to work systematically and authoritatively, requires something less than the truth. Their disagreement is clarified by Shoshana Felman, who explains that because justice must seek "a force of resolution" in its practical operation, it can tolerate only as much truth as will lead to a decisive verdict, whereas literature aims not at "finality" but at "meaning":

A trial and a literary text do not aim at the same kind of conclusion, nor do they strive toward the same kind of effect. A trial is presumed to be a search for truth, but, technically, it is a search for a decision, and thus, in essence, it seeks not simply truth but a finality: a force of resolution. A literary text is, on the other hand, a search for meaning, for expression, for heightened significance and for symbolic understanding. (Felman 54–5)

Literature gives free play to all the "equivocations, ambiguities, obscurities, confusions, and loose ends " (95) that the law cannot afford to acknowledge if it is to rule effectively. A judicial trial requires just enough truth to reach a legally satisfying resolution, which would be obscured by too much testimony or by evidence improperly presented, even if both are true. Truth must yield to propriety, in which case the word "verdict" ("true saying") seems ironic. If a murderer is found not guilty after a fair trial in which the prosecution fails to mount a convincing case, or the defense raises reasonable doubt, then the verdict is correct. Justice is satisfied in the sense that the legal system has been respected and preserved from abuse, but surely there is something more to say.

   Dimock and Felman expect something more from literature, because their revaluation of poetic satisfaction reflects a deeper disagreement about the primary assumption of *le mot juste* in relation to nature: the belief that world, mind, and word are companionable. As I noted, this faith finds expression in the healing forms of traditional comedy (which is only one kind of comedy), which assures us that the earth is our home. Working together, nature and reason ("Nature Methodiz'd") can remedy our ills. Dimock and Felman want stronger medicine. They share Nietzsche's scorn for justice conceived only as arithmetic: as a calculation that begins by "setting a price on everything and making everyone strictly accountable" (Nietzsche, *Birth* 205). However, their revaluation can be traced to earlier sources. In *An Enquiry Concerning the Principles of Morals*, David Hume speculates that the "cautious, jealous virtue of justice" (Hume 13) emerges not from nature's bounty but from scarcity. It arises as a "public utility" (13) when people painfully discover that nature does not supply "enough" to satisfy them – not enough food, shelter, clement weather, property, etc. In a state of natural abundance, justice would be "totally USELESS," an "idle ceremony" (13). It becomes the ruling virtue only when goods must be shared, divided, and exchanged, when deprivation elicits an awareness of what is fair or unfair, which in turn requires that a distributive system of justice be maintained, violently if necessary.

> Thus, the rules of equity or justice depend entirely on the particular state and condition in which men are placed, and owe their origin and existence to that UTILITY, which results to the public from their strict and regular observance . . . The necessity of justice to the support of society is the SOLE foundation of that virtue. (16, 27)

In this view the earth is still our home, but it is not as hospitable as comedy imagines. It is not perfectly adapted to our needs, and we are not ideally adapted to its harsh conditions. We require and demand more than nature provides, or as Thomas Hardy ruefully observed: "We [human beings] have reached a degree of intelligence which Nature never contemplated when framing her laws, and for which she consequently has provided no adequate satisfactions" (Florence Hardy 163).

   Literary justice is now a matter of exploring and assessing dissatisfactions, a job approached by theorists with a curious mixture of pragmatism and hope. The pragmatism appears in Stanley Fish's essays proving that all principles are groundless "formal abstractions" with "no content of their own," and so must stoop to take both content and energy from politics, that is, from "the very realm of messy partisan disputes about substantive goods of which they claim to be independent" (Fish 142). This messy realm sounds like the world of the novel praised by Dimock. Fish calls it an "agonism" (126), an endless conflict waged rhetorically: "strictly speaking . . . there are no principles, just more or less persuasive uses of highly charged vocabularies by politically situated agents" (233). As the self-disciplining word "just" in the previous quotation illustrates, justice especially – the transcendent principle that would direct all others – cannot escape this fate (143), leaving all our judgments where they have always been, in the midst of things, competing for authority "without a ground of justification more basic or higher than the grounds given us by our moral convictions and determinations of fact" (146). We are all pragmatists, although even pragmatism could not justify itself on principle. According to this ironic view of the human condition, everything is up for grabs, and grabbing (another version of the will to power) is the basic human need.

On the other hand, such aggressive self-limitation provokes the transgressive impulse that continually disrupts law-preserving, but now displaces it inward. Following Benjamin's example, critics detect a utopian or messianic yearning redirected so that it functions, not as a lordly principle, but as an unappeasable dissatisfaction in the asymmetrical structure of justice. Justice is conceived not as arithmetical balance or reciprocity, but as excess, not as a remedy for heretical conduct but as itself impatient, outrageous, even lawless. For Derrida, the most influential exponent of this view, justice becomes an unpresentable "experience of absolute alterity," "overflowing," exceeding "calculation, rules, programs, anticipations and so forth" (Derrida, "Force" 27). For Aristotle, justice was the virtue of virtues, and so it is, *mutatis mutandis*, for Derrida: "Justice in itself, if such a thing exists, outside or beyond law, is not deconstructible. No more than deconstruction itself, if such a thing exists. Deconstruction is justice" (14–15). Formulated in this way, deconstruction is poetic justice.

Since poetic justice is determined by genre, its function too must be reassessed. Earlier I considered genre as a jurisdiction that legislates the conditions it will satisfy. It provides a temporary sanctuary, insecure perhaps, but still offering its blessing to true believers, that is, to those who read with the textual grain. Now we require a more volatile sense of genre, or an increased tolerance for the volatility already at work within their forms. Literary genres offer a lively display of the way in which jurisdictions are simultaneously necessary and arbitrary – necessary, because they have the authority of precedent and the inertia of established convention;

arbitrary, because their laws might have been different and will change. For this reason, genres are never quite satisfied with their own laws, not just in the sense that writers grow tired of regulations and take liberties with them, but also in the sense that genres exert authority by entertaining and defeating hostile elements within them. They illustrate how a regulatory system prevails by being victorious and by taking pleasure in its victory. I have used comedy as a test case, because it releases laughable forms of mischief – foolishness, misunderstanding, youthful disobedience, erotic desire, or any of the humors in the comedy of humors – in order to make a calculated show of taming them. These unruly energies make traditional comedy seem transgressive, but finally it is a conservative form that allows a short holiday from responsibility only to restore its grip more wisely, or that replaces an irrational law with a sound one (Frye, *Anatomy* 169). Because comedies celebrate fertility and replenishment, their worst foe is mortality, which they must either laugh away or defy through mockery, but which they cannot ignore. Shakespearean comedies usually include a brush with death, which is comically averted, for example in the inept sword fights that hurt no one in *A Midsummer Night's Dream* and *Twelfth Night*.

Like the sorcerer's apprentice, however, comedies risk being over-whelmed by the disruptive energies that they engage. If Bottom could not shed his ass's head, or Ariel could defy Prospero in *The Tempest*, then they might become monstrous rather than delightful. Ariel would turn into Caliban. The more problematic the comedy (*The Merchant of Venice*, *Measure for Measure*), the more menacing death becomes, and the more miraculous is the means of averting it. Salvation may then take the form of good luck or a wonderful accident – later I will cite an example from the film *The African Queen* – but these solutions are themselves problematic, since they are produced by mere chance rather than by the rational authority of justice. If the solution requires a true miracle, a supernatural intervention, then comic justice will be impotent and another kind will be necessary to satisfy, or artfully dissatisfy, the audience. According to Frye's scheme of genres, we will then pass from comedy into romance with its pattern of death and resurrection (*The Winter's Tale*, *Cymbeline*). Comedy finds justice within the healing powers of nature, whereas romance is truly transgressive and traces ghostlier demarcations.

SACRIFICE

Comedy is medicinal in the sense that it is a healing genre that finds its medicine in nature, for example in the love potion applied by Puck or in the herbs praised by Friar Laurence in *Romeo and Juliet*:

O, mickle is the powerful grace that lies
In herbs, plants, stones, and their true qualities.
For nought so vile that on the earth doth live
But to the earth some special good doth give;
(2.3.15–18)

The word "grace" reveals the divine source of curative powers, the higher justice that attends on nature, but because Friar Laurence lives in a tragedy, he promptly warns that nature is also the source of poison:

Nor aught so good but strain'd from that fair use,
Revolts from true birth, stumbling on abuse.
. . .
Within the infant rind of this small flower
Poison hath residence and medicine power:
(2.3.19–20, 23–4)

Unlike comedy, romance and tragedy are genres that employ a rhetoric of sacrifice to surpass the boundaries imposed by justice. Although the structure of sacrifice appears to resemble the neat symmetry of justice which aligns cause with effect, crime with offense, virtue with reward, in fact it is asymmetrical. The innocent (scapegoat, lamb, child, hero, Christ) suffer to redeem the guilty, thereby giving characters far better (romance) or far worse (tragedy) than they deserve. Justice permits restoration; sacrifice promises transformation. It offers grace rather than equity but only through poison and cruelty, unlike a judicial execution where the supreme penalty of one's life is reckoned equivalent to one's crimes. Instead, sacrifice provides an unmerited gift, which Derrida calls a "gift beyond exchange and distribution, the incommensurable or the incalculable" (Derrida, "Force" 7). Romance and tragedy are more than satisfactory: they begin in scarcity and end in excess.

Thus Hamlet reprimands Polonius for promising to do only what is fair: "Use every man after his desert, and who should 'scape whipping? Use them after your own honor and dignity: the less they deserve, the more merit is in your bounty" (*Hamlet* 2.2.529–33). His advice begins with an assumption of insufficiency: we are all not good enough for this world. It ends with a prospect of unmerited bounty for the giver as well as the recipient. If all of us deserve whipping, then how great can our honor and dignity be? They will increase only after the undeserved gift is presented by an undeserving giver. Hamlet's liberality distinguishes him from Polonius, a figure of both the precision and folly of the law, but it also marks him for tragedy. The generosity he advocates here is the inverse image of his own fate, which will entail the deaths of innocent and guilty alike. As I will discuss in Chapter 3, he must discover that disclosing the truth about his father's murder cannot redeem past injustice, and only the gift of his own death will resolve the tragedy. If comedy promises something better than truth, tragedy shows that truth is necessary but not enough.

It is hard to imagine what lies beyond truth and justice, or why it might be worth pursuing. In *The Gift of Death* Derrida enters boldly into the heresies of paradox (Johnson's dismissive phrase), where, through a transvaluation of values, ethics becomes "irresponsibilization" (Derrida, *Gift* 61) and hate becomes "the sacrifice of love to love" (64), where "[p]aradox, scandal, and aporia are themselves nothing other than sacrifice" (68). Self-sacrifice requires the voluntary giving of one's life for others or for a just cause. This sounds like the tragic saintliness exhibited by Shaw's Saint Joan, but Derrida is not concerned with the ethical service of such an act, that is, with its justice. Instead, he wants to pinpoint the act itself, apart from any justifying value, as a gift that is purely individual (no one else can do it for you; it can be done only once) and purely altruistic (it has no deeper motive and seeks no higher reward). The effect is to isolate a strange instant when the good reveals itself in its inexplicable purity. Self-sacrifice offers "not some thing, but goodness itself, a giving goodness, the act of giving or the donation of the gift" (41). Justice requires a temporality based on moral coherence, whereas the instant of self-sacrifice is uncanny in the sense of being a temporal anomaly. It is a "temporality of the instant" (65) that is purely present, a moment of presence whose significance does not derive from the past (motives, causes, history) or the future (benefits, rewards, recompense). I noted that the structure of sacrifice appears to resemble the structure of justice but diverges from it in being excessive. Following Kierkegaard's example, Derrida would tear them even further apart by insisting on the absolute uniqueness of the individual at the moment of sacrifice. Quite unlike the scene of joyous reconciliation that concludes comedy, the sacrificial scene is wonderful, awful but cruel: the self affirms its uniqueness only in the instant when it abandons itself and is extinguished. I will examine poetic evocations of this uncanny event in Chapter 5.

Uniqueness – the subject of Chapter 5 – is the one thing that justice cannot tolerate, or even imagine with its general rules and impartial procedures. Justice recognizes only general types defined by established conventions, or in Kierkegaard's words: "The ethical as such is the universal, and as the universal it applies to everyone, which may be expressed from another point of view by saying that it applies every instant."[3] Sacrifice, by contrast, occurs at only one instant, whose singularity the temporality of justice cannot accommodate, which is why it seems irrational, unfair, and absurd. This pure moment has an evil twin in the *acte gratuit* beloved by existentialists, notably in the arbitrary crime that appears in André Gide's novel *Les caves du Vatican* where a murder is committed at random and apparently without motive, but really to make a philosophical point about absurdity. While traveling on a train, Lafcadio abruptly decides that if he can count to twelve before he sees a light, then he will push another man, Fleurissoire, out the door, and he does so. His desire to commit an unmotivated crime gives it a motive, and so offers some satisfaction, at least to philosophers. (A tense, similar scene occurs in Cormac McCarthy's *No Country for Old Men*, where the victim is spared.) However, if sacrificial moments are beyond good and evil in the usual sense, then there should be no moral distinction between them; but surely there is a difference between sacrificing oneself for others and sacrificing others for oneself.

Investigating the quality of absurdity is Kierkegaard's task in *Fear and Trembling*, where he interprets the biblical scene in which Abraham is commanded to sacrifice his beloved son Isaac at God's inscrutable command. If the sacrificial instant is unspeakable, because speaking would taint its purity by reintegrating it in an ethical pattern, then poets can imagine it only by devising a devious literary path that leads toward it or circles around it, in order to imply what cannot be represented. Rhetorically, they gesture at the place where it would be, just as they gesture in order to invoke authority. Bowing to a king makes him regal; circling an enigma intensifies its mysteriousness. This is Kierkegaard's strategy as he repeatedly pictures Abraham leaving his family, ascending Mount Moriah, preparing to do the unspeakable by sacrificing his son. Kierkegaard begins to tell the story four times in succession, and again later, like a theme and variations that can never be repeated often enough. (A musical equivalent is the ever-circling, ever-enriching canon by Johann Pachelbel.) The path up Mount Moriah leads his meditation beyond the rationality of justice, beyond tragic heroism, beyond speech, toward the absurdity of faith.

He mounted the ass, he rode slowly along the way. All that time he believed – he believed that God would not require Isaac of him, whereas he was willing nevertheless to sacrifice him if it was required. He believed by virtue of the absurd; for there could be no question of human calculation, and it was indeed the absurd that God who required it of him should the next instant recall the requirement. He climbed the mountain, even at the instant when the knife glittered he believed . . . [4]

Kierkegaard asserts that at the final moment Abraham cannot be a tragic hero, because tragedy must maintain an ethical claim – its sacrifice is made on behalf of some higher good – whereas Abraham's act demands a leap of faith beyond all ethical calculation.

The difference between the tragic hero and Abraham is clearly evident. The tragic hero still remains within the ethical. He lets one expression of the ethical find its *telos* in a higher expression of the ethical . . . With Abraham the situation was different. By his act he overstepped the ethical entirely and possessed a higher *telos* outside of it, in relation to which he suspended the former.[5]

Perhaps it is necessary to emphasize the obvious: the story is not tragic because the father does not sacrifice his son. Isaac (whose name means "laughter") lives and flourishes but not, Kierkegaard insists, because he deserves it. Derrida claims that the uncanny temporality of the event makes intent and deed inseparable: "it is as if Abraham had *already* killed Isaac" (Derrida, *Gift* 72). Nevertheless, until the final instant, the narrative path up the mountain is tragic. Kierkegaard begins to tell a tragic story, but it leads him to a mysterious place beyond tragedy. Like problematic comedies that cannot digest disruptive elements yet cannot ignore them, tragedy reaches the limit of its jurisdiction. In both cases, the limit is death, although comedy is more concerned with mortality, the ludicrous business of dying, while tragedy focuses on death itself as an encounter with the absolute. In Derrida's account, Kierkegaard's path proceeds through an anxious apprehension of death to the interpretive instant, which cannot be interpreted because it reveals "conceptual thinking at its limit, at its death and finitude" (68).

This limit is said to be beyond philosophy, the science of truth; beyond ethics, the discipline of practical knowledge; beyond justice, the art of responsibility and adequation. Kierkegaard claims that it is also beyond the aesthetic, that is, beyond the scope of poetic justice, but surely its very possibility is made imaginable only by the biblical narrative, followed reverently by Kierkegaard's contrapuntal account of it, followed in turn by Derrida's restless, incantatory word-play.

In this book I examine the scope of poetic justice by focusing on key points where justice, law, and literary forms intersect, where they inform and displace each other through legal fictions, fantasies, challenges, and provocations. Following Frye's suggestion, I begin with the therapeutic alliance between justice and comedy as satirized in the operas of Gilbert and Sullivan. They devise absurd legal fictions to show how the law reaches into fantasy to satisfy its logic of atonement, for instance in a judicial sentence of "life plus ninety-nine years." The very absurdity of the satire becomes so compulsive, however, as to reveal a precarious alliance between logic, music, and magic. The same alliance turns tragic in Chapter 3, which studies how judicial reasoning assumes a temporal coherence (for example linking crime to punishment) whose effectiveness requires an exercise in moral imagination whereby the past can be assessed and, in effect, changed – an impossibility according to Nietzsche. A variety of creative and critical texts illustrate the rewards and insufficiencies of two agents, pain and payment, which claim to redeem the past through aesthetic spectacle. This claim, which is problematic especially in regard to tragedy, is highlighted in two texts: Jean Baudrillard's *Symbolic Exchange and Death* and J.M. Coetzee's *Disgrace*.

Chapter 4 examines the juncture of law and literature through their shared but conflicting appeals to nature and human nature. It uses Huckleberry Finn's itch and other involuntary bodily reactions as an avenue into natural law, considered as a more philosophical account of *le mot juste* with its adequation of natural conditions and human needs. *Huckleberry Finn*, *The African Queen*, and *Billy Budd* provide three examples of how justice appeals to nature but cannot be fully satisfied with the sanction that it finds there. Chapter 5 turns to the ethical and artistic challenge of imagining irreducible singularity: the uniqueness of things and of people that elicits yet also defies judicial scrutiny. Wallace Stevens is the main witness, but a variety of creative and critical authors illustrate the rhetorical means of expressing utter particularity as the vanishing point of ethical perception, of the pure present, and of the limit of all jurisdictions, which appears finally at the instant of death.

Chapter 6 considers the adequacy or inadequacy of truth as a guarantee of justice, and conversely the adequacy or inadequacy of justice as an avenue to truth. The classic detective genre, as deftly subverted in Michael Ondaatje's novel *Anil's Ghost*, illustrates the ambitions and failures of both judicial and literary forms as agents of moral healing. It reveals how truth is a goal that justice demands yet must sometimes sacrifice. In tragedy and other ironic modes, finding the truth is necessary but not enough, in which case literature must use the pathetic failure of truth to gesture beyond justice. Finally, I return to *le mot juste* in order to re-examine the rivalry between its two terms as they contribute to legal fictions. By straddling the border between art and life, such fictions operate as paradigm (intelligible framework), as enabling illusion (heuristic device), and as artefact (system of belief). They articulate the conditions that make justice both conceivable and desirable, but that also put concept and desire at odds.

CHAPTER 2

Life plus ninety-nine years
The fantasy of legal fictions

Ah, my Lords, it is indeed painful to have to sit upon a woolsack
which is stuffed with such thorns as these!

(W.S. Gilbert, *Iolanthe*, in *Plays* 210)

the most rigorously rationalized law is never anything more than an
act of social magic which works.

(Pierre Bourdieu, *Language and Symbolic Power* 42)

Oliver Cromwell died on September 3, 1658 and was buried with all the
ceremony due to the Lord Protector of the Realm. In 1661, after the
restoration of Charles II, the body was dug up and hanged in its shroud
at Tyburn; its head was cut off and displayed outside Westminster Hall for
almost twenty years (Fraser 678–9). This belated punishment can be seen
as the fanciful execution of a justice whose ferocity was entirely symbolic,
since only a decaying corpse remained to exhibit the shame and pain
that Cromwell could no longer suffer. Its gruesome display illustrates how
justice resorts to fantasy in order to render its severest judgments. Cromwell
was given what he deserved, just as he had been buried in accordance with
a more reverent judgment of his merits. According to the new authorities,
however, his crimes were so horrendous that even the supreme penalty of
death was insufficient, and some humiliation beyond the grave had to be
devised. His punishment also demonstrates that justice is always public in
the sense that it is a civic ritual affirming social order and official power.
Justice must be seen to be done, not only to ensure that it is done fairly,
but as part of its larger structure and meaning. Even a prisoner doomed to
solitary confinement in an obscure *oubliette* remains, in a sense, on public
display, out of sight but not out of mind.

As Paul Gewirtz notes, although courts of law must be isolated from the
public world, they must also be open to the public gaze; consequently, "there
is always a struggle between this idealized vision of law – which proclaims

that law is and must be separate from politics, passion, and public resistance – and the relentless incursion of the tumult of ordinary life" (Gewirtz
135). This dialectic of form (detached judgment) and energy (tumult) is
essential to literature as well, and in both, their interaction generates imaginative pressure that affects both the performance and meaning of the law.
The ceremonies of justice are isolated by peculiar costumes and rituals –
robes, wigs, woolsacks, Latin phrases – which make them theatrical and so
invite scrutiny from the public audience that they exclude. Cromwell's head
remained as a dramatic prop until it was eventually rescued by a puritan
sympathizer. Otherwise it might have remained permanently on display, as
if to suggest that no amount of mortification would atone for the wrongs
that its owner had inflicted on Britain. Similarly, a vicious criminal today
might be condemned to life plus ninety-nine years in prison. Ninety-nine
is a magical number whose efficacy is symbolic rather than practical since,
from the prisoner's point of view, life plus one minute would last no longer
than life plus a century. It is an example of how justice, in striving to
be rigorous, reaches into fantasy to satisfy the logic of atonement: only
the most precise calculation can compute the extraordinary punishment
commensurate with an appalling crime. For example, *The New York Times*
reports that after two police detectives were found guilty of serving as
assassins and spies for the Mafia, one was sentenced to life plus 100 years
and fined $4.74 million; while the second, who evidently was less culpable,
received only life plus eighty years and was fined a mere $4.25 million. A
further legal reckoning allows, however, that both will continue to receive
tax-free disability pensions while in prison.[1] Such meticulous discrimin-
ation seems to confirm Pierre Bourdieu's observation: "the most rigorously
rationalized law is never anything more than an act of social magic which
works" (Bourdieu 42).

In this chapter I investigate how logic and magic interact in legal fictions that push justice into fantasy. My examples will be drawn mainly
from the Savoy operas of W.S. Gilbert and Arthur Sullivan, because they
frolic with justice in its different guises: divine, social, literary, dramatic.
They provide satirical insight into judicial logic by rendering it absurd,
thereby exposing the magic within logic. Gilbert, who was called to the
bar in 1863 and appointed Justice of the Peace in 1891 (Stedman 20, 281),
was fascinated by the impudence of jurisprudence. He sensed, as M.K.
Sutton perceptively remarks, that "the law had some primal connection
with humor" (Sutton 23), partly because its theatricality inspires reverence
for fallible authorities, but also, as I noted earlier, because they share a common rhetoric. In virtually every opera Gilbert satirizes abuses of the British

legal system: its maze of regulations, the corruption of power, the folly of obeying incomprehensible rules, the privileges of rank that undermine equality before the law, the charade of courtroom solemnities concealing bias or incompetence. My concern is less with abuses of a just system, however, than with inconsistencies evident within the system when justice and legality are at odds – an oddity that Gilbert exaggerates by lampooning the conventions of romantic comedy. More specifically, I will argue that a logic of proportional substitution, by which crime is matched symbolically with a punishment whose aim is to achieve atonement through suffering, forces the reach of justice to exceed its grasp. Justice reaches in two directions – upward to divinity, and downward to nature – but Gilbert mischievously shows that it cannot find a secure foundation in either, because it relies on the unruly discourses of legality, discourses guilty of the very errors they are intended to correct.

MY OBJECT ALL SUBLIME

My object all sublime
I shall achieve in time –
To let the punishment fit the crime –
The punishment fit the crime;
And make each prisoner pent
Unwillingly represent
A source of innocent merriment!
Of innocent merriment!
(*Mikado*, in Gilbert, *Plays* 331)

For Bourdieu, the law culminates in fantasy because it begins in magic. The magic of the law is its quasi-divine power of command, which compels faith in judicial authority and social assent on matters of life and death: "Legal discourse is a creative speech which brings into existence that which it utters. It is the limit aimed at by all performative utterances – blessings, curses, orders, wishes or insults. In other words, it is the divine word, the word of divine right" (Bourdieu 42). As a divine word, the law can even project itself beyond death, as Cromwell's fate illustrates, but to do so it must draw on the resources of art. An earlier account of how social institutions artfully invest themselves with religious authority appears in Moses Maimonides's *The Guide for the Perplexed*, which I offer as a religious counterpart to Bourdieu's sociology. Maimonides insists that laws are not self-sufficient – they are not just simply because they are legal – but must derive their authority from prophecy, which is inspired by the divine agency of an angel bearing the word of God: "Even Moses our Teacher received his first prophecy through an angel. 'And an angel of the Lord appeared to him in the flame of fire' (Exod. iii). It is therefore clear that the belief in the existence of angels precedes the belief in prophecy, and the latter precedes the belief in the Law" (Maimonides 356). Naturally, belief in God precedes the belief in angels. Maimonides is concerned to anchor legality in morality, and morality in divinity; otherwise the law, left to define itself, might be arbitrary or partial. The law is true and just only because it is God's Law, which, however, is not immediately knowable but requires a line of transmission urged by revelation, recorded in scripture, and sustained by faith. The logic of justice begins and ends in fire.

Bourdieu calls this attenuated process, by which justice is conveyed to humanity, articulated in law, and granted supreme authority, "symbolic power," but he explains its function sociologically rather than theologically. Symbolic power operates not through prophecy but through "ministry": "the delegation by virtue of which an individual – king, priest or spokesperson – is mandated to speak and act on behalf of a group, thus constituted in him and by him" (Bourdieu 75). A group delegates a leader who, in effect, creates the group by representing it, that is, makes it recognizable to its own members by articulating their needs. The complex transaction though which social power is ascribed to an individual who assumes the prior right of command must always be shrouded in mystery if it is to seem legitimate: "that is the very definition of symbolic power" (209) and the cloak by which the law conceals its arbitrariness and partiality. Ironically, when justice is seen to be done, its inner dynamic is not seen at all. It is "misrecognized" through an ideological reversal of cause and effect, a mystification achieved through symbols like Maimonides's angel, which have the uncanny ability to become the power that they represent. Thus a politician or judge

derives his truly magical power over the group from faith in the representation that he gives to the group and which is a representation of the group itself and of its relation to other groups. As a representative linked to those he represents by a sort of rational contract (the programme), he is also a champion, united by a magical relation of identification with those who, as the saying goes, "pin all their hopes on him." (192)

Justice is rational, but in order to work effectively it requires a charismatic champion to sum up a community's aspirations. In order to account for its origins, its power, and the righteousness of its consequences, it must supplement reason with fantasy.

The charismatic champion becomes Gilbert's booby – the foolish judges, admirals, and Lord Chancellors who lord it over his operas. Through them, he discloses the absurdity of judicial power by seizing on moments when rational deliberation calls on magic, in Bourdieu's sense of the word, to devise legal fictions. Rivka B. Siegel suggests that legal fictions are essential to judicial thinking, not just in the case of "a few quaint counterfactuals" but as "the figural terrain" of the social world "on which we fight some of the major social conflicts of our day" (Siegel 228). As an example, she cites the fact that a corporation is legally considered a "person" whereas the unborn are not (227). Gilbert pounces on and elaborates moments when the social standing of legal fictions seems wobbly. These he renders preposterous by word-play and equivocation, by treating figurative expressions literally (insisting on the letter of the letter of the law), or by arranging a conflict of jurisdictions.

As a historical parallel, consider the odd legal fiction at issue in *Francis* v. *Resweber*, "in which the United States Supreme Court allowed the State of Louisiana to attempt to execute a convicted murderer twice" (Sarat and Kearns 213). In May, 1946, Willie Francis was executed in the electric chair, but while he suffered painfully, he did not die, either because the machine malfunctioned or because he was so robust. He then appealed against a second execution on the grounds that it would be cruel and unusual punishment, which is banned by the United States Constitution. In a sense, Francis had already been executed and it would not be fair to execute him again, since the punishment must not exceed the crime. Michel Foucault quotes from the French penal code of 1791 stipulating only "one death per condemned man," and cites a tradition that a "condemned man should be pardoned if the execution happened to fail (Foucault, *Discipline* 12, 52). However, the United States Supreme Court ruled that Francis should be executed twice, although in a dissenting opinion Justice Bruton objected to authorizing "death by installments" (Sarat and Kearns 216), and raised the concern that the electrocution might fail again, in which case the court would have to rule how many executions were enough. Gilbert would have felt right at home in this courtroom. Whatever the legal merits of the case, that the debate should arise at all illustrates how the law risks absurdity precisely when it takes itself most seriously in matters of life and death.

Coincidentally, Gilbert had encountered a similar case in 1895, when he was sent a newspaper editorial, "Dead, Yet Alive," which "dealt with the comic problems of an electrocuted criminal, pronounced legally dead, but resuscitated" (Stedman 306). Although he did not use the story, a year later he mounted his final collaboration with Sullivan, *The Grand Duke*, in which the comic device of a "Statutory Duel" (the duelists draw cards rather than use weapons) allowed him to invent a "legal fiction" whereby the loser suffers only a "social death" by forfeiting his position to the winner, who takes the loser's place with all its advantages and obligations. This scheme is painlessly and mutually beneficial, since "it is a beautiful maxim of our glorious Constitution that a man can only die once. Death expunges crime, and when he comes to life again, it will be with a clean slate" (*Grand Duke*, in Gilbert, *Plays* 575, 576). Justice is done through a contractual exchange of identities that is treated literally rather than figuratively, as the winner is publicly recognized in his new identity, while the loser temporarily remains invisible. All of the operas use legal sleight of hand of this sort, as Gilbert seizes on judicial oddities and pushes them into fantasy.

Behind the nonsense are real legal dilemmas, however, as Willie Francis attests. Any judicial system seeking equity in human affairs, whether through contracts, salaries, benefits, punishments, or obligations, aspires to establish an exact fit between (at least) two acts: crime and punishment, deed and reward, promise and enactment. How are we to measure the nature and intensity of the second act in compensatory relation to the first? Gilbert is famous for stretching this relationship by devising grotesque punishments for trivial faults, like the "billiard sharp" in *The Mikado* condemned to play "On a cloth untrue / With a twisted cue / And elliptical billiard balls" (332). Like Cromwell and Francis, the billiard sharp gets what he deserves, but if there is no angel to guide us, how do we assess the kind and degree of punishment or reward commensurate with conduct judged blameworthy (punitive justice), or praiseworthy (distributive or compensatory justice), or fair (exchange)? Extreme cases call for extreme measures, but measuring accurately may require imaginary solutions – posthumous torture, life plus ninety-nine years, death by installments – to real problems.

TO LET THE PUNISHMENT FIT THE CRIME

A punishment is supposed to reverse an earlier misdeed, for instance by returning what has been stolen or undoing what has been done. To restore the social balance, restitution must be as direct and immediate as possible, as Maimonides illustrates:

The law concerning false witnesses (Deut. xix, 19) prescribes that they shall suffer exactly the same loss which they intended to inflict upon another. If they intended to bring a sentence of death against a person, they are killed; if they aimed at the punishment of stripes, they receive stripes; and if they desire to make a person pay money, they are sentenced to pay exactly the same sum. The object of all these laws is to make the punishment equal to the crime. (Maimonides 345)

Often, however, losses cannot be restored or injuries redressed exactly, in which case a symbolic substitution must be devised as compensation, usually in the form of payment or suffering (344). Justice is an art of substitution, since there is no natural or literal connection between, for instance, the act of parking a car in a proscribed location and a fine of $43. The connection is arbitrary, not only because the fine could be different or some other penalty might be exacted, but because a recognizable social code must maintain the link between crime and penalty. One circumstance entails the other, but the entailment is possible only because the two events are joined through a judicial symbolism that is an elaborate expression of cultural thinking and values. Every society has a repertoire of symbolic relations defining the sorts of act that can serve as punishment and are deemed fair in kind and degree. These include: apology, payment, public humiliation, physical confinement, forfeiture, forced labor, enslavement, banishment, mutilation, torture, and finally, death through various kinds of ceremonial execution.

We can characterize a culture or historical period – or a literary genre – by analyzing its judicial semiotic, although our judgment will inevitably reflect our own scale of values. What seems cruelly unfair to a modern sensibility might have seemed reasonable and just, though no less terrible, to an earlier one. Here is a baroque verdict from seventeenth-century England:

The Court doth award that you be drawn upon a hurdle to the place of execution and there shall be hanged by the neck, and, being alive, shall be cut down and your entrails to be taken out of your body, and, you living, the same to be burnt before your eyes, and your head to be cut off, your body divided into four quarters, and head and quarters to be disposed of at the pleasure of the King's Majesty: and the Lord have mercy on your soul! (quoted in Dick 23)

Even the hurdle is chosen as a suitably demeaning form of transport. This prisoner might find little consolation in learning that his torment is a semiotic exercise constituting a "signifying field" in which "[t]he criminal is punished primarily as a sign, then, a salient example, condensing and displaying in his person an entire structure of prohibition. And, as a sign, he is posted mostly for the benefit of others, held up to serve them due warnings" (Dimock 32). But this should remind us that culture is a tissue of symbols, which are as real as heads and guts. The difficulty in "reading" a judicial semiotic is not just a consequence of different sensibilities or historical distance. Today the same problem arises in feminist criticism, which argues that our judicial system cannot serve women fairly because it fails to articulate their experiences within its symbolic grid of permissions and prohibitions. It fails to see them: "If a victim's claim still cannot be adequately translated, her harm goes unnoticed. If she lies completely outside the current representation of justice, her harm, and indeed her very self disappear" (Cornell 109).

As we will see, Gilbert's strategy is usually the reverse: he employs a judicial semiotic so familiar to his audience that he must defamiliarize it operatically, for example, in Nanki-Poo's sentence in *The Mikado*:

When the day comes there'll be a grand public ceremonial – you'll be the central figure – no one will attempt to deprive you of that distinction. There'll be a procession – bands – dead march – bells tolling – all the girls in tears – Yum-Yum distracted – then, when it's all over, general rejoicings, and a display of fireworks in the evening. *You* won't see them, but they'll be there all the same. (Gilbert, *Plays* 316)

The problem of devising fair punishment for an indefinable crime is also satirized in *Utopia Limited* when the King is baffled by irresponsible journalism: "That's precisely it. I – I am waiting until a punishment is discovered that will exactly meet the enormity of the case" (523).

The difficulty in measuring penalties is complicated by the need for justice to be "righteous" as well as right (Maimonides 345). It demands more than a simple congruence between crime and punishment, because its purpose is threefold: to repay the victim, to punish the criminal, and to act as a public example to deter others. To achieve these ends, justice must be exorbitant. Wrongdoing exacts not only repayment but expiation, which requires an additional burden of cost, labor, or pain from the wrongdoer. According to a more precise moral reckoning, then, the punishment should exceed the crime, since it must not only restore a lost balance – measure for measure – but also must chastise and so redeem the criminal, as well as admonish the public. Hence Maimonides's calculation: "'whom the judges shall condemn he shall pay double unto his neighbor' (Exod. xxii, 8); namely, he restores that which he has taken, and adds just as much [to it] of his own property" (344). The punishment exceeds the crime, but only to the correct degree, in order to serve as just and fruitful recompense.

Maimonides's inventive but precise arithmetic is necessary if justice is to prevail, because "it is impossible for man to be entirely free from error and sin" (332), and sin must be expiated conscientiously. A major premise in this book is that any theory of justice presupposes a view of human

nature, whether it is regarded as created by God, fixed by "nature" or
biology, or devised ideologically. Justice requires a basic model of human
interaction, so that it can control that interaction for the benefit of all.
Maimonides believes that we are imperfect beings in need of correction,
but correction requires "a protracted and burdensome atonement" (365) if
it is to be efficacious. It cannot happen instantaneously:

> the nature of man is never changed by God by way of miracle . . . I do not say
> this because I believe that it is difficult for God to change the nature of every
> individual person; on the contrary, it is possible, and it is in His power, according
> to the principles taught in Scripture; but it has never been His will to do it, and
> it never will be. If it were part of His will to change [at His desire] the nature of
> any person, the mission of prophets and the giving of the Law would have been
> altogether superfluous. (325)

The miracle of sudden redemption would correspond to direct contact with
the divine without the agency of angels or prophets, and therefore without
the discipline of law. If such contact were possible, the attenuated process
by which the revelation of justice expresses itself as legality would not be
necessary. We could have justice without law, because knowledge of right
and wrong would be intuitive, and expiation of wrongdoing instantaneous.

This ideal state recalls the exalted promise of *le mot juste* whose truth,
Flaubert said, should pierce like a dagger; or as Pope wrote: "*Something,
whose Truth convinc'd at Sight we find*" (Pope 146). In Bourdieu's terms,
it would mean the obliteration of logic by magic, which would dismantle
not only law, but society itself. Bourdieu regards society as a restless current
of symbolic displacements through which knowledge, power, and prestige
("cultural capital") are constantly negotiated between groups, which are
defined only in shifting relation to each other. A state of utter self-sufficiency
is inconceivable, because it is counter to the nature of human beings – here
is Bourdieu's primary assumption – as sociable, symbol-wielding, insecure
animals. For Bourdieu, people are not imperfect so much as incomplete,
but we complete ourselves only imperfectly through acts of social magic
such as justice. In a sense, we are always reliving Hans Christian Andersen's
fable of "The Emperor's New Clothes," which shows how political power
commands by pretending to be invisible and by inducing citizens to accept
the pretence. Despite ourselves, we believe in the magical clothes (the
woolsacks, robes, and wigs of authority), so that we can trust the justice of
the Emperor's rule.

Because human character cannot change instantly, because there is no justice without law, we require a recuperative process, at once painful and imaginative, through which to atone for our sins. Pain is essential to both justice and comedy, because it is the agent linking logic to magic. In *Residues of Justice: Literature, Law, Philosophy*, Wai Chee Dimock studies justice as a fundamental mode of thought permitting an ideal adequation in human judgment and language – or at least the illusion of such an ideal – allowing them unerringly to connect causes to effects, actions to consequences. This is justice as a conceptual totality in which equivalences between disparate events can be perfectly calibrated so that the human world is enveloped in reciprocity (Dimock 95). Justice requires fictions that do not recognize their own fictionality; it is a "dream of objective adequation, its dream of a world exactly equal to the verdict it sees fit to pronounce" (197). As I noted in Chapter 1, Dimock prefers literary jurisdictions, especially the novel, because it is so beautifully muddled by accidents and misfortune that it presents "something like a constitutive ground for incommensurability" (168). It stretches justice "almost to its breaking point" (26), the point beyond which Gilbert pushes his legal conundrums. She praises the "illogic" of literature over the instrumental logic of justice (169) and seeks in the former an antithetical mode of appreciation, which is more nuanced than the straightjacket of judicial reasoning:

I want to experiment with a *nonintegral* conception of reason, theorizing it, that is, as a field of uneven definition: more heterogeneous, more responsive to contrary plausibilities, and therefore less harmonizing, less effective as a foundational guarantee. Imagined as the ground for disagreement rather than the ground for commensurability, human reason might turn out to underwrite not a unified propositional universe but many domains of thought, many styles of reasoning. (9)

Here, Dimock plays a merciful Portia to the strict Shylock of jurisprudence. Although she does not quite say so, she hints that there is something more just – more compassionate, generous, and responsive – about poetic justice than there is in the law's rigor. Because, in Drucilla Cornell's words, "the absolute determination of what justice is, is itself unjust" (Cornell 114), displaying its insufficiency in literature is a corrective act, a form of restitution. In this view, literature is the necessary angel of earth, speaking prophetically, not by extolling God's justice (Maimonides) or by championing a society's aspirations (Bourdieu), but by proclaiming the vital multiplicity of the world's particulars.

INNOCENT MERRIMENT, GUILTY PLEASURE

The law has a primal connection with humor because it offers a satisfactory resolution of human misconduct or misfortune, but also because it is apt to get things wrong. Both are conditions of comedy, which strives, with varying degrees of success, to rule those disruptive forces (misunderstanding, rivalry, greed, erotic desire, danger) that it must release in order to make a show of disciplining them. The law's misrule also has an internal source. Robert M. Cover explains in a commentary on the theology of Jewish Law that according to Maimonides "the Messiah himself could do nothing against the law. He would have no power to change or transform the law, but only to oversee its more perfect implementation" (Cover 194). This extraordinary discipline, through which nature constrains even the supernatural, will reappear as a condition of natural law in Chapter 4. Here it recalls the repressive, law-preserving function, noted in Chapter 1, which Walter Benjamin finds to be in permanent conflict with a revolutionary law-making impulse (Benjamin 284). Cover finds the same desire to transform the law in Jewish mysticism, noting that its urge to renounce legality on behalf of justice carries with it "a risk of madness," because "Messianism implies upheaval and fairly total transformation. Law ordinarily requires a cautious discernment among commitments" (Cover 196).

These terms apply nicely to Gilbert and Sullivan's Savoy operas, provided one has a sense of humor that regards madness as loony. My account of their judicial fantasies begins with an unruly rule of this sort, arising from Geoffrey O'Brien's observation that in performance, words and music compete for our sympathies by offering conflicting visions of human nature. Gilbert's witty but misanthropic lyrics offer "mordant variations on themes of vanity and avarice, self-serving unctuousness and moral cowardice," while his characters present a "parade of cynics, toadies, grasping senescent figures, gleefully duplicitous bureaucrats, and self-infatuated romantic leads" (O'Brien 16). If theories of justice always respond to a view of human character, then Gilbert's vision is jaundiced and ironic: "I'm really very sorry for you all, but it's an unjust world, and virtue is triumphant only in theatrical performances" (*Mikado*, in Gilbert, *Plays* 337). Throughout his career he was criticized for lacking "geniality and heart" or for displaying too cynical a view of human motives (Stedman 65, 73).[2] Hesketh Pearson refers to his "ineradicable faith in the corruptibility of mankind" (Pearson 219). In counterpoint to this pessimism, however, is Sullivan's music, which is exhilarating, tender or buoyant, "as if to elicit a compassion otherwise alien to Gilbert's creatures . . . Gilbert and Sullivan respectively reached different parts of one's being, Sullivan offering emotion and worldly color, Gilbert a brilliance spinning in the void, withering to any notion of sincere feeling: the oddity of their collaboration was that they did both in the same instant" (O'Brien 16).[3] G. Wilson Knight neatly called this collaborative rivalry "the mastery of the sadistic by melody" (Knight 300).[4]

In Gilbert's uncharitable world, the law is the source of both stability and instability. On the one hand, it is a tangle of restrictions supervised by punctilious officials who hinder love and freedom. As if to confirm Dimock's claim that in fiction, bad luck confounds the symmetries of justice, Gilbert presents a spectacle of lost identities, mismatched lovers, exchanged babies, missing parents, and disasters caused by noble intentions. "Here's a pretty mess," sing the trio of unfortunates in *The Mikado* (Gilbert, *Plays* 327), voicing a bewilderment felt by all the ineffectual heroes who are led astray by the rules that are supposed to protect them. "Quiet, calm deliberation / Disentangles every knot!" sing a corresponding quartet in *The Gondoliers* (492), only to discover that deliberation is the source of trouble, as they think themselves into a tizzy.

> JUDGE: A nice dilemma we have here,
>   That calls for all our wits:
> COUNSEL: And at this stage, it don't appear
>   That we can settle it.
>   (*Trial by Jury*, in Gilbert, *Plays* 48)

There are so many regulations, contracts, vows, rules of conduct, and "preposterous points of imaginary legal doctrine" (O'Brien 16) that life would sink under their weight if the music were not so buoyant. So Rose discovers in *Ruddigore* when she cites the book of etiquette found with her when she was abandoned as a baby, only to learn that it forbids her to point, whisper, or even speak about her love:

> But here I find it doesn't do
> To speak until you're spoken to.
> Where can it be? [*Searching book*]
> Now let me see – [*Finding reference*]
> Yes, yes!
> "Don't speak until you're spoken to!"
>   (Gilbert, *Plays* 353)

Gilbert's characters need a good dose of Bourdieu. They feel duty-bound to follow stultifying laws whose authority they trust absolutely, but whose value they cannot explain.

On the other hand, his dilemmas are resolved only within the law. In Alan Fischler's analysis, a Gilbertian plot typically begins with "a problematic law which creates a conflict for the sympathetic characters between duty and desire" (Fischler, *Modified* 97); after lamenting, scheming, and singing, they solve the problem, not by flouting the law but by embracing it.[5] The audience is enticed to laugh at the law, but only in a cathartic spirit that "purge[s] their reservations about its adequacy" (51), thereby reaffirming the status quo. Gilbert's art is conservative:

And law, in Gilbert's Savoy librettos, is consistently portrayed as protector and savior; indeed, his characters achieve their ultimate happiness not by overturning or abandoning law in the pursuit of liberty, as in traditional comedy, but rather by appealing to the precepts of law and submitting themselves to its arbitration. The quibbles through which the Lord Chancellor in *Iolanthe*, Ko-Ko in *The Mikado*, and Robin in *Ruddigore* manage to adjust or defend their actions in order to square them with obedience to the law illustrate one means by which Gilbert brings about his happy endings; the decisive revelations of the legal facts of Ralph's identity in *HMS Pinafore* and Luiz's in *The Gondoliers* illustrate another. (Fischler, "From Weydon-Priors" 218)

This assessment sounds too comforting to me, but it shows how Gilbert both foments and resolves problems by summoning the paradoxes of legality.[6] What Bourdieu calls "social magic" – the faith that seeks justice in rules and fallible rulers – is precisely the object of Gilbert's satire. He writes comedies of "misrecognition" in which "legal furies" (*Trial by Jury*, in Gilbert, *Plays* 49) are released to confuse the plot, but eventually are tamed through inventive verdicts, loopholes, and byzantine judgments that turn the law inside out. Nonsense is corrected by nonsense. (The same might be said of Shakespeare's *Merchant of Venice*.) First Rose is condemned to misery by the rules that should make women happy; then her lover, Robin, solves the dilemma through a legal quibble. An ancient curse on the Murgatroyd family dooms each member to commit a crime each day or else die in agony; but disobeying the curse is tantamount to suicide, which is a crime; therefore, not committing a crime is a crime; thus the curse is both obeyed and lifted at the same time. *The Yeomen of the Guard* summons the same frantic logic:

So the reason for the laying on of hands is the reason for the taking off of hands, and herein is contradiction contradicted! It is the very marriage of *pro* with *con*; and no such lopsided union either, as times go, for *pro* is not more unlike *con* than man is unlike woman, yet men and women marry every day . . . (408)

The artful entanglement through which the law logically creates problems that it is supposed to solve, and then magically solves the problems it has created, is satirized in *Trial by Jury*. The pompous Judge and servile jury instantly favor the beautiful plaintiff, Angelina, and condemn her betrayer, Edwin, for breach of promise of marriage. Eventually the Judge resolves the case by committing the same crime himself. He has abandoned his wife who "may very well pass for forty-three / In the dusk with the light behind her" (41), and whom he married only for social advancement, but he ends up marrying Angelina. Earlier, Edwin was scorned for proposing the same solution: "I'll marry this lady to-day, / And I'll marry that lady to-morrow!" (47). Angelina's reaction to her sudden shift in fortune is not specified in the libretto, but in the Finale, when Edwin wonders if "They'll live together / In marriage tether / In manner true," the Usher offers reassurance through one last judicial convolution: "It seems to me, sir, / Of such as she, sir, / A judge is he, sir, / And a good judge too" (49–50). Fischler claims that Gilbert's faith in law reflects the Victorian preoccupation with "the disappearance of God": "In the absence of divinity, law – imperfect though it may be – embodies the only reliable set of objective ethical standards left to society" (Fischler, "From Weydon-Priors" 219). An uncharitable spectator of *Trial by Jury* might conclude, however, that Angelina and the Judge know exactly what the other expects from marriage, and ethical standards have little to do with it.

Fischler is right, however, in suggesting that the angel of justice has disappeared. Although divinity is largely absent from the operas, the connection between transcendence and justice is still important to Gilbert, but (as always) with a twist. Gilbert shares Maimonides's assumption that people are inherently flawed and need correction, but he is unsparing in his satire of all standards of correctness. On the one hand, he shows that "man cannot bear perfection long" (Stedman 294) and is happy only when properly discontented. In *Utopia Limited*, the lotusland of Utopia is civilized to perfection by importing English institutions, but the resulting peace is so stultifying that it has to be enlivened by fractious party politics, another English legacy that produces "sickness in plenty, endless lawsuits, crowded jails, interminable confusion in the Army and Navy, and, in short, general and unexampled prosperity!" (Gilbert, *Plays* 559). On the other hand, Gilbert shows that the means of improving the human lot are as corrupt as humanity itself. The attenuated link between divinity and legality is not broken but given a devious turn. Instead of divinity inspiring justice, we find legality befuddling divinity. There are several angels and prophets in

the operas, but they are as confused as everyone else. Here is Mercury, mes-
senger of the gods, reduced to a drudge in *Thespis*, Gilbert and Sullivan's
first collaboration:

> Oh, I'm the celestial drudge,
> From morning to night I must stop at it,
> On errands all day I must trudge,
> And I stick to my work till I drop at it!
>
> (5)

A group of actors whose names express their fallen nature (Sillimon, Stu-
pidas, Timidon, Preposteros) wander up Mount Olympus and temporarily
substitute for the gods, who descend to earth for a taste of humanity. The
actors expect "to set the world in order" (16), but succeed only in making
a mess of things: "A premier in Downing Street, forming a Cabinet, /
Couldn't find people less fit for their work!" (23).

As a practical man of the theatre, Gilbert was less concerned with theology or sociology than with producing plays suited to the public tastes.[7]
When he shows humanity and divinity stumbling into each other's territory, he is following the popular forms of the London stage, including
the "fairy play," which deals with "magical conditions or situations"; the
"lozenge plot," in which magic potions or spells alter characters' behavior;
and the "invasion plot," in which outsiders invade and comically upset
an established society (Stedman 82, 83, 70). By employing these dramatic
forms, however, he invokes a set of artistic laws, which he is then free to
obey or flout. Because he uses – and artfully misuses – established dramatic
conventions, his plots exhibit conflicts that are inherent structurally in
them. The chief conflict is the rivalry between head and heart that arises
when love (another angel) bursts into the world from some mysterious elsewhere (heaven, eternity, paradise), disrupting ordinary laws. "Never mind
the why and wherefore, / Love can level ranks, and therefore" sings the
chorus in *H.M.S. Pinafore*, appealing beyond logic and social distinction
to the higher "jurisdiction" of love (Gilbert, *Plays* 109). In the end, however, romantic justice is reconciled with social propriety through Gilbert's
trick of treating legal fiction as literal fact, when Captain Corcoran and
the lowly sailor, Ralph, learn that they were interchanged at birth. They
promptly exchange identities so that Ralph becomes captain and is worthy
of marrying Corcoran's daughter, who previously was his social superior.
If this logic were followed strictly, she would now be his inferior, perhaps
even his own daughter (if he can shift identities, why can't she?), so the
dilemma would only be compounded.[8] But to quibble in this way is to

become a Malvolio who refuses to enjoy the play's redemptive spirit. I will return to Gilbert's spoilsports later.

Another misguided angel who tries to reconcile law and love, form and energy, appears in *Iolanthe*, which disastrously mingles the human and superhuman through a marriage "against ... fairy laws" (203) between a man and a fairy. The fruit of their illicit union is Strephon, "a fairy down to the waist – but his legs are mortal" (204). His joy is hampered by the law, since he is prevented from marrying Phyllis, a Ward of Chancery under the protection of the Lord Chancellor, who wants her for himself. He is Bourdieu's social minister portrayed as a booby:

> The Law is the true embodiment
> Of everything that's excellent.
> It has no kind of fault or flaw
> And I, my Lords, embody the Law.
> The constitutional guardian I
> Of pretty young Wards in Chancery
>
> (208)

Legal language pervades this play but manages only to confuse things by creating a frantic conflict of jurisdictions, represented by Strephon's divided nature. "My brain is a fairy brain," he explains, "but from my waist downwards I'm a gibbering idiot" (205). He attempts to take command by becoming a Member of Parliament, but since his top half is Tory and his bottom half is Radical, he is unsure how to vote "on a division" (205). Disastrously, his dual character permits him to lead both parties in Parliament and so to pass every bill, no matter how silly, including opening the Peerage to competitive examination. In its farcical way, *Iolanthe* reveals the arbitrariness of the law when it is not sanctioned by divine authority. Anything can be made legal, provided it is passed into law with due ceremony, but what ensures that laws will be just if there is no higher source of ratification? The Lord Chancellor is the play's legal expert, but he is cast into a quandary when he discovers a split in his own authority. How can he judge himself for betraying his position by falling in love with Phyllis?

What is his position? Can he give his own consent to his own marriage with his own Ward? Can he marry his own Ward without his own consent? And if he marries his own Ward without his consent, can he commit himself for contempt of his own Court? And if he commit himself for contempt of his own Court, can he appear by counsel before himself, to move for arrest of his own judgment? Ah, my Lords, it is indeed painful to have to sit upon a woolsack which is stuffed with such thorns as these! (210)

The fairies come to the rescue, but to no avail, since they all blindly obey rules that have no justification apart from legal inertia. All are slaves to duty; that is, they are obedient to the principle of obedience. When the Fairy Queen unfolds a scroll and announces, "the law is clear – every fairy must die who marries a mortal" (244), she appeals only to the unquestioned authority of a text whose source is not identified. Fortunately, observes the Lord Chancellor, "[t]he subtleties of the legal mind are equal to the emergency" (244). The solution is simply to rewrite the text by adding a single word – in pencil, the stage direction says – so that what was forbidden now is mandatory. Marriage between mortal and immortal becomes the law, rather than a crime. This is "The Emperor's New Clothes" with a twist.[9] Instead of dispelling the illusion of political power, the characters find a new tailor to weave a new legal fiction. Effortless solutions to intractable problems, such as abruptly reversing a statute or cutting the Gordian knot, always seem at once trivial and magical. Instead of submitting to a cumulative judicial process through which suffering gradually earns atonement, the miracle of comedy provides instant redemption through love and laughter. Similarly in *The Pirates of Penzance*, the mere mention of Queen Victoria's name is enough to disarm the pirates; then the revelation that they are all "noblemen who have gone wrong" (154) is enough to set them right.

COMIC JURISDICTIONS

At the heart of Gilbert's nonsense is the dilemma that there is no justice without law, but laws may be unjust – a problem for which he devises fantastic solutions. The fact that something is legal does not make it fair; it must be sanctioned by something more secure than a set of edicts written in pencil. I have noted two ways of anchoring legality in justice: through Maimonides's faith in a divine sanction, conveyed prophetically; and through Bourdieu's Nietzschean reversal of priorities, whereby justice is really the legality of the dominant social class, administered through the mystification of symbolic power. Gilbert relies on artistic versions of both prophecy and ministry, but he does so simply by writing plays in which poetic justice satisfies a bizarre fictional world. For divine law, he follows the rules of romantic drama (farce, burlesque, melodrama, comedy), which entice the audience to embrace a joyful distribution of reward and ridicule simply because it is too delightful to be doubted, at least for the duration of the opera. Literary justice is a function of genre, and comedy is a healing genre, with love and nature as its salves. More specifically, comic laws decree that love and nature – the heart's truth and natural justice – constitute a higher authority that triumphs over wrongful social regulations. The truth of true love provides a sure measure by which the audience can judge the rightness of things:

> Love that no wrong can cure,
> Love that is always new,
> Love is the love that's pure
> That is the love that's true.
> (*Patience*, in Gilbert, *Plays* 187)

In performance, songs like this appear at once sublime and quaint. The laws of sentimental romance direct the plot to its happy end, but they are also improbable, and Gilbert heightens their improbability by lampooning their exaltation of love and nature as healing agents. Even as he exposes their rule as illusory, however, Sullivan's music ensures that the illusion retains its beauty, its melodic guarantee of rightness. This leaves the audience in an awkward position, because the comedy's jurisdiction is insecure. Gilbert likes insecurity. He began his career by writing burlesques satirizing the Victorian faith in a providential justice that rewards beautiful people for falling in love (Sutton 67). Then in his nonsense poems, *The Bab Ballads*, he "wanted to challenge the convention of poetic justice in popular fiction and melodrama," reports Sutton, who quotes from Gilbert's parody, "The Triumph of Vice" (1867): "Cunning, malice, and imposture may not flourish immediately they are practised; but depend upon it, my dear children, that they will assert their own in the end" (Sutton 34). Note the reassuring voice here: malice is as natural and as heartfelt as love, yet it is hardly a basis for justice.

By stressing Gilbert's moral ambiguity, I do not mean to postmodernize him, and I do not dispute Fischler's claim that he is fundamentally conservative. Still, I am not sure that he can subdue the misrule of the "legal furies" (*Trial by Jury*, in Gilbert, *Plays* 49) that he releases in the name of love. He pushes dramatic conventions to their breaking point, as if daring the audience to believe, for instance, that "in marriage alone is to be found the panacea for every ill" (*Sorcerer*, in Gilbert, *Plays* 62), but then making the medicine taste sour. He casts doubt on the justice of his own plays, until the audience is soothed by the charm of Sullivan's music. In an early play, *Creatures of Impulse* (1871), Gilbert slyly defeats the audience's expectations by arranging that no characters marry in the denouement (Stedman 88). In *Patience* and *The Gondoliers* he proposes a lottery to pair off lovers, as if chance is as reliable a matchmaker as is affection. In *Patience* (subtitled "Bunthorne's Bride"), he leaves the phony aesthete, Bunthorne, unmarried, embracing his solitude:

> In that case unprecedented,
> Single I must live and die –
> I shall have to be contented
> With a tulip or li*ly!*
> (Gilbert, *Plays* 197)

Justice prevails even here, perhaps, since Bunthorne is punished for his narcissism with solitary confinement. But Patience's faith in pure love as the measure of truth is twisted into a Gilbertian knot. According to another romantic precept, which she dutifully obeys, love so pure must be utterly selfless, which means that she must renounce the man she loves (174). To remain pure, love must sacrifice itself and remain unsatisfied. A particularly nasty tangle in the love knot appears in *Iolanthe* where marriage triumphs over love, since the amended fairy law not only permits but demands that mortals and immortals marry: "Let it stand that every fairy shall die who doesn't marry a mortal" (245). According to Roger Scruton, marriage is the ethical form of love (Scruton 75), but in *Iolanthe* the sanctity of true love is evidently not sufficient, or even required. Is this a happy ending? At a more caustic moment in the opera marriage was derided as "penal servitude for life" (Gilbert, *Plays* 207).

Only when lovers are "matrimonially matrimonified" (*The Grand Duke*, in Gilbert, *Plays* 602) can their story end satisfactorily, but several operas conclude with unwelcome marriages, as a foolish man is dragged to the altar by a middle-aged woman (the "Dame" role): Ko-Ko and Katisha in *The Mikado*, the Captain and Buttercup in *H.M.S. Pinafore*, the Duke and Jane in *Patience*, Sergeant Meryll and Dame Carruthers in *The Yeomen of the Guard*. While Dame Carruthers hastens to make the matrimonial bond official by bringing "love's votary" to "the notary," Meryll leaves no doubt about his feelings: "Ghastly, ghastly! / When man, sorrowful / Firstly, lastly . . . Goes a-marrying" (444–5). Although this is hardly a happy ending, a sour note is not incompatible with comedy, where the pressure of reconciliation is so strong that minor characters are drawn into the festivities by getting married, whether they want to or not. Usually the man is the more reluctant partner: Sir Toby is obliged to marry Maria in Shakespeare's *Twelfth Night*. At the end of Gilbert's *Ruddigore*, the hero's rival, Richard, discovers that he cannot marry Rose, but since the Finale is already underway, he instantly switches his affection to Zorah, a professional bridesmaid who happens to be handy. Comic justice decrees that even these characters get what they deserve. Ko-Ko and Sergeant Meryll get their comeuppance for being so ridiculous, and Richard for being a frisky sailor, while Katisha and Dame Carruthers are rewarded for their patient years of suffering. Some of Sullivan's most poignant songs are sung by older women (contraltos) who contemplate the passing of time, for example Katisha's "Hearts do not break! / They sting and ache" (339) and Jane's "Silvered is the raven hair" (181). Marriage is thus either a punishment or a reward, depending on the character, but in either case it is conclusive.

The case of Phoebe in *The Yeomen of the Guard* is so troublesome that it threatens to shatter the opera's decorum. A kind-hearted maiden who truly loves Lieutenant Fairfax, she finds herself forced to marry Wilfred Shadbolt, whom she despises, and who in the original performance was played as a "repulsive . . . baboonish jailer" (Cellier and Bridgeman 262–3) "with long, forbidding black locks and an ill-shaven chin and cheeks" (Walbrook 94). Their dialogue becomes painfully strained, as she offers him her hand but not her heart, as if to confirm that cunning and malice can successfully enlist legality in their service:

PHOEBE: Oh, father, he discovered our secret through my folly, and the price of his
    silence is –
WILFRED: Phoebe's heart.
PHOEBE: Oh dear, no – Phoebe's hand.
WILFRED: It's the same thing!
PHOEBE: *Is* it? (*Yeomen*, in Gilbert, *Plays* 444)

Poor Phoebe does not deserve her fate, despite her careless lapse in revealing Fairfax's disguise: he was unjustly condemned to death for practicing sorcery, but with her help has escaped and disguised himself as a guard. Poetic justice fails her when she is blackmailed into marrying her beloved's official torturer.

For Gilbert, love, law, and nature are not reconciled, and he pushes to the breaking point the artistic convention that love is nature's blessing. According to Maimonides: "[T]he law always follows Nature, and in some respects brings it to perfection; for Nature is not capable of designing and thinking, whilst the Law is the result of the wisdom and guidance of God, who is the author of the intellect of all rational beings" (Maimonides 352). The law is "Nature Methodiz'd" as Pope said (Pope 146), delicately poised between nature, its source of raw energy, and God, its source of rational design. To obey the heart's law is to follow nature, and natural laws are supposed to be fairer than social regulations, since "Nature never errs"

(*Princess Ida*, in Gilbert, *Plays* 256). On the contrary, for Gilbert the heart always errs – is errant. "Hearts often tack," shifting unaccountably with the winds of chance:

> Ten minutes since my heart said "white" –
> It now says "black."
> It then said "left" – it now says "right" –
> Hearts often tack.
>
> . . .
>
> In sailing o'er life's ocean wide
> No doubt the heart should be your guide;
> But it is awkward when you find
> A heart that does not know its mind!
> (*Ruddigore*, in Gilbert, *Plays* 365)

In *Ruddigore* Richard advises his foster-brother Robin, "Let your heart be your compass" (359), but promptly takes his own advice by betraying Robin and claiming Rose for himself. "I'm bound to obey my heart's dictates" (363), he explains in self-serving justification, even though he had promised to woo her on Robin's behalf. Similarly in *Trial by Jury*, Edwin justifies his fickleness as entirely natural:

> Oh, gentlemen, listen, I pray,
> Though I own that my heart has been ranging,
> Of nature the laws I obey,
> For nature is constantly changing.   (46)

And when Strephon fervently argues the case for natural law in *Iolanthe* –

My Lord, I know no Courts of Chancery; I go by Nature's Acts of Parliament. The bees – the breeze – the seas – the rooks – the brooks – the gales – the vales – the fountains and the mountains cry, "you love this maiden – take her, we command you!" 'Tis writ in heaven . . . (214)

– the Lord Chancellor promptly asks for "an affidavit from a thunderstorm, or a few words on oath from a heavy shower"(215) to show the folly of Strephon's appeal.

SACRIFICE

I have argued that literature illuminates judicial thinking by recasting it as aesthetic form, making its symbolic linkages visible as they conform – or ironically fail to conform – to the conventions of genre. Genres provide an ethical framework to orient the readers' or spectators' judgment by establishing a semiotic of recompense through which fairness can be measured and satisfied. They command assent by defining the way things are, or should be, in the fictional world that they govern. Their laws seem natural, so that even the most contrived tricks become credible, at least for the moment. If comical rules permit baby farming, love potions, inherited curses, and death by proxy, then they, too, figure in the scheme of things. A genre defines how the figuring should be conducted; or conversely, a genre is defined by the sense of justice that it articulates. Even the triumphant discord of party politics at the end of *Utopia Limited* is "in burlesque terms a just conclusion," Knight explains, because "the only system that fits a paradoxical world is one that functions in terms of paradox" (Knight 302). We may resist a genre's jurisdiction by reading against the grain, but to do so while we enjoy Sullivan's gorgeous melodies would make us malcontents – the sort of person Gilbert condemns as "a very dragon of virtue and circumspection" (*Yeomen*, in Gilbert, *Plays* 403).

I have also argued, however, that genres incorporate elements that challenge the laws governing them. Northrop Frye notes that comedic plots approach a catastrophe or ritual death, as if to deliver themselves from the one thing that comic justice cannot accommodate, the one thing that laughter cannot heal (Frye, *Anatomy* 178–9). *The Mikado* makes a joke of this danger by continually threatening to execute its lovers in order to satisfy the Mikado's capricious law against flirting, until the threat evaporates through a legal quibble that argues death into inconsequence. Ko-Ko simply declares a figure of speech to be a literal fact:

When your Majesty says, "Let a thing be done," it's as good as done – practically, it is done – because your Majesty's will is law. Your Majesty says, "Kill a gentleman," and a gentleman is told off to be killed. Consequently, that gentleman is as good as dead – practically, he is dead – and if he is dead, why not say so?
MIKADO: I see. Nothing could possibly be more satisfactory! (Gilbert, *Plays* 344–5)

Logical, ethical, and emotional satisfaction is the ideal reward of both justice and literature. Just as justice is satisfied when its institutions provide exactly enough (*satis*)[10] recompense or punishment to discharge the judicial process, so literary works strive for closure, which they may or may not achieve. This does not mean that all literature concludes neatly, only that proposing and pursuing a satisfactory goal are primary literary motives, which may be fulfilled in a "triumphant matrimonial finish" (*Utopia Limited*, in Gilbert, *Plays* 516), or artfully frustrated in an ending that shocks, puzzles, or vexes us. There can be satisfaction even in frustration

if the effect is stimulating enough. If we are puzzled at the end of Henry
James's *The Turn of the Screw*, we still feel that the screw has been well
turned.

All genres subsume agents of dissatisfaction, who must either be reconciled to the prevailing justice or be excluded as outlaws. In comedies, there
are malcontents and misanthropes who refuse to join in the final festivities
(Frye, *Anatomy* 176) and who continue to mind the why and wherefore
long after others have accepted a comic verdict. Similarly, readers who defy
a work's generic laws are critical malcontents who usually seek a different
order of justice. A feminist or postcolonial critique of a classic work, for
instance, exposing *Huckleberry Finn* as subtly racist, is a case in point.
Gilbert presents several malcontents, whose scepticism probably reflects
his own views. The misshapen King Gama in *Princess Ida*, who insists on
telling the truth even when – especially when – it is most embarrassing, is
one such figure. Another is the villainous Dick Deadeye:

> Both the hunchbacks who appear in the Savoy Operas may be seen as, to some
> extent, Gilbert figures. Dick Deadeye is the one character in *H.M.S. Pinafore* (1878)
> who expresses what is clearly Gilbert's own viewpoint, that "When people have
> to obey other people's orders, equality's out of the question": as Charles Hayter
> notes, he is "the spokesman for the most practical and realistic attitudes in the
> opera."[11]

Comedy ritualistically banishes its malcontents through ridicule, partly to
purge their ill humors and partly because it cannot afford to keep them
in view during the concluding festivities. Like Malvolio, Dick Deadeye
simply fades away after his defeat.

Some characters are so disconcerting, so far at odds with comic justice,
that banishment is not enough and they must be sacrificed. With sacrifice,
we reach a frontier that judicial logic cannot cross even with the aid of
fantasy and pass into a different imaginative order, which will be explored
in later chapters. While the structure of sacrifice resembles the balanced
duality of justice, its character and effect are different. Sacrifice does not
envision the world as a commensurate order, but as unbalanced and unfair
to its victims. Justice is rational; sacrifice is mystical, as its name implies, a
"making holy" through unmerited grace. Justice satisfies; sacrifice blesses.
Frye calls the *pharmakos* or scapegoat a "random victim" (Frye, *Anatomy*
41) who does not fit into the systematic reckoning of justice because he or
she

> is neither innocent nor guilty. He is innocent in the sense that what happens to
> him is far greater than anything he has done provokes . . . He is guilty in the sense

that he is a member of a guilty society, or living in a world where such injustices are an inescapable part of existence. The two facts do not come together; they remain ironically apart. (41–2)

Justice cannot tolerate such irresolvable gaps. It secures social order by restoring an ethical balance, whereas sacrifice is disproportionate in its effects: it redeems society by giving it more than it has lost, more than it deserves. For this reason, Frye associates sacrifice with the revolutionary impulse of romance more than with the conservative consolidation of comedy (Frye, *Secular* 149). As Cromwell's posthumous fate illustrates, justice calls on fantasy to reach beyond death in order to maintain social well-being, whereas sacrifice redeems us from death by promising "a higher world than that of ordinary experience," a world that "transcends the cycle of nature" (150). This promise far exceeds the satisfactions of justice, and Frye sees as its ultimate symbols not the fruitful union of marriage, but virginity (152–3) and fraternity (173). Romance concludes by envisioning a paradoxically "atomized society" (172) combining the solitary and the sociable, an imagined order comparable to the messianic justice-beyond-all-law envisioned by Derrida. He too foresees a wonderful sociality of discreet individuals:

This "idea of justice," seems to be irreducible in its affirmative character, in its demand of gift without exchange, without circulation, without recognition or gratitude, without economic circularity, without calculation and without rules, without reason and without rationality. And so we can recognize in it, indeed accuse, identify a madness. (Derrida, "Force" 25)

Gilbert's characters are loony rather than mad in this exalted manner, and his plots still rely on marriage – the social contract that disciplines the wildest passions – to restrain the transgressive energy that Derrida invokes here. His operas do not transcend law, but they map its cruelties before sinking back into bemused irony. The example of Phoebe forced to marry a man she detests shows how sacrifice may overshadow justice, and when it does, the mood darkens until it is relieved by Sullivan's music. It is funny to see Nanki-Poo perpetually preparing for execution. It is pathetic to see Iolanthe willing to sacrifice her life to prevent the Lord Chancellor from marrying Phyllis. But in *The Pirates of Penzance* it is distressing to see Ruth callously cast off by Frederick, the man whom she raised and loves, and (depending on the performance) it can be unnerving to see her left dangling at the end of the opera. Mabel praises Frederick's "heroic sacrifice" (Gilbert, *Plays* 148) of his love, but she fails to notice who the sacrificial victim finally is, or to accord Ruth heroic stature. Farce does not permit heroism. It is absurd but unsettling to watch the damnation of John Wellington Wells in *The Sorcerer*. Although he is associated with infernal forces when he casts his spell, he is also just a businessman who gives people what they want. He is the means rather than the source of confusion, yet he must yield to an unmerited "public execration" (82) that consigns him to perdition via a trapdoor. Only when he is out of sight can the mismatched lovers be redisposed as they were predisposed. Still, the neat balance of comic justice is troubled by the disproportion of Wells's sacrifice.

Finally, Jack Point in *The Yeomen of the Guard* is Gilbert's most abject character and the one most cruelly sacrificed. Like King Gama, he is one of "Nature's blunders" (*Princess Ida*, in Gilbert, *Plays* 255), a brooding, cynical jester who generally is identified with Gilbert himself (Pearson 181). Hounded by a mob, scorned and jilted, he is finally betrayed by both love and nature:

I am a salaried wit; and is there aught in nature more ridiculous? A poor, dull, heart-broken man, who must needs be merry, or he will be whipped; who must rejoice, lest he starve; who must jest you, jibe you, quip you, crank you, wrack you, riddle you, from hour to hour, from day to day, from year to year, lest he dwindle, perish, starve, pine, and die! (*Yeomen*, in Gilbert, *Plays* 427–8)

All the schemes, accidents and coincidences in the plot conspire against Point, who incongruously dies on stage in the midst of the final festivities, a visible reminder of an agency that justice cannot reward, punish, ridicule, or heal. It may be in accordance with the dictates of the comedy, but it really is not fair.

CHAPTER 3

Time's desire
The temporality of justice

But past who can recall, or done undo?
Not God Omnipotent, nor Fate...
(John Milton, *Paradise Lost* 9.926–7)

Can't repeat the past?... Why of course you can!
(F. Scott Fitzgerald, *The Great Gatsby* iii)

This chapter returns to the question of how literary jurisdictions enforce legal judgments by displaying them as public spectacles. More specifically, it analyzes how such spectacles enact a temporality that would reclaim the past in order to pacify the present and ensure a desired future. I have argued that comedy can be a healing genre: it diagnoses a malady in human affairs and then administers a remedy. This therapeutic pattern is also a judicious one, a timely sequence of logical entailments and ethical discoveries that satisfy most of its characters and most readers, though not all. Tragedy, too, aims at moral and psychological repair, but its medicine is bitter, and as the above quotations suggest, its treatment of poetic justice is more problematic.

Milton and Fitzgerald offer contrary responses to the pastness of the past, and to ethical obligations that are raised but immediately frustrated by a determined backward gaze. After they have fallen into sin, Adam laments to Eve that even God is powerless to reverse the fatal course of events: what was done cannot be undone. Milton may have been recalling Aristotle's warning in *The Nicomachean Ethics* (6:2):

for no one *deliberates* about the past, but about what is future and capable of being otherwise, while what is past is not capable of not having taken place; hence Agathon is right in saying:

> For this alone is lacking even to God,
> To make undone things that have once been done.
> (Aristotle, *Ethics* 139)

49

Nevertheless, Gatsby does deliberate about the past. He believes that the force of his desire can renew the past, not just by winning back the love of the woman he has lost, but by nullifying that loss: what was undone can be redone. In assessing these dilemmas, readers are obliged to make corrective judgments of their own. Pious readers of Milton foresee that only by transcending time can paradise be regained through the intervention and sacrifice of Christ. Sentimental readers of *The Great Gatsby* are cautioned by the story's narrator that Gatsby is deluded, because his life has been haunted by a "meretricious" (Fitzgerald 99) illusion. When he insists that Daisy deny she ever loved her husband, Tom, Gatsby seems at once glamorous, monstrous, and silly. He fancifully reshapes events to his liking, but only through a futile gesture that imposes a corresponding injustice on Tom and Daisy, whom he expects to renounce their shared memories, their own past. He sacrifices others to his obsessive need for an impossible second chance, but if in the novel's final words, we are "borne back ceaselessly into the past" (182), it is into a past, both personal and American, beyond recall.

Earlier I cited Maimonides's caution that God would never change human nature instantaneously, thereby rendering superfluous "the mission of prophets and the giving of the Law" (Maimonides 325). Instead, we must pay for what we have done by enduring "a protracted and burdensome atonement" (365). In order to compensate for the pastness of the past, punitive or corrective justice must devise an arduous process whose physical and moral cost allows us to transcend the irrevocable in ways that satisfy both the ethical and aesthetic demands of justice. Justice should "manifestly and undoubtedly be seen to be done," in Lord Hewart's famous ruling,[1] not only to ensure that it is done fairly, but as part of its public structure and meaning. The "seeing" of justice ensures that it is always a spectacle, even when shrouded in mystery (in which case the mystery intensifies the spectacle), and as such it exerts an aesthetic appeal. All justice is poetic justice, not in Rymer's sense of an ideal apportioning of reward and punishment, but in the sense that its satisfaction derives from the crafting of moral imagination, the only faculty that can restore time. The logic and spectacle of the law should confirm each other, although they need not, but in either case their interplay becomes visible as a temporal current through which we deliberate about the past. As examined here, this intricate symbolic exercise will employ two agents – pain and money – which offer two ways of calculating and paying debts. As Gatsby's fate hints, however, the alliance between legality, morality, and imagination is a risky one, and I now wish to explore how literature displays those risks.

DREAMING BACK

Justice requires a reciprocal accountability between past and future, for instance between a crime and its consequent punishment, whose duration and severity are calculated to atone for the misdeed. The punishment not only follows the crime chronologically, and follows from it logically, but answers to it ethically. By imposing ethical coherence on a sequence of actions the temporality of justice sanctions that sequence through a cumulative design that is rationally ordered, morally effective, and complete. One familiar judicial pattern runs as follows: a malicious intention is enacted as a criminal deed; the perpetrator is apprehended and tried properly before a impartial authority in accordance with just laws; an effective method and period of punishment follow until the debt is repaid and the fault requited. At each stage, an accepted standard of fairness must be maintained in order to propel the process on to the next stage. An error in procedure at any point (for instance, improper collecting of evidence or testifying to it) can nullify the whole sequence. The progression finally circles back symbolically to the beginning: the punishment effaces the crime so that the criminal deserves to be set free. Ideally, according to Hegel, the punishment is already contained in the crime, so that retribution "signifies only the turning back of crime against itself . . . So it is the criminal's own deed which judges itself" (Hegel 100).

Thus the temporality of justice is not linear but symphonic, both retrospective (recuperating the past) and prospective (ensuring the future). It is also redemptive: if the past cannot literally be changed, it can imaginatively be reclaimed for the benefit of society. Such, at least, is the ideal – logical, elegant, satisfying – when viewed at a safe distance from its messy execution. Comedy is the genre that best expresses this ideal by depicting the rectification of error as a triumph of love over injustice. Comedy not only sets things "right," usually by uniting lovers in marriage, but makes the audience feel that they can know what *is* right, and so will be satisfied when it is achieved. The truth of "true love" and the fruitfulness of marriage are offered as adequate responses to faults, wrongs and even death. A fanciful and, for my purposes, revealing evocation of comic justice appears in movies where ghosts and angels permit characters to amend the past by reliving their lives;[2] or where "back to the future" fantasies of time-travel permit characters to fix earlier mistakes so as to alter their consequences for the better. The three *Back to the Future* films (1985, 1989, 1990) directed by Robert Zemeckis play with this form until they lull the audience into overlooking its inherent injustice, the same injustice that Gatsby imposes on Daisy and Tom. After three clumsy attempts, the hero (Marty McFly) reorders the present to his satisfaction and to the dismay of the villain (Biff Tannen), but the effect on other lives is either assumed to be benign or conveniently ignored. The desire motivating these films, and gradually nurtured in the audience, is that things are being ordered as they should be, or as they should have been. The solution assumes a transcendent "rightness," which hints at a benevolent fate behind all the mishaps, and to which characters realign their lives.

Robert M. Cover suggests that law has its own guardian angel. Even as it goes about its everyday business, law acts as a "bridge to the future" (Cover 182) connecting imperfect, present legalities to a vision of justice fulfilled. This vision is expressed in sacred stories and canonical myths, whose aspirations must be restrained by the prudent practicalities of history. According to this dialectic, myth gives purpose to history, while "[h]istory corrects for the scale of heroics that we would otherwise project upon the past. Only myth tells us who we would become; only history tells us how hard it will really be to become that" (190). I propose, however, that we do project heroics upon the past and that we correct history through judicial spectacles, which are always haunted by ghosts and angels. The *Back to the Future* films conflate logic with magic in their sentimental recasting of a mystical pattern that appears most explicitly in W.B. Yeats's fantasy *A Vision*.

In his elaborate charting of the progress of the soul beyond death, Yeats distinguishes a phase called "dreaming back." The second of six stages that the soul passes through in preparation for rebirth, it is followed immediately by "the Return." As the body is buried in the earth, the spirit is forced to review its past life:

In the *Dreaming Back*, the *Spirit* is compelled to live over and over again the events that had most moved it; there can be nothing new, but the old events stand forth in a light which is dim or bright according to the intensity of the passion that accompanied them. They occur in the order of their intensity or luminosity, the more intense first, and the painful are commonly the more intense, and repeat themselves again and again. In the *Return*, upon the other hand, the *Spirit* must live through past events in the order of their occurrence, because it is compelled by the *Celestial Body* to trace every passionate event to its cause until all are related and understood, turned into knowledge, made a part of itself. (Yeats 226)

The past is redeemed first through passion (intensity, luminosity), then through knowledge (causality, relation). Only by reliving the past can the soul master itself and so be worthy of advancing. In the *Back to the Future* films, passion is represented by its impetuous, romantic hero, knowledge by its inspired scientist; both must repeat the past until they get it right. Passion and knowledge are the two main stimulants to imagination in this chapter as well, the first appearing as pain, the second as money or, more precisely, as the ability to negotiate values. Pain and profit are set imaginatively against mortality. By imposing suffering and payment in the correct degree, judicial verdicts establish a redemptive link through time that symbolically redresses past wrongs, or at least offers the satisfying fiction of doing so.

Tragedy configures pain, knowledge, and responsibility differently, and so offers a different kind of satisfaction. In his essay "Guilt and Justice in Shakespeare," David Daiches explores an ethical misalliance whereby "innocence often achieves evil" (Daiches 2). In several Shakespearean tragedies, noble intentions produce nasty results, because the best motives only give a further twist to a spiral of unforeseeable disasters. Action and inaction prove to be equally unavailing, making characters responsible for their lives yet helpless to correct them. "Sin grows with doing good," warns Becket in T.S. Eliot's play *Murder in the Cathedral*, as he faces a similar predicament resolved ultimately by martyrdom, which transcends the brutal, causal sequence. Faced with the temptation to do the wrong deed for the right reason, or the right deed for the wrong reason, Becket determines to do neither, proclaiming: "I shall no longer act or suffer, to the sword's end" (Eliot, *Murder* 53). Unlike Gatsby, who believes that his will is stronger than necessity, Becket abandons his will to the will of God:

> For every life and every act
> Consequence of good and evil can be shown.
> And as in time results of many deeds are blended
> So good and evil in the end become confounded.
> It is not in time that my death shall be known;
> It is out of time that my decision is taken . . .
>
> (79)

Hamlet and Becket want to do the right thing for the right reason to achieve the right result, but through their best efforts, authority over rightness slips from their hands.[3] They are trapped in what Daiches calls a "tragedy of moral frustration" (Daiches 7):

Justice demands appropriate action where a crime has been committed, but in fact *no action is ever appropriate*. The tragedy of *Hamlet*, as in some degree of *Othello*, is that moral outrage as seen by the innocent demands action, when no action can be of any use. (6, Daiches's emphasis)

For Hamlet, no reparation, redress, restitution, or retribution can make up for his father's loss – each word indicating in its prefix a futile desire to undo the past by canceling its errors. No revenge will satisfy him, because it cannot restore his father to life or compensate for the loss of the true King. One life is not commensurate with another, not just because one is more noble, but because each is unique. In a tragedy of moral frustration, justice is impotent to compensate for the singularity of a life whose untimely loss it is supposed to redress. At first, Hamlet assumes that he only has to heed the ghost's command and expose his father's killer for justice to be done. The time is "out of joint" but can be repaired. Instead, he learns that there can be no "fitting" of present to past because ultimately the truth is unavailing. Knowledge, no matter how passionately sought, cannot respond to the absoluteness of death.

Tragedy reveals how the temporality of justice is both driven and baffled by competing desires. Ghosts and angels that grant an impossible second chance in comedy, or impose an unbearable burden in tragedy, represent a command from the past conferring a duty to set things right, a duty that can be discharged only through a fiction that is never quite satisfying. A striking modern example of this clash of desires and duties appears in Thomas Hardy's novel *The Mayor of Casterbridge*. Like Gatsby and Marty McFly, Michael Henchard wants to change the past in order to reclaim the love that he lost. He honestly tries to expiate his drunken crime of selling his wife and daughter, but in Hardy's cruel universe, nothing can redeem the past. Henchard discovers that he can never suffer enough, and at his death he embraces disaster by leaving the following will:

That Elizabeth-Jane Farfrae [his daughter] be not told of my death or made to grieve on account of me.

> & that I be not bury'd in consecrated ground.
> & that no sexton be asked to toll the bell.
> & that nobody is wished to see my dead body.
> & that no murners walk behind me at my funeral.
> & that no flours be planted on my grave.
> & that no man remember me.
> To this I put my name.
> Michael Henchard   (Hardy, *Mayor* 254)

This is both a quasi-legal document and a poem defying legality. Henchard's request to be forgotten ignominiously, which "was respected as far as practicable" (254), is self-defeating, since ignominy, duly enacted in the rituals abjured here, ensures remembrance. It is ironic that he should announce in a document, which has the force of law even if it is unorthodox in form, that he must be forgotten, and then should authenticate this decree by signing the very name that is to be obliterated. In this case the irony is more pathetic than uncanny, but it again registers a disjunction between legal and aesthetic motives, the former seeking justice, the latter rendering it ungraspable.

TORTURE: ELOQUENT PAIN

Justice is done (completed) when it provides forms of redress that are both ethical (fair) and aesthetic (satisfying). Its temporality measures what Paul Ricoeur calls a "just distance" between crime and punishment, and the effect of rehabilitation is progressively to diminish that distance until the past is, so to speak, within reach (Ricoeur, *The Just* 133–4). In practical terms, it offers continuity through a symbolic substitute that compensates for wrongs in the form of payment, embarrassment, imprisonment, or torment. If the punishment is death, a different sense of completion is attained: the criminal "pays" with his life. Even this dead end, however, requires aesthetic confirmation. When the Oklahoma City bomber, Timothy McVeigh, was executed for an attack that killed 168 people, members of his victims' families were permitted to witness the execution on closed-circuit television. This spectacular conclusion offered satisfaction to the families and to the American public, who could read about the execution in precise detail in the press. According to a CNN report, one witness, who held a photograph of her slain daughter, said afterward: "It's a demarcation point . . . It's a period at the end of a sentence. It's the completion of justice and that's what I'll remember about today." Similarly President G.H.W. Bush echoed Hegel (perhaps) when he said that McVeigh "met the fate he chose for himself six years ago . . . Under the laws of our country the matter is concluded."[4] The sense of closure is conveyed by its dramatic enactment, with the photograph of the slain child functioning like the apparition of the ghost in *Hamlet*: it registers a vivid, almost magical accusatory presence at the moment of retribution.

There is something spooky and distressing about this performance. In *Discipline and Punish*, Michel Foucault describes how Western jurisprudence gradually disguised its violent character by retreating behind walls, by shifting its spectacle from execution to trial, and by psychologizing what was previously a matter of fierce public display. The McVeigh execution reverses this process, suggesting that brutal crimes with widespread political importance still require a vivid spectacle to give them significance. If the

punishment must not only fit the crime but provide an intimate, redemptive link to it, then such a horrific offense requires something sharper than
a solemn verdict followed by a discreet execution. Viewed in the theatre,
such a performance would be "just" in the dual sense of being morally apt
and aesthetically pleasing. Viewed in life, however, it is disconcerting. I
hope that I show no disrespect for the victims' families in saying that the
very theatricality of McVeigh's execution makes it suspect. By dramatizing
a political event so publicly, and publicizing it so dramatically, it offers aesthetic satisfaction (a poignant death scene) as adequate response to complex
social problems that cannot be resolved by the death of one criminal. I am
not arguing against the death penalty, which is another fractious issue, but
against the performance, which makes sense only as a form of theatrical
torture.

To put it in perspective, compare the execution in Iran of Mohammad
Bijeh, a serial killer who murdered at least twenty children and was flogged
100 times before being hanged publicly. According to a BBC press release
of March 16, 2005, a "brother of one of his young victims stabbed him as
he was being punished. The mother of another victim was asked to put the
noose around his neck." Finally, the "killer was hoisted about 10 metres
into the air by a crane and slowly throttled to death in front of the baying
crowd." The BBC report explains: "Hanging by a crane – a common form
of execution in Iran – does not involve a swift death as the condemned
prisoner's neck is not broken . . . Spectators, held back by barbed wire and
about 100 police officers, chanted 'harder, harder' as judicial officials took
turns to flog Bijeh's bare back before his hanging."[5] To a tender, Western
sensibility this theatre of cruelty seems gruesome, but it displays explicitly –
and with considerable dramatic flair – what was implicit in the McVeigh
execution: execution is not only a judicial spectacle, but a magical way of
restoring the past. The carefully staged participation of the mothers, one
holding a photograph, the other holding a noose, must have an uncanny
power if it is to make the killings effective. Granted, the standards of
propriety are different in the two cultures, but in each case, because the
murdered children cannot be comforted, their suffering is re-enacted on
the criminal's body, and so given release for the onlookers.

The role of the audience is crucial, because spectacles require spectators.
For the criminal, the agony is intensely present, but for the audience, its
meaning is retrospective and recuperative. Elaine Scarry argues that the
strange virtue of pain is to fill and define the present: to the torture victim,
the present instant is utter agony, disconnected from everything else. As
it occurs, intense pain is an experience only of itself – the hurting hurts.

It is objectless, non-referential, focused in the moment of its occurrence, but this very isolation gives it symbolic force in the temporality of justice. Pain and imagination are complementary: one is pure sensation, the other is pure extension. Scarry then makes a daring inference:

The only state that is as anomalous as pain is the imagination. While pain is a state remarkable for being wholly without objects, the imagination is remarkable for being the only state that is wholly its objects . . . while pain is like seeing or desiring but not like seeing *x* or desiring *y*, the opposite but equally extraordinary characteristic belongs to imagining. It is like the *x* or the *y* that are the objects of vision or desire, but not like the felt-occurrences of seeing and desiring . . . Physical pain, then is an intentional state without an intentional object; imagining is an intentional object without an experienceable intentional state. (Scarry 162–3)

Scarry speculates that through their "peculiar" relationship, pain and imagining may be extremities framing "the whole terrain of the human psyche" (165). I am concerned only to show how the present torment of the criminal symbolically reaches into the past to provide grim satisfaction to the witnesses. Torture as a means of judicial punishment teaches a painful lesson. For centuries, torture was an accepted judicial technique and political instrument; it is becoming so again. Although Scarry insists throughout *The Body in Pain* that torture is "anti-human" (31), she recognizes pain as one of the formative experiences defining our humanity by perversely invigorating our culture. Intense pain is "world-destroying" (29), whereas culture is world-creating, but the latter is inspired by the former. She explores in detail how cultural artefacts, beliefs, and fictions are devised as expressive responses to the inexpressibility of pain. Although she insists that torture is never justifiable, she also shows perversely that it is fascinating because it stimulates imagination and because it plays a central role in cultural semiotics. Because pain marks the intensity of an inescapable present, culture responds with symbolic rituals and narratives through which pain is remembered, anticipated, articulated temporally, and so mastered. The imaginative alarm provoked by pain grants it power to recapture the past imaginatively, but in order to succeed, it must be eloquent.

Since pain itself is not eloquent, it must be poeticized, for instance in the form of tragedy, elegy, or, to admirers of country music, "hurtin' songs." Any meaningful connection between present and past must be symbolic, but symbolism is all the more effective when it hurts. The interfusion of the judicial and aesthetic is easy to overlook amid the decorum of modern courtrooms. By contrast, in eighteenth-century France punishments were designed as "an almost theatrical reproduction of the crime in the execution of the guilty man – with the same instruments, the same gestures. Thus justice had the crime re-enacted before the eyes of all, publishing it in its truth and at the same time annulling it in the death of the guilty man" (Foucault, *Discipline* 45). Foucault cites several examples of how crimes were re-enacted in carefully choreographed torments, so that each punitive act could respond to and annul an earlier fault. The symbolism must be as palpable as possible, F.M. Vermeil explained in an essay from 1781: "In the case of the poisoner, 'the executioner will present him with a goblet the contents of which will be thrown into his face; thus he will be made to feel the horror of his crime by being offered an image of it; he will then be thrown into a cauldron of boiling water'" (quoted by Foucault, *Discipline* 105). The effect of this performance was, in Charles Taylor's words, "to undo the crime at a symbolic level" through a symbolism so excruciating that it takes on "symbolicomagical power" (Taylor 131). Foucault calls this design "a sort of reasonable aesthetic of punishment" (Foucault, *Discipline* 106) because it is scrupulously calculated yet flagrant. Insofar as the McVeigh execution required more fire, it became more theatrical, less reasonable, and more magical, less an exhibition of justice and more one of sacrifice.

PAYMENT: SUBSTITUTE COUNTERFACTUAL

Judicially inflicted pain must seem both eloquent and reasonable if it is to be justified, that is, if it is to articulate an effective link between pain and value. Suffering must be worthwhile. President Bush's response (He "met the fate he chose for himself six years ago . . . Under the laws of our country the matter is concluded") was meant to affirm this link, but his assessment is not convincing. Judicial forms promise closure through small gestures (banging a gavel: this case is closed) and large ones (execution), but something is never quite concluded by these ceremonies, especially in hard cases. Adam's despair that sin is irremediable, Hamlet's anguish that nothing can compensate for his father's loss, Becket's ecstatic vision beyond secular justice – all subvert judicial logic by denying its efficacy. If there is no adequate redress, justice can never be satisfied; if there is no satisfaction, there can be no closure. McVeigh paid with his life, but could he ever pay enough? How can one wicked man's death – even if it were as painful and splendid as Mohammad Bijeh's – requite the obliteration of 168 innocent lives? Even more distressing is the Eichmann trial in Israel, where the prosecutor, Gideon Hauser, insisted that documented facts of the case, shocking as they were, could not convey the horror of the Holocaust. To "do justice to six million tragedies," facts had to be illuminated by survivors' personal testimony: "Put together, the various narratives of different people would be concrete enough to be apprehended. In this way I hoped to superimpose on a phantom a dimension of reality" (quoted by Felman 134). Here, too, the past is made "concrete" by summoning a ghost, but what performance could possibly enact sufficient payment?

To "do justice to six million tragedies": calling each murder in the Holocaust a tragedy illustrates how an aesthetic form is required to articulate a judicial process, but it is also suggests that no form would suffice. No form could encompass six million separate tragedies, in which case there can be no justice. In this horrific instance, aesthetic and judicial values diverge, but their alliance was always tenuous. As we have seen, they cooperate most cozily in comedy, but even then their partnership is menaced by destructive or irrational forces that must be kept at bay. When these forces become overwhelming, as they do when one is assessing the Holocaust, the rhetoric of jurisprudence becomes woefully inadequate and is only subverted further by the rhetoric of tragedy.

The divergence of aesthetic and judicial principles – of poetry and law – is sharpest in tragedy, the genre that loves woe. Tragedy is outrageous as it litters the stage with the corpses of both guilty and innocent parties. With an ecstatic mixture of horror and delight, the audience discovers that the deaths of Ophelia, Desdemona, and Cordelia cannot be compensated by the ruin of guilty characters, because tragedy is not a reasonable aesthetic. It provides a vision of catastrophe, not repayment. According to Shoshana Felman, law is "a discipline of limits and of consciousness" that ensure accountability, whereas tragic art speaks "the language of infinity – to mourn the losses and to face up to what in traumatic memory is not closed and cannot be closed" (107). The verdict at a trial discloses only enough truth to secure a case, but a literary text can reveal what Hamlet discovers: truth is not enough, because "truth [is] an abyss between incommensurable realities, a schism between different ways of seeing, between incommensurable ways of looking at the same facts" (92).[6] Following Daiches's example, I proposed that a tragedy of moral frustration reveals the radical incommensurability of human lives opened by the purity of death. One life is not equivalent to another, because each is irreplaceable. When the scales of justice are used to measure what cannot be measured, the effort is an embarrassment to justice but a source of cathartic pleasure in tragedy.

To avoid this embarrassment, inconvenient truths must be banished from the courtroom by making their banishment part of the performance. Bradin Cormack notes that legal jurisdictions are temporal as well as spatial – they configure power historically – and argues, as I do, that "literature critically opens law onto the complex temporality that is the scene of the law's own jurisdictional activity" (Cormack 17, 30). One form of activity he captures in his neat phrase, the "future elegiac mode" (30) of the law. This is an anticipated disappointment at the inadequacy of legal verdicts, a regret that can be expressed, for example, as a ceremonial apology. Legal judgments often admit their inability to represent what Alan Hyde calls "the sympathetic body" – "the body that is the uniquely differentiated home of a unique human person, the body that is the sole medium through which that person has a world, relates to others" (Hyde 199). On the one hand, because each person is unique, no substitute can replace him or her; on the other hand, justice demands that people be subsumed into common logical, social, and legal categories. Faced with this dilemma, judicial rulings sometimes begin with a ritual confession of powerlessness. For example, in a suit brought by Richard and Mary Ann Rodriguez against Bethlehem Steel for an accidental injury that ruined his health and their marriage, the judicial ruling first concedes that no compensation is really fair:

"Money . . . cannot truly compensate a wife for the destruction of her marriage, but it is the only known means to compensate for the loss suffered and to symbolize society's recognition that a culpable wrong – even if unintentional – has been done." That the law cannot do enough, in short, is an unacceptable excuse for not doing anything at all. (103)[7]

Something is better than nothing, although it will always fall short of a just reckoning. Hyde, who quotes from this judgment, calls the money damages awarded by the court "a substitute counterfactual" (103), a phrase whose cumbersomeness nicely expresses its awkward effort to buy back the past.

Recourse to financial compensation reveals a second imaginative means of negotiating ethically with the past. Far older than modern materialism is the belief that money provides a universal solvent, a medium for equating and exchanging disparate activities. In his account of rectificatory justice, Aristotle notes that money provides for a "proportionate requital" (Aristotle, *Ethics* 118) between unlike things. By measuring the relative demand (price) for all goods and work, it establishes a ratio between things that have no intrinsic connection.

Money, then, acting as a measure, makes goods commensurate and equates them; for neither would there have been association if there were not exchange, nor

exchange if there were not equality, nor equality if there were not commensurability. Now in truth it is impossible that things differing so much should become
commensurate, but with reference to demand they may become sufficiently so.
There must, then, be a unit, and that fixed by agreement (for which reason it is
called money); for it is this that makes all things commensurate, since all things
are measured by money. (120–1)

Money acts as a substitute counterfactual because its value is entirely symbolic, and as a freely adaptable symbol, it can accommodate any object or
activity. Aristotle explains that the Greek word for money (*nomisma*) derives
from the word for law, because its value depends on social convention, not
on intrinsic worth: "it exists not by nature but by law (*nomos*) and it is in
our power to change it and make it useless" (119). Money is worth only what
we agree it is worth, but for this reason, it can also be universally useful. As
practical examples of unlike objects, Aristotle mentions shoes, food, and
houses, whose relative values can be computed in the common currency
of money; but the same symbolic equivalence can be established between
past and future actions, for instance between a crime and its punishment
in the form of a fine. Although the judgment in *Rodriguez* admits that
nothing is commensurate with the harm done to Richard Rodriguez when
a 600-pound pipe fell on his head, sufficient money will offer recompense
in a way that a sincere apology would not.

It is a mystery why money is so powerful. That a scrap of paper or
metal can accomplish so much while having no essential merit of its own
makes money seem magical. Its power arises from the shared belief of those
who credit its value ("credit" also being a financial term), but as Aristotle
indicates, it can be devalued or revalued in an instant. It incites passionate
desire, not for itself but for what it promises to deliver, a desire that it may
or may not satisfy. In this respect it functions symbolically like a ghost.
Both are haunting presences of something strangely absent, either lost in
the past or anticipated in the future. Beside an image of the Queen on the
English five-pound note is the inscription: "I promise to pay the bearer on
demand the sum of five pounds." The note is not itself five pounds, only
a royal promise to deliver it, a promise that presumably will be kept when
the time is ripe. The power of money to redeem errors and accidents works
in a comparable way: it reaches back to ransom the past.

Hegel elaborates on the spectral grasp of money by defining "value"
as an ideal currency that mysteriously flows through and between things,
linking them imaginatively. The phrase "material value" would be an oxymoron for Hegel, because value is the common spiritual ground that makes
unlike things comparable. It is "the inner identity of things specifically

different . . . By it the imagination is transferred from the direct attributes of the object to its universal nature" (Hegel 99–100). Money is only one manifestation of value, although Hegel later calls it "not a special kind of wealth, but the universal element in all kinds" (307). More specifically he is concerned with its ability to establish a rectificatory bond between temporally disparate actions. It provides moral continuity through the logic of retribution: "Retribution is the inner connection and identity of two things which in outward appearance and in external reality are different" (100). Crime and punishment find equivalence not literally or superficially, but "in the inherent nature of the injury, namely, its value" (98), which must be matched by the equivalent value of a fitting punishment. When justice demands compensation for something that cannot be restored, it must establish an "equality in value" expressed in various forms (money, work, time in prison). The exception to this calculus, however, is the worst crime of all – murder. Because life is "the total context of one's existence, and cannot be measured by value" (101), it is inestimable. It is beyond evaluation. Consequently, its punishment cannot be measured by value either, "but must consist in the taking of another life" (101). As Hegel describes it, this punishment sounds justified, but it is not exactly fair, since capital punishment is the attempted alignment of two lives, that is, of two incalculables. If they "cannot be measured by value," then they cannot be equal. For this reason, Timothy McVeigh's execution can never adequately pay for his destroying 168 lives, or even one other life. Even the Rodriguez couple can never be adequately recompensed for their ruined lives.

Still, something must be done, although it strains the resources of moral imagination to envision what eloquent pain (an eternity in hell for Faust) or what transcendent value (martyrdom for Becket, the mystical cycle for Yeats) might succeed.

SACRIFICE

"But past who can recall, or done undo?" A character in Peter Ackroyd's *Hawksmoor* laments that time can be restored only "in the Imagination" (128), but the novel's devious temporality, which superimposes modern and historical London, reveals that literature teaches new ways of imagining. As described above, the temporality of retributive justice redetermines the past imaginatively through passionate knowledge that apportions culpability in order to secure the value of requital and redemption. Through a symbolic drama of deserved pain or repayment it gives aesthetic force to ethical judgments not merely to make justice more vivid, but to make it intelligible, efficacious, and satisfying. The literary examples cited above suggest at least four modes in which moral imagination can be aligned or artfully misaligned with the past:

1. Poetic justice: in Thomas Rymer's sense of a satisfying vision in which justice is both done and seen to be done.
2. Pathetic injustice: a vision like Hardy's in which injustice prevails, but the reader or audience appreciates how unfair fate has been. Justice is seen not to have been done.
3. Moral outrage: a vision of frustration described by Daiches, which leaves the reader in distress, because justice cannot be seen at all.
4. Moral transcendence: a redemptive vision like Becket's, in which no just reckoning suffices, but its failure testifies to a different mode of apprehension.

An easy alliance of aesthetics and ethics is assured only in the first mode, but in the others the lack of assurance may itself be provocative. Literature can relish a spectacle of failure in which the truth does not suffice, but judicial logic cannot, because it requires that something with at least the semblance of fairness must be done, although any "semblance" will require another spectacle. However, in extreme cases of trauma, crimes against humanity and genocide – the crimes of modernity – no retributive economy is adequate and may even seem futile. In such cases where even outrage seems insufficient, judicial discourse either becomes operatic or falls silent. I will examine examples of each.

The most famous stretch of moral imagination, which would revalue the temporality of justice, is offered by Nietzsche, whose prophet, Zarathustra, reaches the same impasse that frustrates Adam, Gatsby, Hamlet, and Henchard. The all-powerful will has one fatal weakness: it cannot will backwards.

To redeem the past and to transform every "It was" into an "I wanted it thus!" – that alone do I call redemption!

Will – that is what the liberator and bringer of joy is called . . . Willing liberates: but what is it that fastens in fetters even the liberator?

"It was": that is what the will's teeth-gnashing and most lonely affliction is called. Powerless against that which has been done, the will is an angry spectator of all things past.

The will cannot will backwards; that it cannot break time and time's desire – that is the will's most lonely affliction. (Nietzsche, *Zarathustra* 160–1)

Hamlet and Becket discover that eventually time always desires death, to which there is no adequate response because, in Daiches's words, "[t]he punishment can never fit the crime, for it can never undo it" (Daiches 7).

Nietzsche's response is not, like Becket's, to renounce the will in favor of a higher, spiritual power. Instead, in *The Genealogy of Morals* he generously affirms a mercy that would rise above the vengeful demand of justice that every misdeed be repaid by a compensating punishment.

> Justice, which began by setting a price on everything and making everyone strictly accountable, ends by blinking at the defaulter and letting him go scot free. Like every good thing on earth, justice ends by suspending itself. The fine name this self-canceling justice has given itself is *mercy*. But mercy remains, as goes without saying, the prerogative of the strongest, his province beyond the law. (Nietzsche, *Birth* 205)

This is not transcendence in Eliot's mystical sense, but it, too, invokes a spiritual nobility that offers to transform judicial temporality. By contrast, Gatsby's futile desire to erase the past seems paltry. We catch the same exalted tone in Jacques Derrida's *Specters of Marx* when he imagines a "quasi-messianic day" beyond vengeance and recompense: "Not for calculable and distributive justice. Not for law, for the calculation of restitution, the economy of vengeance or punishment . . . but for justice as incalculability of the gift and singularity of the an-economic ex-position to others" (Derrida, *Specters* 21, 22–3). The singular gift, in this special sense, asks for no return, and so escapes the economy of symbolic equivalence on which punitive justice is based. Its form is not satisfactory but excessive. According to Ricoeur, pardon "outruns the law" by expressing "not just a suprajuridical but a supra-ethical value." Especially in cases of murder, pardon confounds "the infinite debt, the irreparable wrong" by proposing a "logic of superabundance" that is neither deserved by the criminal nor owed to the victims but that is granted nonetheless: "Pardon is a kind of healing of memory, the end of mourning. Delivered from the weight of debt, memory is freed for great projects. Pardon gives memory a future" (Ricoeur, *The Just* 144).

Here is a third way of willing backward so as to attune time's desire to our own. For Nietzsche, what I have called the ghost of justice is really a vengeful spirit that has infiltrated our very conception of time in order to enforce ethical obligations that we cannot meet, and that will only confirm our impotence. Martin Heidegger explains that for Nietzsche the unappeasable demand for "justice" expresses the will's revulsion against what has vanished beyond recall, a revulsion that arises only because we have trapped ourselves in a temporality that renders the will helplessly self-punishing. Revenge is an embittered response, not against the mere passing of time, but against a specific temporal order that insists on the value of the present only in relation to a lost past: "The revulsion turns not against the mere passing, but against that passing away which allows what has passed to be only in the past, which lets it freeze in the finality of this *rigor mortis*" (Heidegger 103). Retributive justice confounds itself through an alliance with death that cannot be revoked by any spectacle of impartial, rational judgment. The spectacle will merely confirm the same self-defeating logic. Deliverance from revenge depends not on seeking comfort in hateful conditions (an eye for an eye, a life for a life) and not on liberation from all will (which "would lead to nothingness" – 104), but on reconceiving time in a way that reconciles the desires of past and present.

The will becomes free from its revulsion against time, against time's mere past, when it steadily wills the going and coming, this going and coming back, of everything. The will becomes free from what is revolting in the "It was" when it wills the constant recurrence of every "It was."... As the will of the eternal recurrence of the same, the will can will in reverse. (104–5)

Or in Zarathustra's words: "To redeem the past and to transform every 'It was' into an 'I wanted it thus!' – that alone do I call redemption!" (Nietzsche, *Zarathustra* 160).

Achieving such redemption will require a special kind of magnanimity and sacrifice, which I will examine in two examples, one that I find unconvincing, and one that I find challenging.

Transcending the symbolism of judicial pain and payment is the subject of Jean Baudrillard's *Symbolic Exchange and Death*, which argues that "symbolic exchange," the economic principle that once governed "primitive" social relations, has been displaced by a modern "code" or "law of value." The former operates in the courtesies and rivalries of "the gift," a cultural ritual that imposed complex, reciprocal obligations on individuals and communities; the latter controls the market of modern commodities and their postmodern simulations. The code gradually invades all human judgments, until everything becomes exchangeable for something else or, in Baudrillard's hypermodern view, for the illusion of something else. This is a familiar Marxist notion: exchange value becomes the measure of all values. Nevertheless, according to his oracular analysis, the ghost of symbolic exchange continues to haunt modern discourses, especially the judicial system, and it emerges – here he displays a fine sense of poetic justice – just when they claim to attain "perfect operativity," that is, when they aspire to total mastery (Baudrillard 4). This not a case of the return of the repressed, he claims, because Freud's rule does not escape the law of value. It is something more catastrophic provoked by the threat of death felt as an absurd disruption, or a disruptive absurdity, that the law of value cannot compute. Because nothing is equal to a human life, "death and death alone, the reversibility of death, belongs to a higher order than the code. Only symbolic disorder can bring about an interruption in the code" (4). What distinguishes the law of value from symbolic exchange is that the former is irreversible, whereas the latter exhibits "meticulous reversibility" even with regard to death:

> Everywhere, in every domain, a single form predominates: reversibility, cyclical reversal and annulment put an end to the linearity of time, language, economic exchange, accumulation and power. Hence the reversibility of the gift in the countergift, the reversibility of exchange in the sacrifice, the reversibility of time in the cycle, the reversibility of production in destruction, the reversibility of life in death, and the reversibility of every term and value of the *langue* in the anagram. (2)

This is Baudrillard's version of dreaming back. What's undone can be redone, because once upon a time people could negotiate successfully with the dead. For them, time is reversible and the past can be reclaimed because their ghosts are "real" (that is, primitive symbolism and ritual effectively made ghosts real), whereas for modern consciousness, ghosts are merely quaint fictions (our symbolism makes them quaint).[8] Bradley Butterfield explains this distinction further:

> According to Baudrillard, the dead in primitive societies played integral roles in the lives of the living by serving as partners in symbolic exchange. A gift to the dead was believed to yield a return, and by exchanging with the dead through ritual sacrifices, celebrations and feasts, they managed to absorb the rupturing energy of death back into the group... Modern Western cultures have largely ceased to exchange with the dead collectively, partly because we no longer believe in their continued existence, and partly because we no longer value that which cannot be accumulated or consumed. The dead have no value by our measurements. (Butterfield)

It is hard to know if Baudrillard is writing anthropology or a postmodern variant of the modernist fable of lost authenticity. In any case, he dares us to imagine a kind of restitution that justice cannot provide but must instead be envisioned as sacrifice and amnesty. Justice, with its principles of balance, equity, and rightness, depends on the law of value; whereas sacrifice demands excess – a prodigal offering of oneself on behalf of others – not because the others deserve it, or have earned it, but because only by transcending the rationality of justice can the past be redeemed. Sacrifice, "the violent artifice of death" (Baudrillard 165), engages a dramatic symbolism that makes transcendence credible by proposing "a beyond of value, a beyond of the law" (1). Like justice, sacrifice is enacted through pain and payment, but the pain is absorbed into oneself in order to free others, not imposed on others to satisfy some abstract system of accountability. Henchard illustrates the former, Gatsby the latter.

In effect if not intent, Baudrillard follows Becket, who abandons his own desire by making a gift of himself to higher powers, and by so doing brings those higher powers into existence, that is, makes them symbolically accessible. Instead of mystical transcendence, however, Baudrillard invokes the transgressive force of secular acts such as suicide, auto accidents, and hostage taking. More recently in a controversial article after the 9/11 attacks, he considers terrorism, which his own theory seems to welcome if not recommend as the most spectacular postmodern catastrophe. His response to the horror is not to punish the attackers, since no punishment could suffice, but to humble them by out-martyring them. He wants to transcend the absoluteness of death by opposing a counter-absolute of his own through the "irruption of a more-than-real death: symbolic and sacrificial death – the absolute, no appeal event."[9] Presumably, this will meet Nietzsche's challenge that justice should not try to redeem the past through a futile attempt to will backward, but rather should dare to transcend itself. Instead of evaluating everything, and so devising a way to punish everything, justice should find the courage to suspend itself in the name of mercy.[10]

All of the acts that inspire Baudrillard are spectacular, because they are meant to impress an audience. The paradox of martyrdom is that it is an utterly solitary act – there is nothing so private as one's own death – yet it must be observed: one sacrifices oneself not just on behalf of others, but for their horrified admiration. While the 9/11 suicide attackers may have seen themselves as martyrs, they did not absorb the pain ecstatically or tragically into themselves, like Becket or like Henchard, whose legal will addresses an audience. They diffused it as widely and randomly as possible, unlike the monk in Vietnam who set himself on fire to protest against the government's treatment of Buddhists.[11] Baudrillard's operatic style – "In this vertiginous cycle of the impossible exchange of death, the terrorist death is an infinitesimal point that provokes a gigantic aspiration, void and convection"[12] – reveals his own desire to aestheticize politics. It suggests that his vision of the postmodern sublime may be a mirror image of the McVeigh execution, striving to express through its very extravagance the futility of conventional justice.

My second example, from J.M. Coetzee's novel *Disgrace*, seeks moral repair through silence and restraint. I take the phrase "moral repair" from

Margaret Urban Walker's discussion of the Truth and Reconciliation Commission in South Africa, which was convened to confront the crimes committed under apartheid (Walker 115). Its mandate was not to achieve justice
in the sense of disclosing "the whole truth" and then imposing a proportionate response to it. On the contrary, it was an exercise in repair rather
than reparation, conducted in a way that the conventional judicial system
does not allow. The validity and success of the commission have been disputed widely, especially because from a legal point of view its procedures
were irregular, their idiom too religious, their appeal too aesthetic, and
because they allowed the guilty to go unpunished.[13] According to Walker,
however, through this appeal they reveal that in extreme circumstances

> different kinds of justice delimit each other, and that justice alone in any form is
> not enough. Justice alone – retributive or otherwise – is not adequate to nourish
> all the trust and hope that moral repair needs to create or restore. Beyond truth
> and justice, the TRC clearly aims to heal and to inspire, to uplift participants and
> observers and reconnect its citizens in the plane of equal dignity. (Walker 119)

As I understand her, she is not proposing a soothing rhetoric of moral
uplift to compensate for past horrors. The commission did not pretend to
redeem the past, only to confront it. Justice is neither done nor seen to be
done; indeed, its inadequacy is continually re-enacted through the testimony of torture and murder. What is seen, however, is a public spectacle
of confrontation and consolation: confrontation acknowledges irremediable suffering; consolation tries to move on nevertheless. The commission
challenges rather than soothes. If there is something that transcends truth
and justice, then the participants must take the risk of relinquishing their
demand for satisfaction. It must therefore be seen as a companion to the
tragic vision of moral outrage, which it does not correct or nullify but
merely complements in uneasy partnership.

Just how uneasy this partnership is appears in Coetzee's *Disgrace*, another
ghost story that provokes outrage but also aspires to something beyond
justice.[14] It deserves detailed analysis, but I will merely sketch the way
it displaces authority over "rightness" until readers are forced to imagine
what might lie beyond it. The story presents two rapes, to which there are
radically different responses, one operatic, the other silent.

David Lurie, a middle-aged, South African professor of English,
believes – as only an academic could – that his affair with a young student,
Melanie Isaacs, was a matter of mutual attraction and impulsive, Dionysian
"rights of desire," although he admits that his advances were unwelcome:
"Not rape, not quite that, but undesired nevertheless, undesired to the

core" (Coetzee, *Disgrace* 89, 25). Even as he accepts disgrace and dismissal, he calls himself "a servant of Eros" and regards his guilty plea before a "secular tribunal" as an empty ritual, whereas true repentance "belongs to another world, to another universe of discourse" (52, 58). After he takes refuge in an Eastern Cape farm with his daughter Lucy, he gets a shocking view of this other universe of desire when she is brutally assaulted by three Africans, while he is set on fire. Coetzee avoids imposing a moral temporality on his plot, so that while there are many parallel events, they are not equivalences. For example, Lurie's burns are not punishment for his crime. Readers must resist the temptation to interpret his pain as fitting retribution, just as Lurie had scorned the ineffectual symbolism of his tribunal. Of the two crimes, his seems the less heinous, but he later feels obliged to perform a dramatic act of contrition to Melanie's parents:

> With careful ceremony he gets to his knees and touches his forehead to the floor.
>   Is that enough? he thinks. Will that do? If not, what more? (173)

How much is enough to redeem the past? This question applies to the far more problematic history of apartheid. There is no obvious answer. Lurie's penitence is theatrical, but we already know about his love of opera (in another parallel, he is composing an opera based on Byron's illicit love affair with the young Teresa Guccioli), so that his performance is undermined by its very flamboyance. It may be partly sincere, but it is also staged by Lurie to cast himself in an abject but heroic role, even as he admits a "current of desire" for the younger sister, Desirée. Whatever his motives, why should his having the right feelings make a difference? Do we redeem the past merely by adopting an appropriate attitude to it? Lurie's gesture is both authentic and inauthentic, sincere and hypocritical, just and unjust.

By contrast, Lucy barely speaks about her trauma. Because the narrative avoids her point of view, she is an enigma, her silence evoking something other than outrage.[15] She refuses to describe the attack, which the novel does not record, and makes no effort to contact the police or punish her attackers. It may seem reasonable to prosecute them, if only to prevent them from doing further harm, but Lucy's reticence invites us to respect her unexpressed motives. No longer a romantic rebel, Lurie demands the conventional justice that he earlier scorned, but her silence suggests that it would be unavailing. There is no way to set things right because, while there are obvious wrongs, there is no discernible right path to follow, no way to rectify either the singular injury to Lucy's body and spirit or the historical trauma of apartheid. The many discourses through which rightness might be articulated (legal, historical, aesthetic, mythical, erotic) have all been explored and found inadequate. They suffer what Pamela Cooper calls a "representational breakdown, where familiar forms of language collapse and new figurations hover" (Cooper 26). *Disgrace* therefore shows the urgent need for moral repair, but leaves us puzzled as to how to figure it. Lucy, now pregnant, wants to find a viable place for herself in the new South Africa by becoming the third wife of Petrus, the African who tended her dogs and is related to the rapists. If we choose to see her emblematically as a sacrificial victim expiating the sins of white South Africans, then this equivalence too is broken, because Coetzee disrupts the judicial link between pain and value. Suffering afflicts everyone in this story, but it is not redemptive. Suffering today cannot heal the suffering of yesterday; we have seen how atrocious this logic is, because it merely perpetuates suffering.

The novel ends with an image of sacrifice, but instead of being transcendent, it is displaced downward onto the stray dogs that Lurie helps to kill mercifully and for which, with helpless tenderness, he finally feels love. My objection to Baudrillard was that he seems to love spectacle more than he loves people; one might also object that Lurie learns to love animals more than he loves people. But there is a difference and, Coetzee implies, perhaps this is a start.

CHAPTER 4

One touch of nature
Literature and natural law

> to the natural law belongs those things to which a man is inclined
> naturally: and among these it is proper to man to be inclined to act
> according to reason.
>
> (St. Thomas Aquinas, *Summa theologica*, 2.1, question 94[1])

> Between law and action there always is a space to be filled by decisions
> which cannot be written into law.
>
> (Yves Simon, *The Tradition of Natural Law* 83)

Any theory of justice must draw on basic assumptions about nature and
human nature. These assumptions will be historically and culturally vari-
able, and they may be regarded as guaranteed by God, imposed by fixed
biological imperative, or conjured up by shifting ideological motives; but
in any case, there must be some working model of human needs, desires,
powers, virtues, and frailties in order to formulate an authoritative system to
judge and regulate conduct. Similarly, any literary theory must presuppose
some commonly held view of human nature in relation to the natural world
that sustains it. There is no literature without convention, no convention
without consensus, no consensus without community, however fractious,
and no community without justice. The interaction of justice and literature
therefore becomes salient if we consider their common ground in "nature,"
a word that we must treat cautiously but cannot escape. This chapter uses
natural law for that purpose.

Natural law has a long and chequered history from Stoic philosophy,
to Roman law, Thomistic theology, and early modern efforts to define
"nature" in relation to a polity that seeks moral direction from a natural
order.[2] Although repudiated as unnecessary or unhelpful by advocates of
positive law,[3] in literature it has never lost the allure bequeathed by romantic
theory, which seeks the blessing of nature in order to permit people to flourish within a just community. In *Émile*, for example, Jean-Jacques Rousseau
proposes as "an incontrovertible rule that the first impulses of nature are

always right; there is no original sin in the human heart" (Rousseau 56). Perversity is plentiful in human affairs, but it is rooted elsewhere and can be corrected by justice and goodness, which are "true affections of the heart enlightened by reason, the natural outcome of our primitive affections" (196). I wish to examine how several literary texts display the allure of natural law by tracing a path from legality back to the underlying, primitive affections that stimulate the moral imagination. As in earlier chapters, I understand "law" in its broadest sense to comprise any rule-bound behavior, whether as legal statutes, moral precepts, social conventions, or literary forms. Literature offers a vibrant, artistic jurisdiction for testing the conditions of natural law, satisfying them in some forms, contesting them in others. Literary forms often call on natural law for moral guidance and restitution, but they may also open a problematic gap between nature and law, energy, and form.

In order to establish terms for discussion, I begin with the touch of nature in the lowly form of an itch.

ITCH AND URGE

At the beginning of *Adventures of Huckleberry Finn* when Huck is being "sivilized" by the Widow Douglas, he dutifully submits to her well-meaning but "dismal regular and decent" rules governing punctuality, table manners, and Bible teaching, until his skin starts to itch.

Seemed like I'd die if I couldn't scratch. Well, I've noticed that thing plenty of times since. If you are with the quality, or at a funeral, or trying to go to sleep when you ain't sleepy – if you are anywheres where it won't do for you to scratch, why you will itch all over in upwards of a thousand places. (Twain 42–3)

Lured by the call of an owl, Huck throws off his scratchy clothes, gets into his "old rags," and "lit out" for the woods and the river. Like Piglet in *Winnie-the-Pooh*, he needs a good roll in the dirt to cure him of the baleful effects of his bath (Milne 109). In Huck's case bathing is associated not just with unnatural hygiene, but with the civilizing effect of women, of domesticity, and of social regulation in general, which threatens to stifle a more compelling and rewarding natural order. Both compulsion and reward – the glorious discovery that one can be compelled to be happy – are features of natural justice at its most optimistic, although it has darker moods as well. When Huck's skin itches, it speaks not just of its needs or frailties, but of an authenticity that civilization, even with the best of intentions, denies.

Huck's itch introduces a familiar romantic opposition between authentic nature and inauthentic culture, an attractive but naive and even dangerous polarity that Mark Twain seems to celebrate but finally views skeptically. Peter C. Myers argues that despite its enticing depiction of life on the Mississippi, the novel disrupts "a simple opposition between a repressive, alienating realm of convention and a natural realm of goodness and simplicity," because it refuses "to bring our governing conventions into conformity with the principles immanent in the natural condition" (Myers 558). Twain invokes but gradually disputes the primary assumption of natural law that the social order finds a sanction in the rationality of the natural order. More ingrained than any sustaining order is an irrationality that cannot be legislated: "Humankind, in Twain's observation, tends naturally to gravitate to the extreme poles of anarchy and submissiveness, at best displaying only the potential for rational liberty" (558).[4] However, Myers's use of the word "naturally" illustrates that even when nature proves to be untrustworthy, we cannot resist appealing to it for clarity; even to speak of human "flourishing" (flowering) is to invoke a natural model. Huck's itch is telling us something important, if ambiguous. It is one of many literary expressions in which the body abruptly speaks in its own tongue, often to protest against a stifling propriety or false rule. Perhaps the most famous example is Pinocchio's nose, which grows whenever he tells a lie and so signals the truth, or at least its absence. Similarly, an anonymous internet commentator reports that "in Hungry [*sic*], God's confirmation that a statement someone is making is true is often based on the person's sneezing after making the statement."[5] If sneezing vouches for truth, then perhaps we should reinterpret the lexicon of body language, as Leibniz sardonically observes by quoting (or misquoting) Suetonius' report that the Emperor Claudius proposed an edict whereby "in a free state the passing of wind and belching should be free" (Leibniz 47).[6]

Jane Austen's gracious world is more restrained, yet even its etiquette is shattered by a cough in *Pride and Prejudice*.

> "Don't keep coughing so, Kitty, for heaven's sake! Have a little compassion on my nerves. You tear them to pieces."
> "Kitty has no discretion in her coughs," said her father; "she times them ill."
> "I do not cough for my own amusement," replied Kitty fretfully. (Austen 4)

Not every literary twitch or eructation conveys a moral judgment, of course, but the spontaneous intrusion of nature into culture through the physiological reflex of an itch, cough, sneeze, or fart is often comical, sometimes ennobling (Piglet), and sometimes horrifying, as in science

fiction movies where bodies mutate grotesquely. Prickly skin may just signal danger, for instance in *Beloved* when Sethe feels her scalp itch fiercely
in response to the slave-owner (Schoolteacher) listing her "animal characteristics" (Morrison 193), a phrase she does not understand but whose
affront she senses. I am more interested in moments when the body suddenly proclaims its needs, marking an instant when choices must be made
or – as Huck and Pinocchio discover – seem to have already been made
somatically. "Man is the Only Animal that Blushes. Or needs to," quips
Twain,[7] implying that moral sentiments can begin in the flesh. In response
to such earthy intrusions, propriety reasserts itself through rituals of apology, embarrassment, or decorum: *Gesundheit*, Pardon me, Bless you. These
responses invoke an accord with nature (health) that promises a social benefit (pardon, sociability, social health) or a supernatural reward (blessing).
Harmonizing these natural, social, and transcendent conditions is a reward
promised in literature, especially in genres that summon natural law as a
means of resolution, but as I will show, their harmony is not assured, and
may be ironically or tragically disrupted.

All three levels are ironically conflated in Malcolm Lowry's *Under the
Volcano*, when the dissolute Consul, Geoffrey Firmin, apologizes after
discovering that his fly is open: "looking down the Consul discovered
his open fly. *Licentia vatum* indeed! 'Pardon me, j'adoube,' he said, and
making the adjustment continued, laughing, returning to his first theme
mysteriously unabashed by his recusancy" (Lowry 137). The signals here
are absurdly mixed. The embarrassment of an unzipped fly reminds us of
the prohibition against exposing or touching parts of our bodies in public,
but Firmin is not really embarrassed. His excessive display of *politesse*
overcompensates for the lapse first by claiming the divine inspiration of
poetic license for an unpoetic act, and then by evoking a formula from the
elegant game of chess. The expression "j'adoube" ("I adjust" or "I arrange"
in French) must be pronounced before a player touches a piece so as not to
be required to move it.[8] Firmin does not touch his piece, but his display of
good form is really a sly expression of indifference, as is the pedantic term
"recusancy." Although he pretends to be a recusant rather than a slob, his
attentiveness to social niceties really expresses his scorn for them, a scorn
that he increasingly directs at himself in his quest, not for blessing but for
damnation.

Firmin, Huck, and the Bennett sisters in *Pride and Prejudice* illustrate
both the virtues and dangers of natural spontaneity by, in different ways,
indulging primitive affections that both elicit and defy the rule of law.
Huck's escape to the river is associated with lush emotion, sensuality,

unfettered freedom, and superstition; these are precisely the energies that law is designed to control or to redirect to profitable ends. Huck associates the law with prohibition, whereas nature encourages him to indulge his wonder and pleasure as expressed in the sublimity of the American landscape during a thunderstorm (Twain 75) and the generosity of the Mississippi, which yields a six-foot catfish for dinner (102). Society is concerned with property (land, money, slaves) and propriety, whereas nature alleviates concern by washing up whatever Huck and Jim need. The law is about control through exclusion: it divides proper from improper, permitted from forbidden, adult from child, one race from another. Nature is promiscuous: it is about inclusion through a fertile mixing. Huck prefers things when they are blended together like a stew: "In a barrel of odds and ends it is different; things get mixed up, and the juice kind of swaps around, and the things get better" (38). Elizabeth Bennett is no Piglet, but when natural affection drives her to help her sick sister, Jane, she tramps through the mud to the dismay of the Bingley sisters but to their brother's admiration:

"To walk three miles, or four miles, or five miles, or whatever it is, above her ankles in dirt, and alone, quite alone! what could she mean by it? It seems to me to shew an abominable sort of conceited independence, a most country-town indifference to decorum."

"It shews an affection for her sister that is very pleasing," said Bingley. (Austen 30–1)

In Austen's world, it is important to know exactly when and how to break the rules, but it is dangerous to ignore them by yielding too readily to instinct. Excessive scrupulousness is an unsociable display of "cold civility" (36), but excessive spontaneity, as in Lydia's case, is a disaster. Lydia has "high animal spirits, and a sort of natural self-consequence" (39) – a decorous way of talking about sexuality – which lead her astray when she elopes with Lieutenant Wickham in a selfish act that threatens her entire family.

A comparable danger arises in *Huckleberry Finn* through Huck's father, Pap, who like his son is a man of instinct. He, too, lives in response to his body's urges, but in his case they are depicted as disgusting rather than enchanting:

There warn't no color in his face, where his face showed; it was white; not like another man's white, but a white to make a body sick, a white to make a body's flesh crawl – a tree-toad white, a fish-belly white. As for his clothes – just rags, that was all. (Twain 59)

When do rags signify carefree independence and when are they repulsive? Pap shows no respect for the law except when he manipulates it to gain authority over Huck and his money. Ironically, the judge to whom Pap appeals refuses to interfere with the natural bond of kinship by breaking up a family, and so consigns the boy to the brutality of his father (62). If nature asserts itself through both Huck and Pap, but to drastically different effect, then their kinship poses a problem that the novel is never obliged to address or to redress: what will happen to Huck when he grows up? He seems to be caught in American literature like Peter Pan, fixed in ageless youth. Could he turn into his father?

Huck, Piglet, and Lizzy are all romantics who trust in feeling. Following Wordsworth's advice in "Tintern Abbey," they are loyal to elemental urges that inspire moral wisdom "[f]elt in the blood, and felt along the heart; / And passing even into my purer mind" (Wordsworth 97). But how does one pass safely from heart to mind, and does the motive to do so lie in the pure mind or the impure body? The problem for Huck and Lizzy, if not for the pig, is how to link heart to mind so that neither betrays itself by serving the other. In its own small way, then, Huck's itch expands into adventures that illustrate how nature inspires law yet cannot submit to its regulation, while law arises from natural inclinations that it cannot trust. Literary itches, coughs, and belches announce the lowest common denominator of humanity, the "one touch of nature [that] makes the whole world kin" according to Shakespeare's Ulysses in *Troilus and Cressida* (3.3.184). Insofar as natural law is signaled by a touch or itch, its call is direct, sensory, compelling; insofar as it makes us all kin, it is sociable and just (or unjust; that is, it provides a structure whereby just and unjust can be distinguished). When the touch of nature stimulates sociability, it becomes tactful, but what ensures that it will not be tactless? The cynical Thersites expresses the same danger in *Troilus and Cressida* that Pap displays in *Huckleberry Finn*, and that Lowry's recusant Consul mocks in *Under the Volcano*. He reminds us that promiscuous touching can be degrading as well as ennobling: "How the devil Luxury, with his fat rump and / potato-finger, tickles these together! Fry, lechery, fry!" (5.2.68–9).

TOUCH AND TACT

To my question, does the motive of natural law lie in the mind or body? Immanuel Kant answers emphatically: it lies only in the purity of a "good will." He insists that native inclinations or affections may govern personal motivation (maxims) but cannot provide a necessary or sufficient basis for general moral precepts, which must be grounded in the rationality of law as compelled by duty (Kant, *Groundwork* 60–1). One may be inclined to do the right thing, perhaps even urged by an itch, but inclination is not enough. One gets the impression that Kant prefers duties to be painful so that they will not be performed too easily or for the wrong reason. "True moral worth" is exhibited not when one acts "in conformity with duty," but when one acts "from duty" (59), so that even the general rule to secure one's own happiness does not sound like much fun, because it, too, takes its motive "not from inclination but from duty" (61).

> Now an action done from duty must wholly exclude the influence of inclination, and with it every object of the will, so that nothing remains which can determine the will except objectively the *law*, and subjectively *pure respect* for this practical law, and consequently the maxim that I should follow this law even to the thwarting of all my inclinations. (62)

Huck finds duties painful, but his inclinations instruct him with a certainty that reason cannot. Whereas Kant dismisses any faith in empirical principle, human nature or moral sentiment as a basis for moral laws ("it is indeed superficial when those who cannot *think* believe that *feeling* will help them out" [100]), *Huckleberry Finn* offers the hope that inclination and duty might be effortlessly in accord. This hope wanes as the novel proceeds, but that it is raised at all is possible only because Huck has something special to help him out: readers. The role of the reader, who is sympathetic to Huck's plight yet prudently detached from it, is crucial in explaining the novel's appeal to natural law and its promise, only partially successful, to harmonize feeling with duty. I do not mean that the novel fails; on the contrary, its problematic appeal to nature is carefully calculated, first to enchant and then to distress the reader. I will consider its distress in the next section. First I wish to explore why for Huck, the natural choice is bound to be the right one, but only as long as the laws of comedy align touch with tact, and only if the reader remains prudent.

Appeals to natural law arise from the worry that laws can be unjust and require some ethical sanction beyond the artifice of legality, a sanction that must be both natural and rational if it is to be firmly grounded yet practicable. Law cannot legitimate itself, since to legitimate is simply to invoke the authority of another law or social convention. Appeals to natural law always claim authority at some higher level of generality by moving beyond specificities of time and place (positive law) in search of a permanent foundation for justice in procedural fairness,[9] in rationality, in human nature, in the world at large, or in divine will. Thus Aristotle urges that equity represents "a higher order of justice," which is "permanent and unchanging, and the universal law likewise – for it is the law of nature; whereas the written laws are subject to frequent change" (Aristotle, *Rhetoric* 80). Unfortunately, principles of justice are permanent only because they are so abstract that they offer little guidance on how to treat specific cases, especially ambiguous or unforeseen ones. General rules are always shadowed by what H.L.A. Hart calls a "penumbra of doubt," a "fringe of vagueness or open texture" that is the inevitable cost of adapting indeterminate language to changing circumstances (Hart 123, 128). The beauty of Huck's itch and Pinocchio's nose is that they overcome this difficulty by instinctively signaling deviations from the norm, provoking action, and pointing characters in the right direction: follow your conscience by following your nose. Literature always grants symbolic power to mundane experiences, often pushing them into comedy or fantasy. The effect of this imaginative push is to reconcile the natural and rational aspects of natural law, to turn a bodily reflex into a blessing. But itch and nose also expose the difficulty of accomplishing practically what they do effortlessly. By playfully bridging a gap between two worlds, they remind us that such a gap exists. Natural laws are abstract truths, yet are felt intimately in the blood. They are general, yet somehow strike us with the urgency of immediate sensation. They are timeless, yet mark the pressure of the present moment felt in the body.

Natural law must link two worlds, whether the gap between them separates *physis* (nature) and *nomos* (law), inclination and duty, fact and norm, or power and authority.[10] Observing this gap, Yves Simon finds a dilemma that besets, though it need not stifle, the rationality of law:

The individual case with which practical judgment ultimately has to deal may always be in some significant respect unique, unprecedented, and unrenewable. Thus, the last conclusion of the practical discourse [i.e. judging specific cases fairly] is marked in essential fashion by features of strict singularity and of contingency. These features contradict in several ways the already established characteristics of law. In fact, a practical judgment fully adjusted to the circumstances is not so much the work of the reason as that of an inclination. It cannot be connected logically with any first principle . . . Between law and action there always is a space to be filled by decisions which cannot be written into law. (Simon 82–3)

Critiques of natural law propose different ways to fill the cognitive space between law and action or, as I have called them, tact and touch. At one extreme, according to Jean Porter, is the scholastic view to which natural law theory is indebted. It finds no real disjunction, because social norms stem from human nature, whose impulses are consonant with God's creation, as long as they are supervised prudently (Porter 19). Medieval theologians regarded natural law not as a set of specific moral rules but more generally as an intrinsic "capacity or power to distinguish between good and evil" (13), a faculty of "moral discernment" (16) that must be expressed through moral precepts and then codified as law (40). Through this productive sequence, facts and values are providentially intertwined so that by following our inclinations we fulfill both our needs and our duties: "reason shapes our prerational inclinations into determinate social practices and institutions, through which natural aims and exigencies can be pursued" (72). They must be pursued through prudence, which is a virtuous habit distinguished from reason in that it commands particular actions rather than general truths; it is "right reason about things to be done" (Aquinas, 2.1, question 94).[11]

The gap between touch and tact is bridged in the passage from Aquinas cited in the epigraph of this chapter by treating rationality as a human inclination: "to the natural law belongs those things to which a man is inclined naturally: and among these it is proper to man to be inclined to act according to reason." This implies, I assume, that other inclinations "proper to man" must be resisted through the same rational exercise. In either case, a suitable exercise is necessary to follow one's inclination, an effort expressed in Aquinas's Latin phrase "per industrium rationis inventum," which Terry Hall translates as "a rationally guided reflection" (Hall 140). Perhaps this is why literary evocations of natural justice often take the symbolic shape of a journey or an immersion – to the woods or river, into the mud or water. The effort required reveals that the compelling truth of natural law is not apprehended instantly. As David F. Forte explains, natural laws are recognized not "as a set of values that comes to us intuitively," but only after due consideration, because "a self-evident truth is one in which a value (knowledge, for example) is seen, upon reflection, as self-evidently good – a good that is not instrumental, not merely a means to some other thing, but something that is good in itself" (Forte 6).

Inspired by Aquinas, Simon offers prudence as the faculty bridging the gap between principle and practice because, Janus-like, it combines insight (awareness of principles) with foresight (a practical sense of outcomes).[12] Especially revealing for my purposes is the way Paul Ricoeur sets a pruden-tial limit on provocative impulses by tracing a trajectory from an anterior to a posterior ethic, "the anterior ethic pointing to the rootedness of norms in life and desire [inclinations, touch], the posterior ones aimed at inserting norms into concrete situations [devising and applying laws, tact]" (Ricoeur, *Reflections* 46). He seeks to "stitch" the natural to the social with the thread of "moral sentiments" such as shame, modesty admiration, veneration, and indignation. He means "stitch" in the sense of sewing, but I would like to recall the painful jab signified by the English word, a connotation that keeps the sensory urgency of Huck's itch in view. In fact, Ricoeur acknowledges this physicality by stating that moral sentiments are a "vast affective domain irreducible to pleasure and pain" but impelled by the urgency that pleasure and pain impart, allowing sentiments to stitch "norms and moral obligation" to the "desire" that motivates them (49). If the sentiments were mere sensations, they would have no ethical cast; if they were mere precepts, they would have no sensory push. This is his more philosophical way of reconciling touch and tact. Mark Twain's remark about man as the only blushing animal epigrammatically captures the process: blushing spontaneously proclaims a moral sentiment, as if our body involuntarily passes judgment before our good will has a chance to assert itself.

Bridging the gap between touch and tact is precisely the effect of poetic perception, an effect that I have associated with Flaubert's *mot juste*, and Pope's wit: "*Something* whose Truth convinc'd at Sight we find" (Pope 153). Wallace Stevens illustrates the same fusion of sight and insight in the final couplet of "Man Carrying Thing," where a rational ordeal yields startling certainty, a revelation achieved beautifully by Stevens's own imagery:

> We must endure our thoughts all night, until
> The bright obvious stands motionless in cold.
> (Stevens, *Palm* 281)

Huckleberry Finn dramatizes this dual process in a poignant scene where the reader's aesthetic pleasure enhances, and is enhanced by, Huck's moral revelation. I mean the famous episode where Huck argues with his conscience, which, he thinks, obliges him to return Jim to slavery, whereas his heart tells him otherwise. Ironically, his intellectual ordeal hampers, rather than aids, his moral discovery. After he has written a note to Miss Watson revealing Jim's whereabouts, he reports: "I felt good and all washed clean of sin for the first time I had ever felt so in my life, and I knowed I could pray now. But I didn't do it straight off, but laid the paper down and set there thinking" (Twain 271). Huck's thoughts take two forms: citing the law concerning property, since Jim belongs to Miss Watson; and recalling the pleasure and love he enjoyed with Jim, in which the reader has delighted. In contrast to the abstract principle, his memories convey a tactile immediacy:

I'd see him standing my watch on top of his'n, 'stead of calling me, so I could go on sleeping; and see him how glad he was when I come back out of the fog; and when I come to him again in the swamp, up there where the feud was; and such-like times; and would always call me honey, and pet me and do everything he could think of for me, and how good he always was . . . (271)

The instant of decision is again marked by a bodily tremor:

I took it [the note] up, and held it in my hand. I was a-trembling, because I'd got to decide, forever, betwixt two things, and I knowed it. I studied a minute, sort of holding my breath, and then says to myself:

"All right, then, I'll *go* to hell" – and tore it up. (272)

Perhaps this scene suffers from being too famous; Hal Holbrook used it, along with Huck's lying on Jim's behalf, as the climax of his stage performance "Mark Twain Tonight." It may sound sentimental to some readers (in a novel that lampoons sentimentality), but a rough definition of sentimentality might be the welcome appeal of easy solutions to complex problems. The problems are real even if the solution is handy, not for Huck, who agonizes over it, but for the reader, who must assume the job of being prudent whenever Huck loses his way. The luminous truth in this scene, felt in the blood, derives not just from Huck's sound instincts, but from the reader's superior perspective on the boy's naive narrative. Ironically, he is right because he is imprudent, although this irony will be appreciated only by a prudent reader. Reading might be called a prudential process in the sense that I introduced in Chapter 1 when I wrote of reading with or against the grain of a literary jurisdiction, that is, in concert with or opposition to the judgments implicit in a text. While explaining how prudence is necessary to discern self-evident truths, Simon adds that before such clarification occurs, before prudence is fully realized in law (jurisprudence), "we have to rely on a grasp by inclination, which is never superfluous and which is sufficient so long as the rational grasp has not been achieved . . . When moral problems are considered concretely – in all their concreteness and individuality – the last word belongs always to sound inclination" (Simon 117, 129). The adjective "sound" reminds us that not all inclinations are tactful and many are selfish. The irony of Huck's case is that reflection is superfluous, while impetuous action is sure to be right, but this is evident only to readers, who judge the episode in accordance with their own inclinations and moral sentiments. In this case, their verdict seems secure, at least at first.

Viewed more broadly, however, *Huckleberry Finn* shows how the textual grain can shift or become ambiguous, in which case readers, like Huck, must reassess their moral bearings. Have their inclinations been sound? The great delight of comedy is its certainty: it offers natural justice as an aesthetic destiny. But this scene, like subsequent episodes, is hardly comic. Let me clarify the novel's alignment of aesthetic form with moral sentiment by adducing a simpler example: the rivalry between touch and tact, and their delightfully melodramatic union, in the movie *The African Queen*, which appropriately begins with a belch and ends in the water.

After the opening scene, the coarse riverboat captain, Charlie Alnutt (Humphrey Bogart), who like Huck lives mostly amid the freedom of a river, is invited to tea by an English missionary in Africa (Robert Morley) and his sister (Katharine Hepburn). The directions in the screenplay show Charlie trying to respect social niceties in this unlikely setting, until he "begins to get a little squirmy, like a child in church" and his belly growls loudly.[13] As his hosts pretend not to hear nature taking its course, Charlie tries to defuse the awkward moment by drawing attention to it: "Just listen to that stomick of mine . . . Way it sounds, you'd think I'd got an 'eye-ener inside me." The pantomime continues in a silence punctuated by gurgles, until "his insides give out with a growl so long-drawn and terrible" that he announces in a tone combining embarrassment with sly pleasure: "There ain't a thing I can do about it." The gurgling stomach is the voice of nature teaching a lesson in humility, which will be repeated later when Rose, disgusted by Charlie's drinking, empties his supply of gin into the river. As she reads the Bible in accusatory silence, Charlie prowls around the boat like a dog, tomcat, lion, goat, and rooster (according to the script), nervously scratches himself, and complains, "Feller takes a drop too much once in a while. T's only yoomin nyture," to which she replies, "Nature, Mr. Allnutt, is what we are put into this world to rise above."

What makes *The African Queen* comic is the ease with which these opposing views of nature are reconciled by allowing its two characters to redeem each other through love. Their healthy immersion in the world (including its leeches, which feed on Charlie's flesh) and their respect for each other produce a blessing. Charlie, unlike Huck, is gradually "'sivilized,'" while Rose is humbled, taught to appreciate Charlie's coarse but generous humanity. He shaves and respects the "clean 'abits" that a lady brings to his boat. She is thrilled by her wild adventure: "I'd never dreamed that any – any mere – er – physical experience could be so – so stimulating." At the end of the film, their reconciliation is expressed by the image of them immersed in water, swimming and singing,[14] but only after they have been legally married ("matrimonially matrimonified," W.S. Gilbert would say) by the captain of a German warship, which fate promptly destroys. Fate takes the form of their wrecked boat, the *African Queen*, which Charlie has armed with an improvised torpedo and which fortuitously drifts in the path of the German vessel just as the newlyweds are about to be executed. The film ends with a bang, a swim and a song, but also with a blessing. The *African Queen* is the agent of providence, if not the providence of a benevolent God who favors middle-aged lovers over soldiers, or the English over the Germans in the First World War, then of a comic fate that rules the genre of the film, which is a romantic melodrama. Charlie and Rose are saved because they have earned salvation in accordance with the laws of the genre in which they live. They get their just reward because, ultimately, the dilemma of natural law is resolved aesthetically.

THE DEADLY SPACE BETWEEN

I like to think that Charlie and Rose are rehearsing a debate about natural law raised in scholastic and early modern studies, especially in response to a question posed by Leibniz:

It is agreed that whatever God wills is good and just. But there remains the question whether it is good and just because God wills it or whether God wills it because it is good and just; in other words, whether justice and goodness are arbitrary or whether they belong to the necessary and eternal truths about the nature of things, as do numbers and proportions. (Leibniz 45)

Francis Oakley explains that what is at issue here is the question of whether "the constitutive moment and obligating force of law" are grounded "in indicative rational norm or in imperative legislative command" (Oakley 24). Is natural law "immanent in the very structure of the world and springing from the natures of the beings that compose the world" (the constitutive view); or is it "imposed on the world from without and reflecting the mandates of an omnipotent creator God" (the legislative view) (43–4)?[15] Is reason prior to will, or will to reason? Listening to his eloquent stomach, Charlie takes the latter view, while Rose takes the former, until they reach a loving compromise. His generous sensuality combined with her faith wins them a providential rescue. She initially mistrusts human nature as fundamentally corrupt, whereas Charlie's attitude is more forgiving and earns the film its comic resolution. In the comic mode, the job of prudence is not to discipline nature, but to accept and remain loyal to its best prompting.

I have argued that literary evocations of law depend on genre, each with its own jurisdiction, its own way of proclaiming and satisfying the law. We now see that directing classic comedy are two aesthetic conditions that express two corresponding features of natural law. One is a teleology whereby people are best – truest to their own natures – when they cultivate their native energies (health) so as to live amicably (justice) by perfecting their inherent virtues (blessing). Human nature orients people to certain ends, which they are free to achieve fruitfully or frustrate miserably. According to this teleological view, Hart specifies, "this optimum state is not man's good or end because he desires it; rather he desires it because it is already his natural end" (Hart 186). Our very constitution incites us not only to be happy, but to be good. Similarly, the goal of traditional comedy is to allow characters to thrive by fulfilling their true natures and destinies usually, in romantic comedies, by finding their true love. These goals are achievable because of a second, generous assumption. This is the beneficent vision of nature earlier illustrated by Rousseau, according to which the earth is our home: it provides all the materials for human flourishing, because our capacities of body, mind, and language are perfectly suited to its enabling conditions. By merging natural with moral imperatives, by reconciling "must" with "should," natural law makes a virtue of necessity. This stoical formula, best known as the advice offered by Dame Philosophy to the suffering Boethius in *Consolation of Philosophy* and often echoed by Chaucer,[16] cautions that we must patiently make the best of the world we live in; but it can also suggest more hopefully that the world is so constituted as to elicit what is best in us.

The same congruence of natural conditions and human faculties takes various forms in literary theory. It is often expressed as an ideal that I derived from Flaubert's faith in *le mot juste*, according to which the structure of the world, the ordering power of thought, and the articulation of language are all harmonious, so that any dissonance between them can be corrected. In the first chapter I noted how Wordsworth and Emerson praise poetry as the discourse that most eloquently links nature to human nature. Better still, as Wordsworth asserts – and Huck confirms – what stitches them together is pleasure, without which there can be no sympathetic knowledge, no sustaining bond between people, or between them and nature (Wordsworth 18).[17] For Emerson, too, poetry blends feeling with knowledge: the "wild delight" of nature (energy) with the "decorum and sanctity" (form) of humanity (Emerson 24). Although he prudently checks his enthusiasm by advocating "temperance" as the attitude most receptive to nature, he does not worry that poetic delight might become so wild as to disrupt the decorum of our bond with nature, or with each other. This, too, is the faith of comedy whose plot proceeds, first, by disrupting the harmony of body, mind, nature, and language (comic error or entanglement); then by showing how we have betrayed this harmony through misunderstanding, intolerance, or foolishness (comic recognition); but finally by reintegrating the errant parts (comic resolution) through commonsense, humility, and the intervention of a wise authority or, in *The African Queen*, of a comic miracle. For all its waywardness, comedy is a prudent genre that does not permit its wildest natural agents, such as Pap in *Huckleberry Finn* or Lydia in *Pride and Prejudice*, to usurp the plot.

In the modern primitivism of *Huckleberry Finn* we glimpse a comic view of natural law, but only a glimpse through the eyes of its untrustworthy young narrator. At first Huck is like a mixture of Puck and Piglet – mischievous, inventive, soiled – but his raft cannot save him in the way the *African Queen* providentially rescues its lovers. The raft carries him and Jim only into deeper trouble down the river. When Tom Sawyer finally reveals that Miss Watson felt ashamed (a moral sentiment) that "she ever was going to sell [Jim] down the river and set him free in her will" (Twain 381), he seems to be announcing a comic miracle to set things right, a miracle legally certified in the will. But Jim cannot be saved by the very laws that enslave him: Miss Watson can free him only because he was hers to set free (manumission), that is, only within the institution of slavery. *Huckleberry Finn* never disguises the ferocity of human inclinations, which can pervert any human activity, even the best-intentioned. Huck encounters and himself exemplifies an American wildness that Emerson invokes only to restrain, a violence ingrained in human nature as much as in the treacherous currents of the Mississippi, which Twain lovingly describes in *Life on the Mississippi*. In "The Poet" Emerson proclaims that poets "love wine, mead, narcotics, coffee, tea, opium, the fumes of sandal-wood and tobacco," but then immediately cautions American bards to maintain a "clean and chaste body" by drinking only "water out of a wooden bowl" (Emerson 234). He could be advising Huck not to follow his father's example.

Attentive readers of *Huckleberry Finn* are increasingly troubled by the nastiness of events, which forces them to reassess the novel and its jurisprudence. They detect another tradition of natural law, according to which the gap between inclination and rationality remains troublesome. The happiest implication of the Thomistic view is that following our basic urges will lead to a satisfying, good, sociable life, provided that we do not mess things up by acting unnaturally; but Christopher Wolfe notes a contrary assumption: "natural law theorists have a healthy awareness of the darker side of human nature. Whether this awareness derives from theological notions of sin or from simple empirical observation of the human race, the deep and widespread disorder in and among human beings is evident" (Wolfe 159). The point is not just that people prove unworthy of the riches provided by nature, but that nature itself is treacherous, like the Mississippi river. We find this darker tradition echoed in the French moralist La Rochefoucauld, for whom our first and most abiding passion is self-love (*amour propre*), which infiltrates all virtues as rivers flow into the sea (La Rochefoucauld 34). We find it in Hobbes's famous account of the fractious state of nature (Hobbes 185–6). And we find it later in Schopenhauer: "Man is at bottom a dreadful wild animal" ruled by "a colossal egoism ready and eager to overstep the bounds of justice . . . moral freedom is never to be sought in nature but only outside of nature" (Schopenhauer 138–9, 142).

In *Huckleberry Finn* there is no "outside of nature" and insufficient safety within it. If Pap did not die so early in the story, he might continue to disrupt our faith in the benevolence of natural impulses, but a parade of other characters, such as the king and duke, the feuding families, and the iron-willed Colonel Sherburn continue to have this debilitating effect. Myers analyzes in detail the inconsistencies that leave Huck, for all his generous impulses, "in a moral fog" (Myers 570), and comments:

> Beneath its seeming presentation of Huck as an innocent mirror of human cor-ruption, Twain's story shows more subtly the impotence and even moral unfitness of Huck and Huck's desired society as models for the reform of human society and human nature. However appealing we may find his romantic longings and protests, true reform requires the civilizing of Huck, no less than the naturalizing of civil societies. (567)

Myers draws the good Kantian conclusion that even our noblest inclin-ations and moral sentiments provide an inadequate basis for judgment: "uninstructed compassion can neither replace nor provide reliable support for a principled devotion to justice . . . Huck's compassion cannot provide support for the principles of natural human rights, as it is fueled by personal experience that generates no larger reflections" (571). After peering into this "moral abyss" (584) in which nature and culture are equally treacherous, Myers finally rescues *Huckleberry Finn* by discerning in its narrative a liberal-republican-literary education that benefits readers more than the characters. I wish to contemplate the abyss differently by pursuing Huck as he finally heads west into "the Territories," that is, the Indian territories beyond the Mississippi, which are doomed to be "sivilized" by a manifest destiny that Huck cannot resist. Eventually there will be no room for him in America.

Rose and Charlie complete their adventure by swimming back toward a normal life, but when Huck blurs into legend he joins company in the American imagination with another feral boy – Billy Budd. There are so many similarities between the two that I will just summarize a few in order to mark an important distinction. Billy is a childlike man, Huck a manlike child. Both are touched by nature and display the agility of animals. Both are feminized in the company of rough men, where they reveal the strength yet vulnerability of natural virtue amid a corrupt society. Both are sailors adrift on a watery element. Billy's ship is not a refuge in same way that Huck's raft is – Billy's angelic perch on top of the mast is a better parallel – but both vessels are isolated jurisdictions in which natural law briefly has a chance, as the word "jurisdiction" suggests, to speak. Huck, who has the Irish gift of the gab, is the better speaker, whereas Billy can sing (Melville 18) but stammers uncontrollably when under stress. At key moments both are inarticulate, and then readers must correct the boys' defects. In both stories the narrative perspective is manipulated (although in different ways) to make readers feel intellectually superior yet morally inadequate, which is how adults often feel when confronted with a child's naive wisdom. Each of these similarities is accompanied by notable differences, the most important being that *Huckleberry Finn* diverts the reader from a comic to an ironic mode, whereas *Billy Budd* rises into tragedy. Huck recedes into romance; Billy ascends into myth, poetry, and music.

Following Yves Simon's suggestion, I have been probing literary expressions of a gap not only between natural and positive law, but between the natural and rational demands of natural law. Contrasting the universality of law with the particularities of its enactment, Simon warns that "universally, law admits of no immediate contact with the world of action" (Simon 85). Immediate contact, or, "touch," is precisely what makes natural law feel so compelling, or, in fiction, so thrilling; but it is also what divorces intuitive nature from "tact," or rational deliberation. Nature inspires law yet cannot submit to its regulation, while law arises from natural inclinations that it cannot trust. Simon bridges this gap through prudence, which he calls "the power of sound inclinations" (85), that is, of a sensibleness that precedes rationality. (One might almost rename natural law "sense and sensibility.") *Billy Budd* presents a diabolical conflict between duties and inclinations whose soundness it is impossible to judge, because we can judge them only by relying on other inclinations. Trusting one's feelings is a problem in *Huckleberry Finn*, but a disaster in *Billy Budd*. Billy's stammer is something like Huck's itch – a bodily reflex or "organic hesitancy" (Melville 19) that imposes itself, disrupts Billy's thinking, and spurs him to action. Claggart, too, acts on impulses whose motive he cannot understand, so that the two sailors clash in ignorance of themselves and of each other. Like all antagonists, they share common features from which they diverge, but which continue to bind them together. An exaggerated form of Pap, Claggart displays a "natural depravity" (39) that draws him to Billy "magnetically" (42), yet forces him to express his attraction as hostility. Both characters confute Rousseau's claim that "the first impulses of nature are always right" and elicit from Melville's narrator the story's most enigmatic phrase, "the deadly space between" (38). Here is a cognitive and discursive gap that cannot be negotiated prudently, only contemplated. When he uses these words, the narrator admits that Claggart's spontaneous antipathy is inexplicable psychologically except as an *immoral* sentiment perversely provoked by Billy's "harmlessness" (38). In the battle of impulses and judgments that follows, innocence and guilt change places (64), and duty conflicts so sharply with inclination that Captain Vere is trapped in the same vicious ordeal. He feels obliged to condemn and hang "an angel of God" (62) after conducting a hasty trial of doubtful legality. Thus the conflict between inclination and duty passes from character to character, and finally to the reader, who is drawn into the ordeal as both witness and judge.

The narrator begins by claiming that his story is realistic and historically precise, then admits that he must summon the resources of romance to delve into its characters (38) but increasingly stresses its tragic course as shaped by the twin necessities of "fate and ban": "Claggart could even have loved Billy but for fate and ban" (51). "Ban" refers to all the legal prohibitions that keep the two men apart: social class, military rank, the Mutiny Act (72), heterosexual imperatives. The "vice of fate" refers to all the forces that press them disastrously together, forces associated with nature (animal instinct, the "secret fire" in their "fervid heart" [79]), and with chance or "the jugglery of circumstances" (64). As conflicting drives, fate and ban might be compared to the pity and fear of tragic catharsis, where pity attracts the audience sympathetically toward suffering characters, while fear forces them away in terror. This simultaneous push–pull effect helps to explain the extraordinary power of tragedy. If comedy expresses a faith that nature is intelligible, reason is adept, and language is articulate, then tragedy arouses a fascinated horror when these conditions fail. The horror repulses the audience, but the fascination draws them closer, implicating them in the failure. If in *The African Queen* natural law triumphs through a comic plot that finally enlists chance to confer a blessing on deserving characters, then in *Billy Budd* it is engulfed by a tragedy that culminates in a sacrifice that they do not deserve.

Sacrificial imagery pervades *Billy Budd*, so I need only point out that both Claggart (51) and Billy (78) are associated with Christ's suffering, and that the trial scene is a ceremony culminating in public execution.

Tragedy exerts an eerie power because, as a sacrificial ritual, it defies justice. Whereas justice aspires to restore natural balance (health) to a disrupted social order, sacrifice draws on natural energies to redeem natural faults. As I have observed earlier, although sacrifice appears to resemble the judicial structure of symmetrical exchange whereby two events are balanced so that one (payment, punishment) serves as fair or natural recompense for another (trespass, crime), in fact the calculation is quite different. The structure of sacrifice is asymmetrical: the innocent suffer for the sake of the guilty, and the redemption is not proportionate to the crime, but far exceeds it. On its completion, justice offers closure, whereas sacrifice ("to make holy") evokes an astonishing new possibility not yet achieved. Like grace, which is its uncanny partner, sacrifice is excessive: it gives us more than we deserve. Whereas grace intercedes from above, sacrifice emerges from below, usually by using nature as an intermediary to link the human to the divine, through the agency either of pain, loss, or conflagration (burnt offering, auto da fé), or of animal and even human slaughter.

If Billy is a sacrificial lamb, what blessing does he confer on a world at war? All aspects of *Billy Budd* are open to dispute: the justice and authority of the drumhead court, its assessments of guilt and innocence, the role of the narrator, the deadly spaces within the narrative. It is hard to find a blessing in Billy's calamity or even in his final words, "'God bless Captain Vere'" (82), if by blessing we understand a spiritual power that absolves us of natural faults by transcending them, a power that forgives us for being human. Nevertheless, the tale ends by evoking a numinous energy that arises from nature but cannot be confined by natural forms, notably in the portrait of Billy awaiting execution in a serene trance like "a slumbering child in the cradle" (78); and in the final, exquisite moment when he "ascended, and, ascending, took the full rose of the dawn" (83). In both scenes, he seems to defy fate and ban through a purity of character (though not of action) associated with childhood and virginity, as displayed in "the faint rose-bud complexion of the most beautiful English girls" (80). As Northrop Frye notes in his study of romance, virginity is associated with an untouchable core of being, an identity constantly threatened by worldly contamination but protected from it by its own strange integrity (Frye, *Secular* 152–3). In a sense it is both natural and unnatural, a condition of birth that we must sacrifice, whether literally or figuratively. According to Frye, as a genre romance magically renews this purity, whereas comedy celebrates its passing by guiding characters toward marriage, sexual fulfillment, and social integration. By contrast, tragedies cast their heroes into ever deeper solitude, where they painfully affirm their identity just as it is extinguished.

Thus the chaste Antigone is confined to her cave; Virginia Woolf's Mrs. Dalloway retreats to her solitary room to feel "a virginity preserved through childbirth which clung to her like a sheet" (Woolf 27). Tragedy is the genre that loves soliloquies or, in Billy's case, an intense inner silence. As he approaches death, he is rendered both girlish and boyish, evoking a virginal purity proclaimed ecstatically through his ritual slaying. In executing Billy, Captain Vere offers a life for a life, but no life is commensurate with any other, because all are unique. I noted Simon's concern that laws always risk being unjust to individual cases, which are "unique, unprecedented, and unrenewable" (Simon 82) and so elude the generality of the rule. This is the fate played out in a tragic jurisdiction. What is affirmed through Billy's sacrifice is a singular selfhood, celebrated in song but lost forever. Here is the fragile, irreplaceable touch of nature that law aims to protect yet cannot articulate in its generalities. I will examine this intense singularity in the next chapter.

CHAPTER 5

The course of a particular
Justice and singularity

The leaves cry. It is not a cry of divine attention,
Nor the smoke-drift of puffed-out heroes, nor human cry.
It is the cry of leaves that do not transcend themselves,
In the absence of fantasia, without meaning more
Than they are in the final finding of the ear, in the thing
Itself, until, at last, the cry concerns no one at all.
(Wallace Stevens, "The Course of a Particular," *Palm* 367)

In the first chapter I noted how David Hume traces the provenance of justice to an experience of natural scarcity. The notion of equity arises, he speculates, as a practical means of coping with a world where there is not enough food, shelter, or property to satisfy everyone, prompting the need for a regulatory system governed by principles and enacted through laws. A state of permanent abundance – recall the bounty of Huck Finn's six-foot catfish – would make justice irrelevant, since there would be no need either to be possessive or to share. At the other extreme, a state of utter deprivation would impose a perpetual emergency in which justice would be ineffectual. The former would have no need for justice, the latter no use for it. In both, "[b]y rendering justice totally *useless*, you thereby totally destroy its essence, and suspend its obligation upon mankind" (Hume 16). It is useful only in a social setting that falls somewhere between perfect ease (the absence of necessity) and perfect dis-ease (inflexible necessity), that is, in an ethical setting where freedom can be allied with social obligation. If we look to literary equivalents for these two limiting cases, we find that abundance elicits few literary forms, because it allows for no conflict, no plot, no ordeal. Hume observes that "the *poetical* fiction of the *golden age*" corresponds to a condition of perfect abundance, but few stories can be set in such a wonderfully uneventful world. It leaves us with nothing to say except "and they lived happily ever after." On the other hand, "the *philosophical* fiction of the *state of nature*" corresponds to the condition of perpetual want, which produces a Hobbesian "state of mutual war and violence, attended with the most extreme necessity" (17). Here there may be stories of conflict and suffering, but no laws, therefore no laws to break, and therefore no comedies or tragedies. Literature lives between the two extremes of ease and want, limits that the literary imagination recognizes but often aspires to transgress by envisioning an abundance or scarcity beyond freedom and justice. What forms might that vision take?

Tragedy is a genre of introspection and isolation expressed through the dramatic convention of the soliloquy – the cry that concerns no one but oneself, to borrow Wallace Stevens's phrase. By contrast, comedy is a sociable genre seeking to unite its characters; its soliloquies are often overheard, as if even solitude must be shared. For example Beatrice and Benedick, the reluctant lovers in Shakespeare's *Much Ado about Nothing*, discover their passion for each other in monologues, but without realizing they are being overheard by friends who are conspiring to unite them. Beyond both the lonely tragic cry and the shared comic cry is the empty cry evoked by wintry leaves in Stevens's poem "The Course of a Particular." It provokes a shift in mood from robust assurance that "one is part of everything," to a deepening loneliness, and finally to a depleted sense of the world drained of meaning. These dispositions – one expansive and gregarious, the other contracting to the vanishing point of consciousness – suggest two complementary responses to literature. I will be concerned with the latter, which tries to acknowledge the uniqueness of a literary work, but it must first be set against the "fantasia" whose plenitude it renounces in order to trace a path of diminishing returns. My purpose is to explore the rhetoric of singularity in order to detect its "final finding," that is, its aesthetic and ethical limit. My hope is that artistry and ethics will converge: the course of a literary particular leads to ethical discovery.

According to Stevens, however, such a discovery "concerns no one at all," an inconclusive conclusion that Joseph Carroll glosses as follows:

In the absence of fantasia, these two aspects of particularity, the self and the world, are equivalent in their meaninglessness. Stevens repudiates essential unity, but he does not then revert to a celebration of the parts of the world. The failure of transcendental affect leaves him at the nadir of the cycle from Romanticism to indifferentism. (Carroll 306)

Indifference hardly sounds like a just or moral position, and defining that position in relation to the artistry that exposes it will be my subject. In English the word "just" is used to mark a natural, conceptual, or moral limit, as in the expressions "that's just the way things are," "just so," "just because I say so," and "it's just right." In pursuit of some extreme literary moments when things "are just" because they "just are," my path in this chapter will run from the numerous to the singular. I intend, first, to contrast a criticism of plenitude with a criticism of austerity; then to inspect some rhetorical devices through which singularity is indicated; then to show how this rhetoric isolates the here-and-now in the instant of its inception and deception, its appearance and dismissal; and finally to examine how this singular aesthetic raises a comparable ethical challenge that sets judicial generality against the dignity of the unique.

THE SHIPWRECK OF THE SINGULAR

We have already encountered the problem of acknowledging singularity in relation to judicial thinking. All laws are general rules based on basic principles governing categories of behavior, yet they must cope with a bewildering variety of specific cases, each of which, as Yves Simon advised in the previous chapter, "may always be in some significant respect unique, unprecedented, and unrenewable" (Simon 82). Justice must be blind, which means it must not be unfairly discriminating, but if it cannot discriminate particulars, how can it be fair? Literature faces the same problem, but takes more delight in the risk involved.

When studying any literary work, we customarily nudge it in two directions, though not in equal measure. Usually we relate it to other texts in an expanding pattern of interdependence within larger contexts and communities. Whether the terms of explication are historical, cultural, biographical, national, generic, or religious, a work gains significance within a wider field to which it contributes, however modestly. No artist or artefact has its meaning alone, T.S. Eliot advises in a famous dictum, because they participate in an "ideal order," a totality that is temporarily complete yet continually altered as new works are added to it (Eliot, *Selected Prose* 38). A text is intelligible through its commerce with other texts: as one elegy in an elegiac tradition, or as an American lyric, or a novel by Virginia Woolf, or an example of women's writing. At the limit of this expansive view lies a glimpse of all literature conceived as one ongoing discourse – a grand intertextual poem, myth, or conversation forever in progress. Northrop Frye provides one of the most daring modern attempts to see literature steadily and to see it whole by fitting every work into a vast network of modes, myths, and genres, all combining in a sublime vision of cultural totality corresponding to what Eliot calls "the mind of Europe" (39). A poem is like a momentary thought within that mind.

As the critic's field of vision expands, however, individual works become more and more significant, yet less and less discernible as they are engulfed by the whole. Ideal readers catch every allusion and influence, but at the cost of losing the shock of first discovery. As a countermeasure, they try to savor a literary work not in relation to other writing but in and for itself. It may be another eighteenth-century, middle-class novel written by a Protestant man for women readers, but it is this particular text, and not another one, read here and now, not elsewhere. How are we to account for its specificity? Even an ardent advocate of intertextuality like Harold Bloom admits, "[t]here can be no poem in itself, and yet something irreducible does abide in the aesthetic" (Bloom, *Western* 23).

Although specific qualities of a literary work may startle us on first reading, they are difficult to define because all the modes of definition at our disposal have the perverse effect of depriving a work of its particularity. Explanations inevitably generalize. Whether we rely on categorization, analogy, paradigm, function, influence, or genealogy, the process of understanding in each case is contextual and systematic. It is relational, whereas specificity is what precedes any relation, and then enters into it. Do the primary units have any identifiable standing before they contribute to a larger structure of meaning, or are they created only by the act of being differentiated within it, just as "left" has no meaning until paired with "right"? Even analyzing a poem into its constituent parts fails to disclose its particularity, because analysis is possible only if we are already able to recognize those parts and their functions. To do so requires that we rely on general structural principles, which specify the parts as parts in the first place. In this case, "to specify" does not mean to isolate what is unique in a poem, but to draw from a repertoire of established practices. To analyze a sonnet into quatrains and tercets is to recognize it as a sonnet, and so to relate it to a conventional, lyrical category.

If the imagined limit of the expansive critical view is a total literary universe where "one is part of everything," the limit of the contracting view is irreducible singularity – "the thing / Itself" apart from all else. Neither extreme is attainable, but the path to the first is far more inviting. The first promises glory, the second threatens ruin. The first is accommodating, because it finds room for everything, whereas the latter founders on what George Oppen calls "the shipwreck / Of the singular."

> Obsessed, bewildered
> By the shipwreck
> Of the singular
> We have chosen the meaning
> Of being numerous.
>
> (Oppen 151)

Meaning is never really a matter of choice, since we cannot live without it, and it is always "numerous" in the sense of being relational and participatory. To understand is to relate, and relations always proliferate. The challenge, therefore, is to renounce the numerous with its fantasy of totality in order to focus on singularity, even if it invites disaster, even if disaster is required to imagine the singular.

So far, we seem to be offered a choice between too much and too little – either the bewilderment of infinite multiplicity or the shipwreck of singularity. In "Notes toward a Supreme Fiction" Stevens succinctly calls the former a fecund "principle," the latter a chaste "particle" (Stevens, *Palm* 215). Principle pushes the imagination to "a point / Beyond which thought could not progress as thought"; particle pulls it to "a point / Beyond which fact could not progress as fact" (229). Because each extreme directs Stevens's mock-hero, Canon Aspirin, toward "nothingness," it is tempting to retreat to a common ground accommodating both. But accommodation is a goal of the expansive critical view, as it aspires to "the whole, / The complicate, the amassing harmony" (229). The challenge to imagine the singular by resisting accommodation still remains.

According to Bloom, we treasure "something irreducible" in each poem, which is all the more precious for the enigmatic immediacy of its appeal. Even Frye, the great systematizer, agrees that criticism can give knowledge only *about* literature, which is quite different from actual literary experience felt on the pulse. Criticism is judicial. It delivers a verdict, whereas the original pulsation has no voice of its own, because critical understanding

is founded on a direct experience which is central to criticism yet forever excluded from it. Criticism can account for it only in critical terminology, and that terminology can never recapture or include the original experience. The original experience is like the direct vision of color, or the direct sensation of heat or cold, that physics "explains" in what, from the point of view of the experience itself, is a quite irrelevant way. However disciplined by taste and skill, the experience of literature is, like literature itself, unable to speak. (Frye, *Anatomy* 27)

The dilemma of critical knowledge is captured in the oxymoron "aesthetic distance." Sensory or aesthetic experience is direct, not distanced. Criticism makes the immediate experience of art intelligible only by rendering it less and less immediate. It speaks about art by preventing it from speaking for itself. This is the dilemma that Flaubert's *mot juste* was supposed to overcome: the just word that pierces like a dagger should link thought directly to reality. Until it does, we must rely on theory, such as the theory of *le mot juste*, which is always belated, trailing after "the direct experience of literature, where uniqueness is everything" (361).

Generalizing on this dilemma, Jean-François Lyotard argues that philosophy can never comprehend the instantaneous "gesture" made enigmatically by art. Aesthetic presence is punctual, whereas philosophical understanding is postponed: "The artist asks of us philosophers that we think the perceptible singularity that is presented here and now: a work or works that are here, now, in the singularity of their occurrence. But we should bear in mind that this possessive of occurrence is only reconstituted by memory after the fact" (Lyotard 75).

Because understanding lags behind the experience that it interprets retrospectively, it will always miss the singularity of its object. It will be baffled by a unique gesture that "no mode of thought is capable of thinking" directly, only of reconstituting in a displaced form:

the fact that there is a gesture in space-time-matter, the fact that it *is* there and is a gesture – constitutes the impenetrability of the work for thought. It is precisely to the level of this enigma that the artist obligates the philosopher to place or displace his thought, and this is so whether the artist is aware of it or not. It is up to the philosopher, in the awareness of his debt, to know this for both himself and the artist. (75–6, Lyotard's emphasis)

How are we to acknowledge literary uniqueness, when any systematic explanation of it must rely on generalities?

In opposition to a critic like Frye, who enlarges his theoretical gaze to accommodate everything, is Paul de Man, who forces poetic thought back toward particularity, knowing very well that it can never achieve its goal. Like Canon Aspirin, both critics undertake pilgrimages to the limit of thought, though in different directions; and both are thwarted by the very nature of literature, whose vitality springs from a uniqueness that theory can only dissipate. But whereas Frye patiently constructs a baroque system culminating in a glorious "anagogic" vision that compensates us for the original loss, de Man follows the opposite course. He devises an ascetic path leading to the expiry of meaning in singularity – the final finding that concerns no one at all. He agrees that literature itself is unable to speak, but he respects its muteness by resisting the inclusiveness of critical thought. According to Tobin Siebers, "[g]enerality is the hallmark of the kind of theory that de Man most opposes" because he believes that "[p]hilosophical generality is the death of genuine self-knowledge" (Siebers 100, 120). He renounces comprehension because it is driven by a will to power through violent totalization. As a corrective, he stubbornly resists theory's philosophical tendency to convert the unique into the general, by summoning the arsenal of rhetorical disfiguration and erasure associated with deconstruction. By these means he retraces the course of the particular almost to the point of nullification. Insofar as something is truly unique, it is unknowable and unsayable, because knowing and saying both rely on signification, which operates through equivalences: this for that, signifer for signified. The unique eludes the web of signification, because it is not comparable or equivalent to anything else. To propose any analogy or relationship, even contrast, which requires some commonality on which to distinguish the contrast, would be to forfeit "something irreducible" abiding in the aesthetic.

I offer Frye and de Man as opposing responses, each daring in its own way, to the need for criticism to respect aesthetic singularity even as it relies on theoretical generality. The word "accommodate" suggests what Frye welcomes and de Man repudiates: the spaciousness of thought. In the comprehensiveness of literary appreciation, Frye finds a sublimity that restores to literature the splendor of the innumerable, discrete poetic moments on which his grand system rests. For de Man, on the other hand, literature's value lies in its uncanny ability to dismantle all equivalences and compensations, until we can almost imagine the uniqueness of being. Where Frye's critical vision culminates in the timeless co-presence of all literature, de Man's confines itself to a random instant. The cost of this austere revelation is devastating, for we must accept, de Man concludes bleakly, "that nothing, whether deed, word, thought or text, ever happens in relation, positive or negative, to anything that precedes, follows or exists elsewhere, but only as a random event whose power, like the power of death, is due to the randomness of its occurrence" (de Man, *Rhetoric* 122).

To Frye, this inchoate world of dislocated singularities would look like hell.

ITS SINGLE EMPTINESS

Given a choice between an all-encompassing totality and an all-excluding singularity, most literary theorists nowadays would probably choose neither. The recent climate of opinion welcomes pluralities of all kinds – multicultural, heteroglossal, polysemic, interdisciplinary – but subject to two competing regulations. First, these pluralities must never be subsumed within a single dominating system; and second, they must never pretend to be autonomous. These logical limitations reflect an ethical worry: both conditions are regarded as authoritarian and so unjust. The first is tyrannical, because it forces its diverse constituents to obey a single rule; the second is irresponsible, because it falsely claims to be self-sufficient, subject only to its own rule. In exploring the rhetoric of singularity, then, I might seem to be backing the wrong horse. I am not eager to follow de Man's ascetic example, which recommends a chastity of thought so severe that it leads to critical self-martyrdom, as Siebers calls it (Siebers 117). However, his rigorous analysis relies on a number of metaphors – asceticism, self-denial, nullification, mourning, sacrifice – that I find compelling. They illustrate how any effort to grasp the specificity of a literary work will require a double strategy in which an analogy, immediately recognized as flawed, expresses a poetic precision that precedes any analogy and will be falsified by it. Because analogy invites us into a "fantasia" of correspondences, we must studiously decline the invitation through a policy of denial, isolation, or annulment. In Stevens's terms, we must reject an abundant principle in order to isolate the scarcity of a particle. Consider some literary strategies.

A simple but intriguing way of evoking singularity is through insistence, as in Gertrude Stein's hypnotic refrain: "A rose is a rose is a rose." Each repetition narrows the focus, as one flower belonging to the large class of roses is finally distinguished as *this* rose and no other. In her lecture "Composition as Explanation," Stein explains (repeatedly) that repetition is her way of "groping for a continuous present" small yet capacious enough to include everything: "I naturally made a continuous present an including everything and a beginning again and again within a very small thing" (Stein 518–19). As her novel *The Making of Americans* mushroomed to a thousand pages, however, she realized that she could cherish a thing's particularity only by marking its difference from all other small things. Her singular style had to show not only that we always live in a present stuffed with innumerable details, but that the present is forever changing – "if it is all so alike it must be simply different and everything simply different was the natural way of creating it then" (519). At the limit of this contracting process she finds an enigma. As a single rose is progressively isolated from everything else, it loses the commonality it shares, first with other flowers, then with other roses, until it stands solitary but indefinable even as a rose. It is the opposite of the symbolists' platonic flower evoked by Stéphane Mallarmé as the forgotten, fragrant ideal ("idée même et suave") in which all flowers are subsumed.[1] Stein's rose utterly depletes this plenitude: it is no longer "this flower" or "this rose," but merely *this*.

The deictic "this" recalls the insistent gesture concluding Stevens's poem "The Man on the Dump": "Where was it one first heard of the truth? The the" (Stevens, *Palm* 164). His question drastically shrinks its focus until it points not at the thing itself, but at the verbal function – the definite article – through which things are specified. Here is an act of specifying without content. We are directed to look at the place where the answer would be. This tactic suggests that the rhetoric of singularity is positional and indicative; that is, it seeks ways of circling and pointing from a distance at an untouchable source – the rose itself, the unique person, the the.

A related gestural tactic is the "hapax legomenon," a term denoting a word that appears only once in the Bible, but is applicable more generally to neologisms or unrecognizable words. Whereas Stevens resorts to the definite article, a word so common that it has no meaning of its own, other writers imagine words that can be used only once. In practice, a word that is truly unrepeated or unrepeatable would be incomprehensible. Iterability makes words both intelligible and ambiguous, because they can be understood only when they are used and shared, yet reiteration also makes them constantly change their meaning in new contexts. If they were never repeated, then they might seem frozen at the moment of utterance, pure but without resonance. A.M. Klein uses the Hebrew form "millot bodedot" (Klein, *Notebooks* 131) to evoke this magical insularity: "Isolated words. Lonesome words. They occur but once in the whole Torah, and are related to no other word. In English, or rather in Greek, they are called hapax legomena, words of single occurrence. Once, only once, do they appear in the Bible, and then are not heard from again" (131). Even to cite a hapax legomenon is, perversely, to destroy it by using it a second time and so converting it into common currency. Instead, Klein accords exclusive value to the word of single occurrence by identifying it with God's divine *fiat* – "let there be light" – a genesis that occurs only once. This utterance is the original verdict, the "true speaking," which creates the world and which the poet imitates by "uttering" a fictional world. Klein's eloquent example from "A Portrait of the Poet as Landscape" illustrates how quickly the single utterance proliferates into a fantasia of correspondences:

> Look, he is
> the nth Adam taking a green inventory
> in world by scarcely uttered, naming praising,
> the flowering fiats in the meadow, the
> syllabled fur, stars aspirate, the pollen
> whose sweet collision sounds eternally.
> (Klein, *Poems* 638–9)

The hapax legomenon is performative – a self-creating word – but as Zailig Pollock shows in his commentary on Klein, it must also be self-destructive if it can be performed only once. There is a demonic parody of the hapax legomenon in the death sentence: the irrevocable verdict that hangs over us all and that, for Klein, finds horrific exclamation as a nuclear explosion or the Holocaust (Pollock 207–8).

Both genesis and death decree, the singular word is ascribed an uncanny power exerted at either the very beginning or the very end of things; or more correctly, it offers a way of imagining how beginnings begin, and where endings end. Because of its proximity to creation and destruction, it is too dangerous to touch. Anne Carson asks why neologisms should be so disturbing, and answers:

> If we cannot construe them at all, we call them mad. If we can construe them, they raise troubling questions about our own linguistic mastery. We say "coinages" because they disrupt the economic equilibrium of words and things that we had prided ourselves on maintaining. A new compound word in [Paul] Celan, for example, evokes something that now suddenly seems real, although it didn't exist before and is attainable through this word alone. It comes to us free, like a piece of new air. And (like praise) it has to prepare for itself an ear to hear it, just slightly before it arrives – has to invent its own necessity. (Carson 134)

A neologism has to justify itself by preparing for its own coming; otherwise it cannot be received intelligibly at all. "Coinage" suggests a fresh minting of meaning, but the image is wonderfully inappropriate, since singularities are not commensurate with other things, and therefore cannot be exchanged for them. Their value is not economic but inspirational, as Klein shows. Perhaps that is why both poets immediately associate the creative burst of language with praise, but also with irrationality.

The same is true of my third example, catachresis, which is the other side of the coin. If neologisms upset the equilibrium of words and things, and the hapax legomenon is a word without a thing, then catachresis is a thing without a word. Also known as "abusio," it is a strained metaphor ("to take up arms against a sea of troubles"), but also a term used metaphorically to point at something with no proper name of its own. Common examples are "table leg," "book leaf," and "mother tongue." Here again, the verbal economy is disrupted. In most metaphors one term is substituted for, or transferred to, another; but there can be no substitution of a figurative term for a literal one if the literal word does not exist. Instead, we have what the witches in *Macbeth* ominously call "A deed without a name" (4.1.49). In the heyday of deconstruction, catachresis was regarded as the abusive, rhetorical deed *par excellence*. Jacques Derrida used catachresis to illustrate the way language strains between sense and reference, meaning and use

(Derrida, "White" 59–60); J. Hillis Miller saw it as a primal misnaming that lurks in all words (Miller 19–20); de Man called it "[t]he trope which coins a name for the still-unnamed entity, which gives face to the faceless" (de Man, "Lyrical Voice" 57), and he warned: "Something monstrous lurks in the most innocent of catachreses: when one speaks of the legs of the table or the face of the mountain, catachresis is already turning into prosopopeia [personification, literally "to give a face"], and one begins to perceive a world of potential ghosts and monsters" (de Man, "Epistemology" 19).

As Klein's Adamic poet illustrates, these metamorphoses quickly proliferate into a hallucinatory fantasia, but only after they have been invoked by an unnameable singularity that remains faceless and wordless. It is the power of speech that has not yet spoken, the inhuman substratum of humanity to which de Man's analysis constantly leads him. In his wintry mood, Stevens annuls the creative *fiat* invoked by Klein by abjuring personification and relinquishing metaphor (even if he must do so metaphorically), in order to return to the instant before light emerges from the first sound:

> In this bleak air the broken stalks
> Have arms without hands. They have trunks
> Without legs or, for that, without heads.
> They have heads in which a captive cry
> Is merely the moving of a tongue.
> Snow sparkles like eyesight falling to earth,
>
> . . .
>
> It is in this solitude, a syllable,
> Out of these gawky flitterings,
> Intones its single emptiness,
> The savagest hollow of winter-sound.
> (Stevens, "No Possum, No Sop, No Taters," *Palm* 247–8)

Here is a form without a shape, a word without a meaning, a deed without a name. "No Possum" pinpoints singularity at the convergence of light, sight, and sound by isolating the present in the precision of its immediacy. It focuses not on a rich, contemplative moment as in Marvell's "The Garden" or Milton's "Il penseroso," and not on Stein's bulky, continuous present, but on the here-and-now, which is always singular, always transient, and always different.

THE LAST ONSET

Right here, right now, Stevens says in "Man Carrying Thing," "[t]he bright obvious stand motionless in cold" (Stevens, *Palm* 281), but the reality revealed so brilliantly stands only for an instant. In the rhetoric of the instantaneous, the bare present, which vanishes as we touch it, is more elusive than the past, which can be exhibited by memory, or than the future, which can be anticipated. Past and future join in the continuity of a "major reality" like Frye's explanatory myths, or like the symphonic temporality of justice examined earlier. Poets entice us to enjoy such comforting fictions, but also warn us to resist them whenever we retreat to the cold, solitary present. These rival dispositions offer a rhythm of elevation and relapse in "As You Leave the Room":

> Now, here, the snow I had forgotten becomes
> Part of a major reality, part of
> An appreciation of a reality
> And thus an elevation, as if I left
> With something I could touch, touch every way.
> And yet nothing has been changed except what is
> Unreal, as if nothing had been changed at all.
>
> (396)

A "major reality" seems fully tactile yet proves to be specious or "unreal." It is a lofty fantasy that appreciates in value under the aegis of imagination, but then must be depreciated imaginatively in its turn. In "The Sail of Ulysses" the "particular thought" is a "difficult inch," coaxed into "Plantagenet abstractions" and "stellar largenesses"; but, Stevens warns, the poet must also resist the "law / that bends the particulars to the abstract" (392) in order to face the present in its strange momentariness. It is the barely imaginable reality that first provokes sensation and cognition. In Stevens's poetics, time, sight, and thought often converge in the image of light, as in the common expression "to see things in a flash."

Singularity, sensed fleetingly as the brilliant intersection of time, being, and thought, finds more familiar expression in the modern fascination with photography, for instance in Roland Barthes's *Camera Lucida*. The click of a shutter and the illuminating flash mark the beginning of another double strategy to reclaim the present:

What the Photograph reproduces to infinity has occurred only once: the Photograph mechanically repeats what could never be repeated existentially. In the Photograph, the event is never transcended for the sake of something else: the Photograph always leads the corpus I need back to the body I see; it is the absolute Particular . . . the *This* . . . the Real, in its indefatigable expression. (Barthes 4, Barthes's emphasis)

Here again is a preoccupation with first and last moments, with cognition and recognition, with first utterance and last breath. Barthes, too, imagines singularity as a mere "this," which he can point to only from a distance measured by the lapse between taking the photograph and viewing it later. The creative instant is characterized by "contingency, singularity, risk" (20), which Barthes sums up nicely in the figure of "surprise" (32), a jolting discovery that lies "outside of meaning" (34) yet is the precondition for any subsequent understanding. He characterizes the second, recuperative moment variously as interpretation, objectification (13), nostalgia, and even justice (70), the most satisfying recuperation of the past; but also, since the past is gone forever, as melancholy, mourning (79), and catastrophe (96).

Modernist poetics explores all of these moods. In its early formulation as Imagism, it especially stresses the singularity of visual or tactile stimuli in conjunction with intuitive thought and spontaneous language. Sensation, sense, and signification all fuse in *le mot juste*. The best-known examples are Erza Pound's definition of the poetic image as an emotional and intellectual complex released instantaneously (Pound 4) and T.E. Hulme's equating of meaning with sight and touch, in contrast to the tardiness of sound (Hulme, *Further* 77–8). A better example for my purposes is the way D.H. Lawrence casts off tradition and aspiration (past and future) in order to formulate a poetry of the immediate present:

But there is another kind of poetry: the poetry of that which is at hand: the immediate present. In the immediate present there is no perfection, no consummation, nothing finished. The strands are all flying, quivering, intermingling into the web, the waters are shaking the moon . . . We look at the very white quick of nascent creation. A water-lily heaves herself from the flood, looks around, gleams, and is gone. We have seen the incarnation, the quick of the ever-swirling flood. We have seen the invisible. We have seen, we have touched, we have partaken of the very substance of creative change, creative mutation . . . Give me the still, white seething, the incandescence and the coldness of the incarnate moment: the moment, the quick of all change and haste and opposition: the moment, the immediate present, the Now. (Lawrence, "Introduction" 85–6)

The present is at once the most palpable and the most intangible of states. Lawrence associates it with the quick of life, which he pictures as a creative spark that ignites change but cannot share in it, since it lives only in the instant of its passing. He condenses this paradox in the word "still," which ambiguously suggests both quietude and continuance, stasis and motion: "the still, white seething."[2] Most revealingly, his imagery links vitality to death (here the trope is as much romantic as it is modernist), because life is felt most intensely at the instant of its loss.

In Chapter 3 I suggested that the temporality of justice is symphonic – an amassing harmony at once progressive and recuperative. By contrast these examples suggest that the course of a particular follows a traumatic temporality in which the present expires as soon as it occurs, and is known only when it haunts us afterwards.[3] Dylan Thomas evokes such a moment in "A Refusal to Mourn the Death, by Fire, of a Child in London," a Second World War elegy that steadfastly refuses to lament a child's death in the Blitz and then concludes: "After the first death, there is no other" (Thomas 192). Because we die only once, contemplating the instant when life ceases – a traditional, devotional exercise – can give ecstatic assurance of the uniqueness of our being, which is most precious at the moment of loss. Following his own double strategy, Thomas draws on religious imagery (Zion, synagogue, sackcloth, "stations of the breath"), which he renounces in order to lament all the more strongly. He evokes a comforting fantasia – the ceremonies of mourning, the solace of religion, and the afterlife – only to reject their comforts through a series of oratorical denials stretching from the first word ("Never") to the last ("no other"). Some readers may interpret this poem as subtly (or not so subtly) reaffirming the religious faith that it makes a show of denying, as it mourns for the dead child by pretending not to. But we might also hold Thomas to his word: after the first death, there is no other.[4]

De Man identifies lyric poetry with two mutually exclusive kinds of mourning. The more familiar is expressed in the lyrical impulse to establish a temporal harmony that humanizes death through a "pathos of terror": to mourn is to cling to the past, and so to preserve it, however painfully, as ongoing testimony to the value of one's grief. The more stringent form of mourning offers no such comfort. It insists on looking death in the face by refusing even to personify a face: "True 'mourning' is less deluded. The most *it* can do is to allow for non-comprehension and enumerate non-anthropomorphic, non-elegiac, non-celebratory, non-lyrical, non-poetic, that is to say, prosaic, or, better, *historical* modes of language power" (de Man, *Rhetoric* 262, de Man's emphasis).[5] As the parade of negations indicates, we are back in de Man's world of random events, which resist being assimilated into any historical continuity. Viewed in this way, Thomas's refusal to mourn is not a way of defying death or of triumphing over it, but one of submitting to its power by relinquishing past and future, and by renouncing even the pathetic continuity of bereavement. The death of a child thus portrays most poignantly what is true of all people: all are unique, mortal, and therefore irreplaceable.

Dying may take a lifetime, but death is instantaneous.[6] The desire to isolate the final second of life by filling it with all the significance that is about to vanish appears in proverbial notions such as prophesying with one's dying gasp, like John of Gaunt in Shakespeare's *Richard II*; or having one's life flash before one's eyes, as in Ambrose Bierce's story "An Occurrence at Owl Creek Bridge," and in A.M. Klein's poem "And in that Drowning Instant," which condenses not only an individual life, but the Jewish diaspora into its glimpse of a "preterite eternity" (Klein, *Poems* 609). Literature is full of fine death-bed scenes, and none more poignant than Bottom's theatrical death-throes in *A Midsummer Night's Dream*:

> Thus die I, thus, thus, thus.
> Now am I dead,
> Now am I fled;
> My soul is in the sky.
> Tongue, lose thy light;
> Moon, take thy flight.
> Now die, die, die, die, die.
> (5.1.296–302)

The joke is that the last moment goes on and on and on, yet when the noblemen scoff,

DEMETRIUS: No die, but an ace, for him; for he is but one.
LYSANDER: Less than an ace, man; for he is dead, he is nothing. (5.1.303–4)

they illustrate how death is painful proof of a uniqueness that language strains to express. Through their word-play, dying becomes gambling – a bet that we all lose – and singularity (the ace, or single spot on the dice) is proclaimed only as it is nullified.

Compare this bombastic display with three other examples. The first concludes Tolstoy's "The Death of Ivan Ilych," when Ivan's prolonged suffering grants a charitable insight that ultimately redeems him from the futility of his life. As he feels his son kissing his hand, he is surprised by a joyful intuition, which is expressed as falling, as light, as release from pain, and as the euphoric temporality of dying:

There was light instead of death.
"So that is it!" he suddenly said out loud. "What happiness!"
All of this took place in an instant, but the significance of that instant was lasting. For those present his agony continued for another two hours. Something rattled in his throat, his emaciated body twitched. But gradually the wheezing and the rattling ceased. (Tolstoy 283)

A similar pattern appears more ironically in Yuri Olesha's story "Lyompa," which also entices the reader toward the unimaginable, in this case by inventing the odd word that serves as the title. Critically ill, Ponomarev turns away from all the bubbling, snorting sounds that animate his house. In contrast to a young child, whose world is expanding explosively as he discovers a bewildering fertility of things that he cannot name, Ponomarev feels reality contracting:

First, the number of things on the periphery, far away from him, decreased; then this depletion drew closer to the center, reaching deeper and deeper, toward the courtyard, the house, the corridor, the room, his heart . . . Death was destroying things on its way to him. Death had left him only a few things, from an infinite number . . . The vanishing things left the dying man nothing but their names. (Olesha 142, 144)

Fading into abstraction, he is left with an absurd hapax legomenon, which he associates with a noisy rat in the kitchen: "He knew that at any cost he must stop thinking about the rat's name. But he kept searching for it, knowing that as soon as he found that meaningless, horrifying name, he would die. 'Lyompa!' he suddenly shouted in a terrifying voice" (145). The word is all the more frightening for naming the unnameable. My third example is Emily Dickinson's poem "I Heard a Fly Buzz – When I Died" (Dickinson 223–4), in which light, sight, and sound again converge at the moment of death. The speaker patiently awaits "the last Onset" (death as oxymoron), wills her "Keepsakes," and finally concentrates on the "uncertain stumbling Buzz" of a fly. Like Olesha's rat, it becomes the focal point of her expiring life, its tiny furious energy revealing all that she is about to lose. Instead of word-play or neologism, Dickinson ingeniously contrives a reflexive doubling that turns insight into blindness, as if a word could be in oxymoronic relation to itself:

> And then the Windows failed – and then
> I could not see to see –   (Dickinson 224)

The rhetoric of singularity is positional: it points from a distance at an untouchable source. In these examples, the configuration fixes on a contracting point – the dead centre – where the powers of speech and vision are confounded at the moment of revelation. This pattern is familiar in mysticism, but it is also a formation that Elaine Scarry ascribes to the perception of pain, as we noted earlier. Although aesthetic experience is usually associated with pleasure – or with the vicarious pleasures of tragic, pathetic, or sentimental suffering – pain demonstrates even more forcefully the severe concentration of particularity. Pain concentrates the present moment with the severity of its command; or as Pascal said with epigrammatic polish: "The present usually hurts . . . it afflicts us" (Pascal

39, my translation). In Scarry's account, as the world contracts for the torture victim (Scarry 32–3), the self is first isolated and then dissolved (47), until the "absolute privacy" of its suffering becomes confused with utter self-exposure (53). An experience of pure interiority deepens until it suddenly is externalized. Pain, she argues, is the one somatic state that has no object in the external world: "desire is desire of x, fear is fear of y, hunger is hunger for z; but pain is not 'of' or 'for' anything – it is itself alone. This objectlessness, the complete absence of referential content, almost prevents it from being rendered in language" (162). For this very reason, however, it incites an imaginative fantasia – a "dense sea of artifacts and symbols" (162) – that never suffices to render the uniqueness of the experience, and therefore circles it restlessly. The name "Lyompa" is such a symbol-without-reference, while Dickinson's self-nullifying phrase "I could not see to see" evokes such an experience-without-object. Scarry's analysis of this phenomenological pattern explains why intense physicality so readily finds expression as intense spirituality. It also illuminates Stevens's final decree that the course of a particular "concerns no one at all." The absolute privacy of pain obliterates everything but the self, suffering here and now; then the strange singularity of death obliterates even the self.

THE SUPREME DIGNITY OF THE UNIQUE

As traced so far, the course of a particular seems to exclude justice by suspending its ethical obligation and rendering it socially useless, as Hume warned, though not for the reasons that he was considering. A religious response would see the course as a moral path leading to God – the unique, creative source – but hampered by the fallibility of human understanding.[7] Alexis de Tocqueville speculates in *Democracy in America* that God alone does not require general ideas because "[a]t a single glance he sees separately all of the beings of which humanity is composed" (de Tocqueville 411). Because the human mind cannot encompass such bewildering variety, it must reduce "the immensity of detail" to inexact generalities:

General ideas do not attest to the strength of human intelligence, but rather to its insufficiency, because there are no beings in nature exactly alike: no identical facts, no rules indiscriminately applicable in the same manner to several objects at once.

General ideas . . . never provide it with anything but incomplete notions, and they always make it lose in exactness what they give it in extent. (411)

A religious sensibility would reclaim the exactitude obscured by general ideas by acknowledging the precious uniqueness of each soul. This goal is expressed in Egyptian mythology where the god Anubis weighs souls after death but never finds two with exactly the same weight.[8] I began this chapter by wondering what moral footing might be offered by an aesthetic insight that, in Stevens's words, grows "less and less human" (*Palm* 264) until it "concerns no one at all" (367). This diminishing process poses an ethical challenge, since in each of my literary examples the unique moment of sensory impact, of illumination, of the here-and-now, of pain and death, is simultaneously a instant of moral awakening and its frustration. Justice depends on the *duality* structured by a practical, principled confrontation between oneself and another person or persons for whom one is responsible, or to whom one is answerable. Each example discloses responsibility – what one owes to others (Tolstoy, Thomas, Klein), to the social and physical world (Olesha, Stein, Lawrence), or even to oneself (Dickinson) – but it does so just as one's power to exercise that responsibility is lost. The ethical moment vanishes just as its demand is felt, its loss only heightening the perplexity of the obligation. In Kant's famous formulation, "ought implies can": we can be morally obligated to perform only actions that are within our power. To be obliged to perform an impossible or unknowable act is meaningless, because "duty commands nothing but what we can do" (Kant, quoted by Stern).[9]

The paradox of literary singularity, which is impenetrable to the critical understanding that explicates it, thus corresponds to an ethical dilemma. Ethical insights, like aesthetic ones, become intelligible only within a larger system framed by general principles and rules that allow one to adjudicate conduct, but that very generality dispels the uniqueness of the insight and the urgency of its call. Individually we encounter not Duty as an abstract principle, but *my* need to act here and now. The ethical imperative occurs instantaneously; only later can we assess its wider implications. Zygmunt Bauman explains the dilemma as a opposition between duty and responsibility:

> Only rules can be universal. One may legislate universal rule-dictated *duties*, but moral *responsibility* exists solely in interpellating the individual and being carried individually. Duties tend to make humans alike; responsibility is what makes them into individuals. Humanity is not captured in common denominators – it sinks and vanishes there. The morality of the moral subject does not, therefore, have the character of a rule. One may say that the moral is what *resists* codification, formalization, socialization, universalization. (Bauman 54, Bauman's emphasis)

Like de Tocqueville, Bauman sees generality as an enabling limitation of human thought that conflicts with the particularizing imperative of ethical being. What I called the expansive critical view, which sees literature as one vast system, finds a partner in the Kantian ethical tradition, with its categorical imperative that submits every personal decision to the stringent test of universality: "What we call good must be an object of desire in the judgment of every rational man, and evil an object of aversion in the eyes of everyone" (Kant, *Practical* 80). Far from concerning "no one at all," desire for the good requires that "one is part of everything" (Stevens, *Palm* 367).[10] For Kant, the test of both aesthetic and moral judgments is universality. The paradox of aesthetic experience is summed up in his notion of "taste," understood as a subjective universal. As the metaphor of sensory taste implies, aesthetic experience is purely subjective, a pleasurable feeling, yet it is also disinterested, without ulterior purpose, and universal – a "necessary delight" enjoyed by all who share the same "common sense" (Boos 20).[11] We can distinguish "good" and "bad" taste concerning the beautiful only within a community of shared responses, a community whose standards Kant treats as universal. Similarly, ethics is rooted in our "sensible nature" (Kant, *Practical* 80) with its urgent demands of the moment. The good, like the beautiful, is commanding: it imposes itself directly; it is thrilling. Nevertheless, morality is intelligible only as a social discipline based on general rules impartially applied. Ethical encounters transpire through the interplay between personal will and social law (81), between discrete experience and universal rule. However, their interplay is asymmetrical rather than harmonious. Slavish conformity to the rule obscures the justice of individual cases; excessive insistence on peculiarity (the exception to the rule) threatens the law's authority. There is always a tug-of-war between generality and specificity.

As we saw when discussing *Huckleberry Finn*, in this contest Kant ensures that the general principle commands the specific particle: rational law must be the *a priori* determination of the particular will. However, maintaining this deductive pattern requires what he calls a "paradox of method": "*The concept of good and evil must not be determined before the moral law (of which it seems as if it must be the foundation), but only after it and by means of it*" (82, Kant's emphasis). Rules are not framed in accordance with what is good; rather, the general law precedes the discrete experiences from which it seems to arise: "it is the moral law that first determines the concept of good, and makes it possible, so far as it deserves the name of good absolutely" (83). Modern theory tends to twist this paradox in the other direction by asserting the priority of the particular over the general, as is illustrated by Ludwig Wittgenstein's comment: "ethics presupposes the *uniqueness* of life" (quoted by Greisch 74). The word "presupposes" suggests that the uniqueness of the moral agent comes first as the precondition of moral generalities, which then follow inductively. Responsibility precedes duty, as Fabio Ciaramelli explains: "Ethical obligation arises not from the logical and ontological universality of reason which discloses to knowledge criteria for freely determined action, but rather immediately from the uniqueness of the moral situation itself... moral obligation takes hold immediately, before understanding or decision on the part of the subject" (Ciaramelli 85). The philosopher who argues most passionately and enigmatically on behalf of ethical singularity as a foundation for justice is Emmanuel Levinas.

From Levinas's richly opaque writing, I wish to stress only how he offers the radical singularity of the self as an enigmatic point of departure for all ethical encounters. He begins with a customary clearing of the rhetorical ground. The unique self ("ipseity") is not displayed in essential qualities: it is not a "distinguishing characteristic, a *unicum* or a *hapax*, like fingerprints"; it is not an ego, agent, consciousness or "individuated quiddity" (Levinas, *Basic* 84). It is not even an individual, since individuality means being one of a kind, that is, one member of a category such as "the human genus" (Levinas, *Entre* 189). Ethics begins before any of these notions have been formulated. The precious "indefeasible unity" (Levinas, *Basic* 84) of each soul is marked, not just when it expires at death, but when it is startled into moral being (a nice parallel with Barthes's figure of surprise) by the cry of an Other. This is the first onset when "the essential, primary and fundamental structure of subjectivity" is constituted through an "assignation" between two solitary selves who realize themselves only through that encounter (95). "The ego is an incomparable unicity" (114) that must be "troubled" from its passivity into moral, intellectual, and social consciousness. This occurs only when the "uniqueness of the I" (55) is reflected in the Other's "face." Paradoxically, "against the logic of the genus," one's uniqueness does not precede the call of the Other but is summoned by it, "as if I... precisely *I* or *me* – the one who, summoned, heard the imperative as an exclusive recipient, as if that imperative went toward me alone" (Levinas, *Entre* 193). "[T]he I qua I is absolutely unique," but it asserts its uniqueness only when called to responsibility by another (Levinas, *Basic* 28).

Before the neighbor I am summoned and do not just appear; from the first I am answering to an assignation. Already the stony core of my substance is dislodged. But the responsibility to which I am exposed in such a passivity does not apprehend me as an interchangeable thing, for here no one can be substituted for me; in calling upon me as someone accused who cannot reject the accusation, it obliges me as someone unreplaceable and unique, someone chosen. Inasmuch as it calls upon my responsibility it forbids me any replacement. (143)

Like de Man, Levinas wants to imagine the disconnected particularities of being before they are rendered intelligible by "the labor of thinking" (153), which disposes them into general categories. The moral moment precedes thought and therefore cannot be thought ("thematized"). Its irreducible specificity is prior to all the systems of definition that I listed earlier (analogy, category, causality, etc.), and according to Levinas it even precedes the fundamental structure of symbolic exchange that makes linguistic signification possible. It is therefore unspeakable and unknowable, although it provides the primary unit from which speech and knowledge will arise. Happily, where this anarchic state made de Man think of martyrdom, mourning, and death, it makes Levinas think of life: "This is the bursting forth of incessant novelty. The absolute novelty of the new. This is the spirituality of transcendence, which does not amount to an assimilating act of consciousness. The uninterrupted bursting forth of novelties would make sense, precisely beyond knowledge, through its absolute and unforeseeable novelty" (155). Stevens imagines the original cry of life as a wintry syllable intoning its single emptiness. For Levinas, it is also "a cry of ethical revolt, bearing witness to responsibility" (147) by sounding the first moral injunction: "The first word of the face is the 'Thou shalt not kill.' It is an order. There is a commandment in the appearance of the face, as if a master spoke to me" (Levinas, *Ethics* 89).[12] The moment when moral power is summoned is also the moment when it is restrained in deference to "the supreme dignity of the unique" (101).

In this dramatic account, genesis (emergence of selfhood), mortality (awareness that one could kill the Other and therefore is oneself mortal), and responsibility (altruism) are all revealed instantaneously. It is also the genesis of justice, first in the specific sense of "*doing justice to* the difference of the other person," and then in the broader sense of social justice, which arises when a third party enters the drama. At that moment the "original sociality," which bound the self to one Other, is multiplied into a public sociability or fellowship (Levinas, *Entre* 194–5). This is a dangerous moment, however, because the rationality of justice now takes precedence over one's pre-rational responsibility for the fate of the Other (104). Inevitably, human uniqueness must yield to individuality, that is, to personal participation in social life, where society assumes the power of fate in the form of law and its institutions. The danger is that justice will forget the charity and love from which it arose. It must judge fairly on the basis of general principles, but in so doing it can become cold and calculating rather than merciful. To soften the arithmetical justice scorned by Nietzsche, which impartially computes all human conduct in order to impose equivalences on everything, Levinas appeals to "a Reason capable of comparing incomparables, a wisdom of love" (195).[13]

"Love must always watch over justice" (108), but how is this to be accomplished? What form of justice can compare incomparables without accommodating them in a uniform system? Levinas's answer is to call for "prophetic voices" to teach that justice must never submerge "the right or the uniqueness of the other" in "the generality of the human" (196). These voices resound in the Bible and in "all literature" (109), as well as in another of Levinas's prophetic phrases, "Nous n'est pas le pluriel de Je" (quoted by Bauman 48) – the solitary "I" is not absorbed by a collective "we." Happily, he expresses this paradox not as scarcity but as abundance. While he shares de Man's ascetic withdrawal into singularity, this act of humility leads to an affirmation of responsibility as startling, prolific, transcendent. Precisely because the atomic "I" precedes any rational, social, or psychological articulation of its character, when summoned into proximity with the Other it is awed by the prospect of limitless responsibility: "I am responsible for a total responsibility, which answers for all the others and for all in the others, even for their responsibility. The I always has one responsibility more than all the others" (Levinas, *Ethics* 99). In defiance of any rational computation of fairness or adequacy, he affirms "[t]his surplus of being, this existential exaggeration that is called *being me*" (Levinas, *Basic* 17).

What poet could achieve more? If we look to literature for prophetic moments when singularity blossoms into its own excess, we find them most readily in romance and in the sublime. We are back in Northrop Frye's territory. Frye treats romance as a transgressive genre that foresees not a return to the stability of family, duty, and political order, but revolutionary transformation. It exhibits not the circularity of comic restoration, but a spiral of creative revelations. Comedy offers justice by granting characters what they deserve; romance grants more than they deserve. Frye finds a remarkable expression of redemptive singularity in the romantic motif of the threat to virginity (Frye, *Secular* 80), which we encountered briefly in *Billy Budd*. While these threats obviously express patriarchal conventions of male dominance and female modesty, for Frye they also point to "a vision of human integrity" menaced by

the one fate which really is worse than death, the annihilation of one's identity ... What is symbolized as a virgin is actually a human conviction, however expressed, that there is something at the core of one's infinitely fragile being which is not only immortal but has discovered the secret of invulnerability that eludes the tragic hero. (86)

Romances depict the loss, sacrifice, and recovery of identity, a narrative pattern circling a unique core of being that cannot be described directly, because it is "a state of existence in which there is nothing to write about," an abundant existence that romances gesture at by invoking an earlier ("once upon a time") and a later ("they lived happily ever after") time beyond record (54). In the meantime, where all stories occur, identity is sensed most acutely when it is threatened. What protects the "beleaguered virgin" or faithful wife (or heals her if she is sacrificed) is not so much the intrepid male hero as "a certain redemptive quality" (87) inherent in her untouchable singularity.[14] Virginity cannot be touched or "known" either conceptually or physically, since what is touched is not virginity, but only its apparent loss. "[W]hat is objectively untouched symbolizes what is subjectively contained" (153), Frye states quaintly of a fertile chastity that is "perpetually renewed . . . in a world where every experience is fresh and unique" (153). This, too, may be a male fantasy, but it also expresses an energy that perpetually animates the novelty of an innocent world. Working within the conventions of romance, it "emphasizes the uniqueness, the once-for-all quality, in the creative act" (184).

The final scene in Shakespeare's *The Winter's Tale*, where the faithful wife Hermione apparently is resurrected, offers an example of aesthetic and ethical creativity corresponding to Levinas's notion of ethical awakening. After Hermione's patient sixteen years in hiding, which enact a kind of chastity, there is a magical rebirth through the re-creation of life through art: the statue comes to life to the sound of music. Her resurrection is a gift in excess of the occasion. Just as the earlier sacrifice of Leontes's innocent son, Mamillius, is far worse than justice demands, his wife's return to life is far better than any reward commensurate with his expiation of his sins. Remorse cannot re-animate the dead. Nor does the found daughter Perdita replace the lost Mamillius, since no unique self is equivalent to any other self. When Levinas speaks of the self as "hostage," he is not referring to a fair substitution of one for the other, but to an "involuntary election" (Levinas, *Basic* 121–2). Similarly, the final moment in *The Winter's Tale* points to a power beyond moral calculation – a blessing. With startling simplicity Leontes's words "O, she's warm" (5.3.109) evoke the shock of aesthetic and moral insight, the sudden gesture whereby a scene that in realistic terms would be absurd, becomes enchanting.

I conclude this chapter by returning to Wallace Stevens, because he is so rigorous in tracing the course of a particular, and because he is particularly drawn to romance, to the poetry of what he calls "transport" – the triumph of delight over bare fact. Finding moments of transcendent particularity in his poetry is tricky, however, because he expresses his triumphs ambiguously, or finds only modest satisfaction in them (Stevens, *Necessary Angel* 42). To be satisfied is to find enough, not an excess. Whereas Levinas prophetically announces "[t]his growing surplus of the infinite that we have ventured to call *glory*" (Levinas, *Basic* 144), Stevens is more diffident. In "Sailing after Lunch" he foresees only a "slight transcendence to the dirty sail" (Stevens, *Palm* 112) of his craft. In "Extracts from Addresses to the Academy of Fine Ideas" he proposes that the world's familiar climate is only just enough:

> There is nothing more and that it is enough
> To believe in the weather and in the things and men
> Of the weather and in one's self, as part of that
> And nothing more.   (183)

And in "Final Soliloquy of the Interior Paramour" he concludes humbly:

> Out of this same light, out of the central mind,
> We make a dwelling in the evening air,
> In which being there together is enough.   (368)

Only the word "together" hints that the unique self is not self-sufficient, but must probe beyond its limits. The same hesitancy appears in section 12 of "The Man with the Blue Guitar," which first proclaims, "The blue guitar / And I are one," but later asks if one can ever remain self-contained:

> I know that timid breathing. Where
> Do I begin and end? And where,
> As I strum the thing, do I pick up
> That which momentously declares
> Itself not to be I and yet
> Must be. It could be nothing else.
>   (139)

The haunting phrase "that timid breathing" recalls the first hint (and last gasp) of life in *The Winter's Tale*, but as it leads to a "momentous" (momentary, crucial, imperative) assignation with an Other, Stevens seems wary of venturing too far, as if the glory might fade if affirmed too romantically.

One can twist Stevens into any convenient shape – Emersonian, Nietzschean, Santayanian, Derridean, etc.[15] – and I would like to avoid contriving a clumsy application of Levinas's ideas to the poetry. Instead, we should hope for a coincidence of mood, image, or situation. The two dispositions with which I began this chapter can lead Stevens, on the one hand, to an omnivorous imagination that consumes whatever it surveys; and on the other hand, to a solipsism that recognizes the Other only as stunted expression of oneself. The former appears in "Anecdote of the Jar" (46), where the artefact placed on a hill in Tennessee composes the landscape (just as "Tennessee," the "anecdote," and the poem itself are all compositions) by taking dominion over it.[16] The latter appears in images of confinement or monotony. His provocative question "Where / Do I begin and end?" is often posed in such way as to leave the reader uncertain how to proceed. Nevertheless in his essay "The Figure of the Poet as Virile Youth," when Stevens asks only for a meager "satisfaction" of reason or imagination, he promptly suggests that "an idea of God" just might satisfy both and so would provide "a sanction for life" (Stevens, *Necessary Angel* 42–3). His coy understatement ("This is an illustration.") cannot disguise the enormity of his intimation: such a sanction (blessing) would "momentously" exceed any egotism. Similarly "Academic Discourse at Havana" begins skeptically by restraining the lusty imagination with its promise of glory ("perfect plenitude," "ornatest prophecy"), but its chastening of thought raises a hope that poetry might achieve "An infinite incantation of our selves" (Stevens, *Palm* 87–9).

"Credences of Summer" (287–92) offers a final illustration of how aesthetic particularity can be troubled into opening an avenue to the ethical promise of romance. Here is an example of Klein's Adamic poet discovering the world, but its peaceful evocation of summer is upset by anxieties expressed in oxymorons and paradoxes. Its celebration of natural abundance ("green's green apogee") is an odd occasion to look for the virginity of the particular, yet the season is so fruitful that its very excess reveals an "essential barrenness": "This is the barrenness / Of the fertile thing that can attain no more." If the instant of death marks the summation of life, then this moment of completion "[b]eyond which there is nothing left of time" is the summation of the year. Stevens stresses the uniqueness of the present by isolating the here-and-now. "Now" the poem begins, here at "[o]ne of the limits of reality," the landscape's festival of light, sight and sound pinpoints attention on "the very thing and nothing else . . . [w]ithout evasion by a single metaphor."[17] Here and now "[i]t comes to this" – the unassigned demonstrative pronoun marking a particularity without defining it – "and we accept what is / As good. The utmost must be good and is."

To find sensory and contemplative joy in a summer day is necessarily to appeal beyond oneself to the earth and its vital gifts. "Dear life redeems you," proclaims Paulina in *The Winter's Tale* (5.3.103), while Stevens's speaker admits more modestly to be "appeased" by the generous scene. While Frank Kermode feels that the subject of "Credences" is "total satisfaction," (Kermode 106), most readers have been less convinced (Jarraway 225). The limit of reality should be a place where belief (credence) is justified and desire is fulfilled ("Exile desire / For what is not"), but by section 5 the rhythm grows restless as the speaker wonders about the goodness that he has just argued himself into affirming. Some dissatisfaction turns his meditation into what Charles Berger calls the "dark countersong" of a "countersublime" (Berger 83, 86), as it questions the relation between "concentred self" and Other, between particular and general. Does the valiant particular dominate generality ("One day enriches a year") as the jar claimed both heroically and absurdly to dominate Tennessee; or does a defining generality ennoble all its particulars ("Or do the other days enrich the one")? Where do I begin and end?

The beginning is the "rock" (section 6) – unique, "extreme," elemental, conveying no secret meaning ("hermit's truth") beyond its bare existence "on this present ground." The end is more difficult to foresee, because Stevens persists in renouncing the traditional solaces of romance or the egotistical sublime (section 7). As he explains of a similar situation in "Angel Surrounded by Paysans": "the point of the poem is that there must be in the world about us things that solace us quite as fully as any heavenly visitations could" (Stevens, *Letters* 661). The visitations in "Credences" arrive with the awakening call of the trumpet (section 8) and cock (section 9), which can be compared to Levinas's "cry of ethical revolt, bearing witness to responsibility" (Levinas, *Basic* 147) at least in the sense that they herald a challenge from the world beyond the self that forever implicates the self. For Levinas, too, ethics is an "awakening" that "designates the improbable field where the Infinite is in relationship with the finite without contradicting itself by this relationship... The Infinite transcends itself in the finite" (146). Stevens would agree with the last sentence. His trumpet does not herald the resurrection of the dead, only of the summer with its virginal fertility. The "resounding cry" urges us to "share the day." It not only startles the mind into awareness of its own precious existence, but makes it "aware of division ... [a]s that of a personage in a multitude." Commenting on these lines, Justin Quinn argues that Stevens's specific landscape in Olney, Pennsylvania, is "already woven through with social meaning by the generations of the people who have lived here," and therefore the multitude refers, not to abstract humanity, but to a local community "with its ceremonies, family ties, and transmission of cultural and ethical values"

(Quinn 119, 118). The scene draws the speaker into its intimacy. The cock, too, is a "civil bird" that momentously makes "a sound / Which is not part of the listener's own sense," and which urges him to speak his part in "[t]he huge decorum, the manner of the time, / Part of the mottled mood of summer's whole" (Stevens, *Palm* 292). What the self earns here is not dominance but a supreme dignity.

CHAPTER 6

Truth, justice, and the pathos
of understanding

and you will know the truth, and the truth will make you free
(John 8:32)

truths are illusions of which one has forgotten that they *are* illusions . . . Art is with us in order that we may not perish through truth.
(Nietzsche, "Truth" 694; *Will* 264)

I began this study with *le mot juste*, Gustave Flaubert's pursuit of a literary
style so precise that it would contribute equally to a justice of expression,
thought, and judgment, each enhancing the others and all sustained by
pleasure. The joyful companionship of truth, beauty, and virtue is an ideal
perpetually sought but never quite found; indeed, Flaubert takes sardonic
pleasure in its failure, which testifies to the banality of bourgeois culture.
However, it also demonstrates his belief that literature is vitally important,
because it can help to cure the ethical and intellectual malaise of his nation.
Faith in the political value of literary language recurs with varying degrees of
confidence in modern theory. It appears in Ezra Pound's complaint that in
the modern republic "the health of the very matter of thought" is weakened
when "the application of word to thing" becomes "slushy and inexact, or
excessive or bloated" (Pound 21). It appears more cautiously in George
Orwell's essay "Politics and the English Language," where he warns that
modern political discourse must be reformed, not just because it is sloppy
but because it deliberately clouds judgment, making the most atrocious
injustice seem normal. He, too, believed that an honest style would sharpen
critical and moral insight (although he excluded literary language from
his analysis[1]): "the present political chaos is connected with the decay of
language, and . . . one can probably bring about some improvement by
starting at the verbal end" (Orwell 157).

Subsequent chapters in this book have shown, however, that the verbal
end is unruly, not just because it is so hard to formulate truth or to interpret
its documented traces, but because the relations between truth, legality, and

justice are always strained. Judicial procedures may claim to seek "nothing but the truth," but because they find "the whole truth" far too much to assimilate, they must exclude testimony or evidence by following a rule of appropriateness that is continually disputed. When, for example, is evidence unduly prejudicial, and when is it merely incriminating? When is a person's past behavior relevant to a case, and when it is unfairly distracting? I have adapted Shoshana Felman's suggestion that criminal trials especially are concerned as much with closure as with truth. They are formally satisfied when a verdict is delivered in accordance with correct procedures, whether the accused person actually committed the crime or not. The so-called "Blackstone ratio" derived from William Blackstone's *Commentaries* – "Better that ten guilty persons escape than that one innocent suffer" (Volokh) – is a calculation that accepts a remarkable margin of error. This chapter is devoted to the margin of error that protects the truth.

When Jesus says, "you will know the truth, and the truth will make you free," He refers to the higher truth of His own divinity and warns of the sacrifice that it will require. Ultimately His radiant truth ("I am the light of the world," John 8:12) will bring a justice that supersedes the Law, but in the meantime the whole truth is obscured to ordinary vision and will appear only after an ordeal of faith. Similarly I noted that literary evocations of natural justice often take the symbolic shape of immersion in water, or an arduous journey through the woods or up a mountain, suggesting that self-evident truths become evident only after a pilgrimage through error. Fortunately, literature loves to explore error and to trace its contours. The wandering path of error (Latin *errare*: to wander, stray)[2] is one way of describing a plot whose erratic course maps out what I have called a literary jurisdiction – a discursive field of definition and rule.

As we saw in Gilbert and Sullivan's operas, in comic jurisdictions truth is often expressed as true love: the right couples are rightly paired off to the satisfaction of both characters and readers. Comic truth is also expressed as clear vision: after a trial of error, characters and readers come to see reality accurately and to accept it as just. Seeing is believing. In the final scene of *Twelfth Night*, Shakespeare uses the simple expedient of placing all his characters on stage without disguise for the first time. Their simply seeing each other is sufficient to permit a dramatic recognition that resolves the comic confusion. The "talking cure" associated with Freudian psychology aims at a similar effect of bringing truth to light (Launer). Encouraged by the sympathetic questioning of a psychologist, a patient speaks freely to disclose the subconscious source of his or her neurosis. Knowing the truth, however painful or shameful, is therapeutic. The same hope motivated

South Africa's Truth and Reconciliation Commission. Even Freud's account of the traumatic "return of the repressed" suggests that the truth will re-present itself as nightmare until it is confronted. That one can be cured by truth is as refreshing a belief as that one can be cured by literature.

If justice cannot tolerate too much truth, how much falsehood can it withstand? Tragedy reveals not only the inadequacy of passion and clear vision in revealing truth, but the inadequacy of truth itself. Discovering the truth is necessary for a tragic hero, but it is not enough, and a more radical purgation is required. Oedipus' severe social and psychological problems are exacerbated by his learning the truth about his parents; Hamlet's revelation of his father's murder brings vengeance but not justice; in *Billy Budd*, the truth is endlessly debatable and ultimately irrelevant. In a more ironic mode, to which I now turn, truth becomes the problem rather than the solution. Neither therapeutic nor purgative, it becomes unbearable, so that it is an act of kindness or cowardice, or both, to conceal it from the weak-hearted. "Human kind cannot bear very much reality," Becket laments in T.S. Eliot's *Murder in the Cathedral* (Eliot, *Murder* 75; the phrase is repeated in "Burnt Norton"). This solicitude prompts the "necessary lie" or well-intentioned deception associated with Socrates' advice in the *Republic* that the populace must be told "some magnificent myth" rather than the unpalatable truth about their social origins (Plato 115–16). The necessary lie reappears in Nietzsche's warnings that "truth" is an erratic, linguistic fiction that makes life seem intelligible and worthwhile to all but the heroically minded:

The world that *concerns us at all is false* – that is to say, is not a fact; but a romance, a piece of human sculpture, made from a meagre sum of observation; it is "in flux"; it is something that evolves, a great revolving lie continually moving onwards and never getting any nearer to truth – for there is no such thing as "truth." (Nietzsche, *Will* 107)

According to these views literature offers "poetic justice," either in Rymer's sense of a reassuring falsehood, or in the sense of a just aware-ness of the fundamental incommensurability and untruthfulness of things. In the first case we read with the grain: we may know that the myths are false but prefer to treat them as if true. In the second we read against the grain: we resist the solace of "romance," but because Nietzsche's explan-ation cannot itself be true ("for there is no such thing as 'truth'") we are left suspended between belief and disbelief. Both conditions are evoked by the final words of Conrad's Marlow, the narrator of *Heart of Dark-ness*, who wavers between illusion and delusion – between Plato's politic misrepresentation and Nietzsche's compulsive mirage. When Marlow lies to the "Intended" about Kurtz's horrifying death, he justifies his deceit by claiming that women are too tender to face the truth and, by implication, that civilization must be protected from the darkness on which it rests: "The heavens do not fall for such a trifle. Would they have fallen, I wonder, if I had rendered Kurtz that justice which was his due? Hadn't he said he wanted only justice? But I couldn't. I could not tell her. It would have been too dark – too dark altogether" (Conrad 77). It is hard to know what kind of justice is being denied to Kurtz by being offered instead to his fiancée. Marlow claims to sacrifice truth to decency, but his tale has been so indecent, so corrosive to all the values that make justice conceivable (rationality, fairness, authority), that his sacrifice produces only more darkness. The heavens have already fallen, and there is no transcendent source of light.

  In this chapter, I examine the erratic, error-prone wandering in search of truth depicted in *Anil's Ghost*, Michael Ondaatje's novel about the civil war in Sri Lanka. It, too, presents a quest for justice in the form of a journey of discovery, and more specifically as a detective story that gets entangled in both political myth and philosophical romance. Although the detective genre usually promises success, in this case it is gradually betrayed by its own conventions. Ondaatje writes one kind of novel in the guise of another, so that what seems to be a familiar murder mystery, in which truth is discoverable and justice prevails, turns into something far more troubling. Ironically, the detective succeeds in her investigation, only to find that she has been betrayed by her own efforts, because the truth is unavailing.

TOUCH

I begin with another tactile, sacrificial image. In one of the novel's most horrific moments, a truck driver named Gunesena is found crucified to the tarmac on a country road in Sri Lanka (Ondaatje, *Anil* 111). The scene summons one of European culture's most revered symbols, but leaves the reader baffled as to its significance in a land where Christianity is superseded by older myths written in an alphabet in which the words "beautiful" and "dangerous" differ only by a single syllable (192).[3] Although it is easy to see that the crucifixion is ironic, it is difficult to interpret its irony. As an emblem of sacrificial suffering, Christ's ecstatic agony on the cross is itself dangerously beautiful, whereas Gunesena is tortured according to the "mad logic" (186) of a political terror without clear cause, purpose, or value. There is no sense to it, yet its very senselessness finds expression in a symbol whose meaning is sanctioned by centuries of devotion. "[E]ven crucifixion isn't a major assault nowadays" (130), remarks Gamini, the doctor who extracts the nails many hours later, as if Christ's fate hardly deserves notice in an undeclared civil war that has cost more than 70,000 lives in twenty-six years.[4]

To readers familiar with Ondaatje's writing, Gunesena's agony will recall the author's fascination with hands and touching as displayed in the torture of Caravaggio, whose thumbs are cut off in *The English Patient*; in the obsession with fingers expressed by the young gunfighter-poet in *The Collected Works of Billy the Kid*; in the "[s]uicide of the hands" suffered by the jazz cornetist Buddy Bolden in *Coming through Slaughter* (Ondaatje, *Coming* 49). Although clear vision is the most common metaphor for understanding ("I see what you mean," "clarity of thought," etc.),[5] Ondaatje often uses the sense of touch to express all that is tactile and textured in human perception. Hands express how we fumble with the cumbersome foreignness of things even as we caress them into human shape through work and art.[6] The sheer physicality of the world is at once inescapable and impenetrable. To handle things, to be handy, is a both a virtue and a horror for his characters. For example, Billy the Kid reaches into the stomach of a wounded comrade to extract a bullet, in a jigsaw puzzle of a poem that interchanges its lines as if to discover how things fit together:

> His stomach was warm
> remembered this when I put my hand into
> a pot of luke warm tea to wash it out
> dragging out the stomach to get the bullet
> he wanted to see when taking tea
> with Sally Chisum in Paris Texas
> (Ondaatje, *Billy* 27)

Touching the quick of the wound permits an unnerving contact with his friend, an intimacy that is also a way of feeling death at one's fingertips with a tangible immediacy impossible to abstract understanding. In *Anil's Ghost* tactile knowledge again confronts impersonal reasoning, but instead of two gunfighters, we have the hand of a surgeon opposed to the hand of a torturer. Between them stands a detective.

At first glance the novel seems to be a forensic mystery story of the sort that, adapting Northrop Frye's terms, we might call an "epiphany of justice."[7] In this genre, a detective solves a murder by interpreting evidence until the guilty party is revealed, usually in a final, dramatic scene. The reader is keen to discover the murderer, but is even more intrigued by the meticulously constructed inferential path that leads the tactful detective through error and doubt toward the truth. This is, or should be, the path of justice. What makes the genre so comforting is its ready association of reason, truth, guilt, and punishment, each advancing inexorably to the next through a moral and narrative dynamic that drives the story to its satisfying conclusion. Solving the mystery grants a enriched sense of resolution, because simply revealing the truth is sufficient to expose the guilty party and ensure the triumph of justice – the epiphany. The genre is redemptive, not only because it celebrates the efficacy of reason in the service of justice, but because it provides an imaginative victory over death. The ultimate secret of the murder mystery is death itself, but even it can be tamed, at least momentarily, by the clever detective (such as Sherlock Holmes, Hercule Poirot, and their many followers) and by the institutions of social order (Scotland Yard, the courts). However, the Sherlock Holmes model suggests complications that Ondaatje will exploit. Even the best social institutions require an inspired outsider like Holmes to help them crack the case, but inspiration is a dangerous eruption of energy, even when it is summoned to enforce social norms. It may produce a criminal genius like Professor Moriarty, and even Holmes, with his moodiness, music, and drugs, has a darker side. Equally dangerous is the complication, especially strong in American literature, that one might have to step outside the law to find justice, either because the forces of law are corrupt or because of the bureaucratic constraints of legality.

Anil's Ghost summons inspiration in its quest for justice, but by giving freer play to the disruptive powers on which it relies it transforms Holmes into a *makamkruka*: "'an agitator. Someone who perhaps sees things more truly by turning everything upside down. He's a devil almost, a *yaksa*'" (Ondaatje, *Anil* 165). While the conventional detective story devises many twists in its search for hidden truths, it rarely suggests that the truth, once discovered, may be insufficient or unavailing or, worse still, that it may provoke further injustice. Truth is supposed to set you free, but what if it is just another source of suffering? Would a soothing lie not be better?

Anil's Ghost begins with a corpse and two astute detectives: Anil Tissera, a forensic anthropologist, and Sarath Diyasena, an archaeologist. Anil has been partly an outsider or "prodigal" (10), since leaving her native Sri Lanka fifteen years earlier to pursue a career in the West. As she investigates atrocities on behalf of the Centre for Human Rights in Geneva, she naively believes that if she can prove government complicity in political murder, then she can demand justice. Although she is examining just one body in a country littered with victims, she trusts that "[t]o give him a name would name the rest" (56). Although her quest is dangerous, she is confident about its essential worth and reassures Sarath: "'Secrets turn powerless in the open air . . . You're an archaeologist. Truth comes finally into the light'" (259). She assumes that truth is enlightening, but he warns her not to trust her eyes: "'I don't think clarity is necessarily truth'" (259). As an archaeologist he regards knowledge as more tactile and earthy, but also as ambiguous: "'I love history, the intimacy of entering all those landscapes. Like entering a dream. Someone nudges a stone away and there's a story'" (259). Stories remain mysterious even when they offer to solve mysteries, and they may lead to unforeseen conclusions. His fears prove justified when, in the novel's calculated anticlimax, the truth proves to be not only useless – "he would have given his life for the truth if the truth were of any use" (157) – but deadly, as it costs him his life. The point is not that they fail in their mission. They succeed, but the secret that they unearth consumes them.[8]

Far from being triumphant, the knowledge that Anil pieces together so ingeniously is pathetic, not just in the obvious sense that the novel elicits sympathy for a tormented nation, but in that it evokes a vexed understanding that both encourages and baffles the pursuit of justice. The pathos of understanding arises from Ondaatje's ambiguous treatment of knowledge as a means of grasping the world through the combined faculties of mind and body. On the one hand, he presents a romance of understanding that transforms knowledge into science, and science into art; on the other hand, he presents knowledge as faltering pathetically behind the reality that it grasps only well enough to be its victim.

TACT

The romance of understanding might also be called the handiness of thought. It requires intimate familiarity derived from the wisdom and expertise cultivated in sciences like anthropology and archaeology in *Anil's Ghost*; or cartography, geology, and geography in *The English Patient*; or engineering in *In the Skin of a Lion*. These disciplines are wonderful because they are at once disciplined and inspired. They elicit all the virtues that Ondaatje treasures: patience, tact, curiosity, encyclopedic information, daring speculation, rigorous logic infused with a sense of wonder. They require a "sweet touch" (307) as well as a nimble brain. Scientists and scholars master the tools of their trade so well that they develop an instinctive rapport with their materials, like the construction workers dangling precariously in *In the Skin of a Lion*, or Kip defusing bombs in *The English Patient*.

To touch is to know intimately. Similarly Anil and Sarath decipher dusty clues that can be teased into revealing the great civilizations of Sri Lanka's past. Their mentor, the blind anthropologist Palipana, is the Homer of *Anil's Ghost*. Part sage and part fraud, he writes "in spite of blindness, in large billowing script that was half language, half pageantry – the border between them blurred" (94). A few scrapes on a bone tell him about the lives of people who lived thousands of years ago. The novel lovingly probes Sri Lanka's ancient history, revealing the richness of its accomplishments, as if nothing human ever dies entirely because the world remains marked with the poetry of its passing, provided we are sensitive enough to read it.

History was ever-present around him. The stone remnants of royal bathing pools and water gardens, the buried cities . . . Still, the patterns that emerged for Palipana had begun to coalesce. They linked hands. They allowed walking across water, they allowed a leap from treetop to treetop. The water filled a cut alphabet and linked this shore and that. And so the unprovable truth emerged. (80, 83)

Mortality – the way things flourish and die – displays itself in signs that express the immortality of human efforts, which endure as pageantry, religion, history, and art. History is ever-present because everything leaves a trace from which the past can be reconstructed. Similarly, Anil's faith is that an intelligible account of the past will disclose patterns of responsibility and accountability through which justice can be affirmed.

Palipana is an epigraphist who loves runes and graffiti etched in stone, and who is honored after his death by having a "yard-long sentence" of his wisdom (107) chiseled into rock, where it is lapped by water.[9] As a poet, Ondaatje exhibits a fascination with words and things, which like water and rock, like flesh and stone, are elementally different yet enhance each other's character: "The water filled a cut alphabet." The fluidity of language delineates the solidity of matter, which, in turn, imparts its substance to words. Ondaatje reveals his continuing debt to romanticism when he dares to imagine a poetic fusion of words and things so intense that language overcomes its mediating function and directly bodies forth the world. Instead of intervening between us and the things that it signifies, poetic language would lyrically embody them. Thus Coleridge longed "to destroy the old antithesis of *Words & Things*, elevating, as it were words into Things, & living Things too" (Coleridge, *Letters* 626), in which case the poetic word would touch us palpably: "it heats and burns, makes itself to be felt. If we do not grasp it, it seems to grasp us, as with a hand of flesh and blood, and completely counterfeits an immediate presence, an intuitive knowledge" (Coleridge, *Inquiring* 101). Tactile language later becomes the *mot juste* of modernist poetry proclaimed in T.E. Hulme's imagist manifestos: "With perfect style, the solid leather for reading, each sentence should be a lump, a piece of clay, a vision seen; rather, a wall touched with soft fingers" (Hulme, *Further* 79); and by William Carlos Williams: "Oh catch up a dozen good smelly names . . . But can you not see, can you not taste, can you not smell, can you not hear, can you not touch – words?" (Williams 10). It is also the effect of Ondaatje's condensed style, which has, in Karen E. Smythe's words, "a linguistic density that evokes an almost physical response – writing that can tingle the senses" (Smythe 3). Similarly, Marni Parsons finds in his volume of poems, *Handwriting*, "[a] yearning for a gone sympathy between word and thing, an erotics of linguistic attachment, a longing to defy postmodern distance between signifier and signified" (Parsons 70).

The defiant romantic and modernist nostalgia detected here is a strong current in *Anil's Ghost*. Palipana is an Ondaatjean hero: a flawed, impassioned scientist so closely in touch with his work that he can read the language of stone and "leap from treetop to treetop" by making daring inferences. He cultivates an intuitive knowledge that probes mysteries ("the unprovable truth") found not beyond but within science. Ondaatje invests these mysteries with value by modulating his tone, so that scientific curiosity gives way to aesthetic admiration, and then to quasi-mystical reverence. This modulation occurs again when Sarath recounts how, while excavating a flooded tomb in China (water and rock), he felt strangely exhilarated by the sixty-four bells discovered beside an ancient coffin. As the bells rang out after centuries of silence, he explains:

"Music was not entertainment, it was a link with ancestors who had led us here, it was a moral and spiritual force. The experience of breaking through barriers of slate, wood, water, to discover a buried women's orchestra had a similar mystic logic to it . . . Each bell had two notes to represent the two sides of the spirit, containing a balance of opposing forces. Possibly it was those bells that made me an archaeologist." (Ondaatje, *Anil* 261)

The bells did not inspire him to look beyond science, but to appreciate its unfathomable depths, not to glimpse a transcendent light of the world, but to hear its inner music. At this point, the detective quest is redirected inward. Instead of raising a buried secret into the light of day, it sinks into a fertile, vivifying darkness, where truth is associated not with "clarity," as Anil expects, but with "cloud" and "nuance" as Sarath suggests in his response to her (259). Ondaatje evokes this downward quest by quoting (actually, misquoting) a line from D.H. Lawrence's poem "Bavarian

Gentians" (119), in which the poem's speaker ignites a flower to illuminate his path into the underworld:

> Reach me a gentian, give me a torch!
> let me guide myself with the blue, forked torch of this flower
> down the darker and darker stairs, where blue is darkened on blueness
> even where Persephone goes, just now, from the frosted September
> to the sightless realm where darkness is awake upon the dark
> (Lawrence, Selected Poems 243)

Viewed romantically, Anil becomes a Persephone-figure, divided between worlds (East and West, the living and the dead) and drawn into an underworld that she hopes to illuminate, but in which she is finally engulfed.

Ondaatje's artful detection goes far beyond Sherlock Holmes's scrutiny of telltale dust and tobacco. By celebrating a "mystic logic" that fuses science and art, knowledge and music, rock and word, he ventures as close to religious reverence as his novel permits. To this end, conventional religious images from Christianity (crucifixion) and Buddhism (contemplation) are absorbed into his evocation of an inspired, sympathetic wisdom that refines our minds and hands until we become ideally suited to the world. He envisions a secular grace in which being, knowing, and doing (existence, cognition, and ethics) are perfectly consonant. Such would be the epiphany of justice, the *mot juste* offered by *Anil's Ghost* if the revelation were allowed to go unchallenged, just as it might be the beatific vision contemplated by the 120-foot-high Buddha, whose stone eyes are restored by the sculptor, Ananda Udugama, in the novel's coda. Those eyes "that had once belonged to a god" (Ondaatje, *Anil* 304) might see what Palipana's hands imagine in their touching.

PATHOS

To leave this optimistic view unchallenged would be to ignore warnings that continually undercut Anil's faith in rationality. Sarath offers a skeptical counsel, Gamini cautions that "in the heart of any faith is a history that teaches us not to trust" (193), and even in his keenest insights Palipana glimpses only an "unprovable truth" tendered by "his unprovable theories" (83). Anil trusts in reason, not just in the sense that she is confident in her analytical powers, but in that she believes reason will dispel falsehood through the very force of its rightness: truth should set us free because it is stronger than deceit. She does not realize that Gamini's warning about naive faith applies both to her own research and, self-reflexively, to history itself. Since history, too, requires faith in a retrospective intelligence that discerns meaningful patterns in the disarray of human events, even it is not trustworthy. History teaches us not to trust historians. It is typical of Ondaatje's vexed romanticism that at the very moment of revelation, truth should slip out of reach by drifting into fantasy, as if modern science inevitably reverts to its magical sources in alchemy and astrology. For example, when radio telescopes turn their gigantic ears to heaven and read "the huge history of the sky," they cast a horoscope in which Anil reads her own destiny: "Who was out there? How far away was that signal? Who was dying unmoored?" (255). Truth, even scientific truth, is always tinged by magic, which, like inspiration, is too unruly to be a reliable ally. Like the sorcerer's apprentice in Goethe's fable,[10] it might release chaos as well as freedom. Although the last question concerns Anil's fatally ill friend, Leaf Niedecker (named in tribute to the American poet Lorine Niedecker), it also applies to Anil, as she is cast adrift between truth and falsehood.

If Palipana is the novel's sorcerer who brings the past back to life by deciphering its codes, Anil is the apprentice who invokes uncanny forces (her "ghost") in the cause of justice but loses control of them. The same fate befalls the novel as a whole. Signification – the power to generate meaning – is unmoored when the "mystic logic" (261) of science and art is confounded by the "mad logic" (186) of political terrorism, which is methodical yet demented. When rebels kidnap Dr Corea and taunt him in an incomprehensible "idiot language" (122), they mimic the lapse into non-sense that threatens *Anil's Ghost*. Instead of a poetic fusion of words and things, the novel risks utter confusion. How we finally interpret its quest for justice depends on how we assess these rival claims to determine meaning. Does one logic dominate the other, can they be reconciled, or does their rivalry remain unresolved?

Although their opposition might be regarded as a simple moral contest between art (mystical, life-affirming) and politics (mad, life-denying), this would be to sentimentalize a much more fraught relationship. Certainly, knowledge would be splendidly tactile if we were all devoted scientists like Palipana or artists like Ananda, but usually we are clumsy with both our thoughts and our hands. We are maladroit, Ondaatje shows, because knowledge comes as an after-thought. The pathos of understanding is that it is belated: it falters behind experience, and usually arrives too late to render justice to it. The most famous expression of this dilemma is Hegel's warning in *Philosophy of Right* that the brilliance of philosophical knowledge is only a "grey" substitute for the vital reality that it comprehends.

Only one word more concerning the desire to teach the world what it ought to be. For such a purpose philosophy at least always comes too late. Philosophy, as the thought of the world, does not appear until reality has completed its formative process, and made itself ready. History thus corroborates the teaching of the conception that only in the maturity of reality does the ideal appear as counterpart to the real, apprehends the real world in its substance, and shapes it into an intellectual kingdom. When philosophy paints its grey in grey, one form of life has become old, and by means of grey it cannot be rejuvenated, but only known. The owl of Minerva takes its flight only when the shades of night are gathering. (Hegel xxx)

The fusion of words and things appears here as a partnership between the ideal and the real "in its substance," while Hegel's heroic definition of philosophy as "the thought of the world" applies nicely to Palipana's inspired science, as he reads sermons in stone in order to rejuvenate antiquity. Although Anil is not so presumptuous as "to teach the world what it ought to be," she is a disciple of Minerva (wisdom) on a moral mission to prove that "*One victim can speak for many victims*" (Ondaatje, *Anil* 176). But what good is knowledge if it comes too late?

The cruel irony that Anil's ingenuity might disclose a truth that speaks for no one is suggested by Gunesena's fortuitous rescue, which, in its own small but painful way, illustrates the pathos of belated understanding. At first she and Sarath drive right past, assuming that he is taking a nap beside his truck; twenty minutes later they recall that no dogs were barking (a clue borrowed from a Sherlock Holmes story) and infer that something sinister has occurred. In this case, knowledge does not come too late. They return in time to save him, but only through good luck. Earlier I argued that when Rose and Charlie are saved in the nick of time by their drifting boat, the *African Queen*, the accident is part of a providential plan transposed into aesthetic design. By contrast, Gunesena is saved not because he deserves it, or because he teaches a lesson about patience or sacrifice, but simply by chance. He could just as easily have perished, and his death by crucifixion would be no more meaningful than his rescue. Applying this lesson more widely, Anil admits that archaeologists make sense of the past only because natural and human catastrophes (Pompeii, Laetoli in Tanzania, Hiroshima) have accidentally preserved evidence to be inspected centuries later. The fruit of past chaos and a lucky chance is the placid understanding of science, which knows but cannot rejuvenate the colorful reality it recasts in shades of rational grey. The pathos of understanding is that it severs meaning from experience, so that being, thought, and action can never be fully consonant:

> Tectonic slips and brutal human violence provided random time-capsules of unhistorical lives. A dog in Pompeii. A gardener's shadow in Hiroshima. But in the midst of such events, she realized, there could never be any logic to the human violence without the distance of time. For now it [her investigation of atrocities in Sri Lanka] would be reported, filed in Geneva, but no one could ever give meaning to it. She used to believe that meaning allowed a person a door to escape grief and fear. But she saw that those who were slammed and stained by violence lost the power of language and logic. (55)

The disjunction between experience and understanding reduces "meaning" to a ghost of the violent reality that it supersedes. It displaces justice into the attenuated form of a document in a file in Geneva, which may some day be unearthed by another detective.

For most of the story, Anil is shielded from the horrors that she investigates by a "door" – intellectual and emotional detachment – that makes "meaning" possible but justice unattainable. The understanding supplied by forensic anthropology arises when she discerns "[p]atterns of death" (279) in the tangle of evidence that she has amassed. Then random clues fall into shape in her hands. But they can be recognized as "clues" only insofar as they are presumed to contribute to a systematic explanation of events, and such presumptuous systems are tenuous hypotheses at best, which may satisfy only our secret desires and which lapse back into "grief and fear" as soon as they lose their explanatory power. Ondaatje offers a poignant example of this faltering delusion when the sculptor Ananda tries to reconstruct the face of the murder victim, only to end up revealing the face of his beloved, dead wife.

The dislocated narrative of *Anil's Ghost*, with its abrupt flashbacks to unrecorded horrors, re-enacts this threat. As the detective structure advances toward a promised resolution that never comes, it is interrupted by digressions revealing that death *without* pattern – without justification or value – is the real trauma of political brutality. Gunesena's crucifixion is a pathetic example of a recognizable pattern that disintegrates as soon as we try to interpret it, and if he represents his troubled country, then its suffering, too, defies the power of language and logic. There is no logic to death as random as the public bombs that devastate crowded markets (127); no political mythology can justify the flood of mutilated corpses washed down rivers and in from the sea (212–13). In its darkest moments, the novel suggests that "'[*t*]*he reason for war was war*'" (43), which is to say, war feeds on itself without reason or justice.

JUSTICE

If "the power of language and logic" is nullified by a pathological violence that is its own *raison d'être*, does that leave *Anil's Ghost* drifting both conceptually and morally, as Brooke Allen complains in a caustic review?[11] What justice does it foresee?

Ondaatje's many commentators agree that he cultivates poetic crises; they disagree over how he resolves them, or whether he even wants to. As he remarked in conversation: "Writing is trying to make order, to understand something about yourself. Orderless situations are, for me, the most interesting things, and I tend to write about the finding out of order" (Kareda 49). Even this casual remark illustrates the crisis. To give an orderly account of orderlessness repeats the pathos of understanding by rendering systematic the chaos that invigorates us precisely because it defies all attempts to harness it. Like a "science" of the unconscious or a "theory" of the irrational, such an account is self-defeating unless it somehow accommodates a transgressive impulse that threatens order (conceptual, social, aesthetic) until it collapses. Ondaatje both imposes and renounces order, although not in equal measure. He either focuses on glorious moments when disorder suddenly assumes a graceful shape, for example when Buddy Bolden channels the fierce energies of racist America into jazz, or, conversely, he focuses on terrifying moments when familiar patterns disintegrate, for example "the one altered move that will make them [the stars] manic" in *Billy the Kid* (Ondaatje, *Billy* 41) and the "false act of madness" that disrupts "the centre of the symmetrical plot" ascribed to some thieves in *In the Skin of a Lion* (Ondaatje, *Skin* 191). These crises, when anarchy and precision pass into each other, are both moments of truth, but of opposite truths, neither of which takes priority. One does not command the other. Palipana weaves falsehood into truth when he fraudulently makes his great archaeological discovery, which may be history, or fiction, or both. The novel's narrative voice concludes hopefully: "perhaps for him it was not a false step but the step to another reality, the last stage of a long, truthful dance" (Ondaatje, *Anil* 81). Truth emerges from a graceful ceremony, not just from factual accuracy. However, the wavering phrase "perhaps for him" functions like the ambiguous "Asian nod" that puzzles Anil, because it "included in its almost circular movement the possibility of a no" (16–17). It might signify affirmation, denial, or hesitancy between the two. It might hint that all our steps, even the best-intentioned, tumble into error.

Similarly, Ondaatje told another interviewer: "All art, for that matter, is self-conscious . . . one has to be on the border where that craft meets the accidental and the unconscious, as close as possible to the unconscious" (Solecki 22). He presents himself as a craftsman who ventures to the verge of the accidental but does not fall in, just as Sherlock Holmes draws on unruly inspiration that he rules intellectually. However, there is no necessary reason why this fertile disorder need submit to artistic direction, especially since its secret energy – its fertility – is uncontrollable. Like the sorcerer's apprentice, he might be overwhelmed by the forces that he releases. The same danger threatens the reader of *Anil's Ghost*, which ends with another Asian nod. M.S. Nagarajan takes comfort in the novel's placid coda, where Ananda restores the Buddha and aspires to share its vision: "The superb ending is on a positive note of affirmation that even with the escalating number of politically motivated murders and arson, there is the coming together of people in breathing fresh life, in recreation . . . there is the life-affirming and life-sustaining spirit that conquers and survives, towering over and above death and destruction" (Nagarajan). While it is comforting to assume that formal order – intelligibility, humane values, justice – will ultimately master the confusion that provides its content, there is no sure reason why it need do so. If we feel that it *should* do so, in other words that literature should be socially productive and morally uplifting, then we share Anil's quest for justice.

This is a noble aim that the novel encourages but gradually frustrates: it promises to solve a mystery, only to recede into a deeper mystery. How can we secure any moral footing in a disjunctive narrative that separates knowledge from experience, and justice from knowledge? Simply insisting on the necessity for a redemptive vision is to repeat Ananda's act of fashioning the remnants of horror into the face of a loved one. Like history, justice is a discourse that retrospectively discerns an intelligible course in events, but it is far more presumptuous. As I argued earlier, the temporality of justice affords not just knowledge, but a recuperative power granted by the adequating and healing agencies of thought. These can succeed only if events can be assessed morally as virtuous or vicious; if the culpability or innocence of ethical actors can be weighed; if fair judgments can be rendered by legitimate authorities; and if punishments or rewards commensurate with the original deeds can serve as reparation for them. History seeks to understand the past, but justice seeks to amend it, and even to "touch" it in the sense of rectifying its errors by offering symbolic compensation for what happened. Only then can the violence of the law (arrest, imprisonment, execution) be a just corrective to the violence (criminality) whose injuries it claims to heal. In this way it provides an imaginative triumph over error, loss, and even death, which, as in the classic detective story, is no longer final but an integral part of the system.

If at a few exalted moments Ondaatje makes this symphonic, judicial semiotic seem within reach, at other times he shows how presumptuous it is, and how pathetic to believe that a neglected document in a drawer in Geneva might be an effective vehicle of justice. Too little, too late. The closer Anil's investigation gets to the truth, the less she trusts the power of truth to rectify the violence engulfing her, because unforgivable violence seems to be man's natural element. For instance:

They had brought him [Gamini] nine-month-old twins, each shot in the palms and one bullet each in their right legs – so it was no accident, a close-range job and intentional, left to die; the mother had been killed . . . You thought, What did they do to deserve this, and then, What did they do to survive this? It was the formal act of evil perhaps, he didn't know. Thirty people had been massacred that morning. (242)

There is no reason for such brutality, and even if it somehow is explicable, there is no adequate response to it. We are left with T.S. Eliot's bewildered question from "Gerontion": "After such knowledge, what forgiveness?" (Eliot, *Collected* 40).

Critics have accused Ondaatje of being recklessly fond of violence, especially in his earlier work, which romanticizes antisocial men who find a fierce refuge in what Lorraine M. York nicely calls "'the male chaotic' – a realm of seemingly random, centrifugal violent energy, associated with males and either opposed or ignored by females" (York 77). His later work has also been criticized for irresponsibility – for exoticizing the East in defiance of political realities (Mukherjee 33–4); or for preferring frisky postmodern aesthetics to social commitment (Beddoes 206); or for substituting moodiness for insight (Allen 63). In reply, critics like Ajay Heble, Christian Bök, and Susan Ellis argue that his earlier writing emphasizes the subversion of order through physical, sexual, and verbal energies, but his later writing uses a more "ex-centric" style to direct violence to productive social ends. Similarly, Marni Parsons finds "a heightened political awareness" that offers "a gesture of resistance" (Parsons 73) to the poems in *Handwriting*. I, too, am looking for a final gesture that might illuminate Eliot's question by re-examining the disjunction between knowledge, justice, and responsibility.

Anil's Ghost is not a political novel of the sort that maps out a cultural milieu, debates social ideas, or even bothers to distinguish between warring factions, apart from mentioning a brutal government fighting guerrillas in the north and insurgents in the south (Ondaatje, *Anil* 42).[12] While knowledgeable readers can probably supply names and dates,[13] Ondaatje exhibits no such interest and prescribes no remedies for Sri Lanka's dreadful wounds. Nevertheless, he imbues his narrative with a powerful compassion by focusing on the war's victims and on the people who tend them. When doctors and nurses operate on maimed patients day after day, all on the same table, they ignore the political or ethnic affiliations of the victims (243) because they realize, as Elaine Scarry has shown, that the only meaning of pain is pain, and their only responsibility is to alleviate it. This is one of the novel's defining ethical moments. Different readers might judge that compassion transcends politics, or that compassion should inform politics, or that compassion is always already political, but in any case Ondaatje depicts a primary ethical encounter between the handy and the needy, between knowledgeable though fallible doctors and suffering victims.

The encounter renders each patient at once unique and anonymous. Each one has specific wounds to be tended appropriately, yet each person is identified only by those wounds and the urgent need to treat them. A comparable moment appears in *The English Patient* when Hana nurses soldiers fighting with the Canadian Infantry Division in Italy, and calls them all "Buddy." She knows their wounded bodies intimately, yet she is afraid of knowing them too well:

She feared the day she would remove blood from a patient's face and discover her father or someone who had served her food across a counter on Danforth Avenue. She grew harsh with herself and the patients. Reason was the only thing that might save them, and there was no reason. The thermometer of blood moved up the country. (Ondaatje, *English Patient* 50).

The last two sentences apply equally well to Sri Lanka, where Gamini is shocked to find himself in exactly the situation that terrifies Hana, when he abruptly faces the corpse of his brother, Sarath, its flesh tortured, its hands broken. In the novel's most pathetic moment, Gamini, his medical expertise now useless, dresses the wounds of his dead brother, with whom he shared an intense, fractious love that can now never be resolved. Ondaatje calls the scene a "pietà between brothers" (Ondaatje, *Anil* 288), and it echoes earlier images of a mother grieving over her child (119, 156), one of which appeared in an ancient rock carving that haunted Sarath: "the mother's back bowed in affection or grief. An unseen child. All the gestures of motherhood harnessed. A muffled scream in her posture" (157).

The pietà image, which brings another Christian icon to Sri Lanka, is the companion piece to Gunesena's crucifixion, but its meaning too is unmoored. It is fraternal as well as maternal, and it evokes not the universality of grief reaching across cultures, but grief's unanswerable particularity. Anil had argued that one murder victim, if accurately identified, could stand for all victims (176), and with respect to her quest for justice she is right. Justice is never concerned solely with individuals, because it is social in scope and general in formulation. Individual suffering may be terrible, but it is "unjust" only insofar as it falls within a system of judicial prohibitions, a system that engineers a response to death. Anil wants her solitary investigation to deploy this larger system; her motto could be "the personal is political." By contrast, Gamini grieves for a single person, whose death agony was his and his alone, and whose murder cannot stand for, or respond to, the death of anyone else. Gamini finds no solace in an adequating rationality (Wai Chee Dimock's phrase) because nothing is adequate: the death of one's child or brother or beloved reveals the utter uniqueness of human lives, which are incommensurable. Nothing is "equal" to Sarath and no retribution is equivalent to his loss. Because all human lives are singular and irreplaceable, the truth about how they died is useless. From this intensely personal perspective, the truth that Anil seeks so assiduously is irrelevant, because no knowledge can answer to the absoluteness of death.

In his account of "the supreme dignity of the unique" (Levinas, *Ethics* 101), Emmanuel Levinas asserts that responsibility is the very structure of subjectivity (95). It is not duty, which must be deliberately undertaken or imposed by a social code, but an unformulated obligation that precedes everything else, even being. Before all being, knowing, or doing, before all political and cultural life, and therefore before any articulation of justice, is the naked presence of the Other in the "rectitude" of its face, which inspires responsibility in me (86). The shocking intimacy of this confrontation is possible only between two unique people; it is not a social meeting or even a personal one, since it precedes any acquiring of personality.[14] The Other makes no demands of me, yet "summons" me to unlimited responsibility, which I cannot decline, because the moment also precedes all willing (Levinas, *Basic* 113). Justice can impose a sentence of precisely "life plus ninety-nine years" on a criminal, but it cannot make unlimited demands because it is a discourse of equity, which requires that responsibility be calculated exactly so that a commensurate response (punishment, reward, compensation) can be justified. By contrast, the pure ethical encounter is incalculable and, strictly speaking, unknowable. Knowledge depends on recognizing correspondence, analogy, or recurrence (67), whereas the "nameless singularity" (85) that Levinas evokes but cannot define precedes all such correlation. It is not like, equal to, or a repetition of anything else. The Other remains anonymous, because its alterity can never be known or even "seen." For Levinas, too, knowledge is inevitably belated, because "seeing" implies observing the Other in a pre-established field of vision. The Other cannot be seen in its uniqueness but only touched, or, in Levinas's vocabulary, "caressed" like a mystery: "It is this seeking of the caress which constitutes its essence, through the fact that the caress does not know what it seeks" (Levinas, *Ethics* 69). Knowing, seeing, and speaking arise only afterward as the result of "a search for adequation" (87) within a contextual field – a search equivalent to Anil's quest for justice – whereas the face is pure "signification" prior to any context or content: "the face is meaning all by itself" (86). It is a "signifyingness anterior to signification" (Greisch 70). It is "the signifyingness of meaning" (Levinas, *Basic* 102) as a power of articulation, itself unarticulated, that generates all subsequent meanings. What makes the good, good? What makes justice, just? We cannot say, since saying comes later, but we have initially been constituted by an enigmatic relationship that makes goodness and justice possible and necessary.

Levinas offers a remarkable recasting of the pathos of understanding, which I venture to apply to *Anil's Ghost*. In opposition to the belatedness of knowledge, history, and justice, he sets a "preoriginal past" (116) from which issues an "intuition of sociality . . . irreducible to comprehension" (7). His intense scrutiny of the primordial, face-to-face encounter that precedes and entails all of our of social and moral life means that all consequent human activity is an aftermath. We are responsible before we know what we are responsible for: "Such responsibility does not give one time, a present for recollection or coming back to oneself; it makes one always late" (143). This temporal dilemma makes us strangely vulnerable yet strong. Knowledge is secondary but, as J.-F. Lyotard and J.-L. Thébaud explain, this is now a source of ethical strength:

when Levinas, citing a much-commented-upon passage of the Talmud, says: "Do before you understand, and the Jews did, and then they understood," he sets the problem exactly right. It is clear that it is not a question of first understanding, no! First, one acts from the obligation that comes from the simple fact that I am being spoken to, that you are speaking to me, and then, and only then, can one try to understand what has been received. In other words, the obligation operator comes first and then one sees what one is obligated to. (Lyotard and Thébaud 41–2)

If in one sense we are always too late, in another sense we are always on time, poised in the midst of an "intrigue from beyond being" (Levinas, *Basic* 101) that gives us moral authority. When we touch the face of the Other, when it intrigues us, then it inspires the "first word," Thou shalt not kill: "the face is what forbids us to kill" (Levinas, *Ethics* 89, 86).

What makes the good, good? What makes justice, just? In seeking moral ballast for my reading of *Anil's Ghost*, I do not appeal to its beatific coda, which may reaffirm the dominance of order over chaos but need not be interpreted so hopefully, since its final position in the narrative ensures not that it triumphs by coming last, but that it comes too late. Instead I appeal to Gunesena's crucifixion and the pietà emblem, which do not gesture upward to a divine transcendence of which the novel offers no assurance, but instead reach backward to what Levinas treats as an archaic reverence arising from the inter-meshing of individual lives through a uniqueness that forever joins them even as it separates them. In response to brutal tautologies – the reason for war is war, the meaning of pain is pain – Ondaatje offers an answering enigma: the meaning of life is life. This does not mean that he seeks a sanction for life beyond the world of touch and tact, of science and art, but rather that he searches within their vitality to offer life as an absolute, secular value, which it is the duty of justice to articulate and protect.

CHAPTER 7

Conclusion
Legal fictions

KO-KO: When your Majesty says, "Let a thing be done," it's as good as done –
practically, it is done – because your Majesty's will is law. Your Majesty says,
"Kill a gentleman," and a gentleman is told off to be killed. Consequently,
that gentleman is as good as dead – practically, he is dead – and if he is dead,
why not say so?
MIKADO: I see. Nothing could possibly be more satisfactory! (W.S. Gilbert, *The
Mikado*, in *Plays* 344–5)

All the nobler aspects of our life are based upon fictions . . . The
higher aspects of life are based upon noble delusions.
(Hans Vaihinger, *The Philosophy of "As If"* 84)

till the poets among us . . . can present
for inspection, "imaginary gardens with real toads in them"
(Marianne Moore, "Poetry", in *Collected Poems* 41)

The Lord High Executioner's devious verdict from *The Mikado* illustrates
W.S. Gilbert's favorite trick of treating legal fiction as literal fact. Ko-Ko
blithely overrules a problem raised by Leibniz, which I cited in Chapter 4.
Whatever God wills is good and just, but "there remains the question
whether it is good and just because God wills it or whether God wills it
because it is good and just" (Leibniz 45). Does reason direct will, or will
direct reason? For Ko-Ko, will is supreme. He ascribes to the Mikado a
divine volition that instantly determines reality, making fact follow fiction,
so that the gentleman at risk, Nanki-Poo, must actually be dead if the
Mikado has proclaimed he must die. Things are as he decrees they should
be, and if that is the case, why not just say so? The word "just" conflates
finality with fairness: the final word of agreement will merely confirm what
the first word of command has already decreed. In this fanciful view even
the word "verdict" (true saying) is literalized, so that saying something
is true makes it true. Such is the magic of legal fictions, whose power is
exaggerated whimsically here but is always at work in the logical and moral
economy of judicial judgments.

138

This book has focused on conceptual jurisdictions – literary territories where justice, literature, and law conspire to speak and rule – in order to examine how legal fictions shape our understanding and sympathies. Each chapter locates a point where the three discourses converge as they pursue their shared concern with satisfaction, transcendence, temporality, nature, singularity, and truthfulness. The analysis in each chapter wavers between two extremes, which mark the distance between justice and its insufficiencies, between its promise to satisfy our moral and sociable needs and its inability to do so, between its prospects of abundance and scarcity, of harmony and cruelty. At one extreme is an ideal that I have followed Flaubert in calling *le mot juste*: a joyful limit at which the world and human comprehension are reconciled through the sweet powers of language. At the other extreme is a sacrificial impulse, equally commanding, that finds in their disjunction other possibilities, whether ironic or tragic, humbling or sublime. Justice may falter, not only through the inadequacy of its agents – incompetent judges, biased juries, false testimony – but through its own inner contradictions. Giving a common ground to all of these interests is the role of fiction as both an organizing principle and a medium of exploration, as a rational principle permitting imaginative discovery. I conclude with some observations on this fictive ground, which marks the border between art and life.

Marianne Moore's imaginary garden containing real frogs suggests the strange alliance of enchantment and reason conveyed by the word "fiction," which must be understood in its twin meanings of artefact and enabling illusion. Its Latin roots (*fingere, fictio*) suggest "to shape, fashion, form, mold"; "to devise, represent, conceive." This first meaning denotes both a structural principle and the understanding that it yields – a thing formed and formulated, rendered intelligible through its adherence to rules. However, this sense does not distinguish between, for example, a true story and an invented one, since both are designed with the same tools. The second more familiar meaning, which links fiction to falsehood, expresses suspicion that our ability to design forms is a creative but corrupting talent. It permits us to invent and so to deceive others and even to fool ourselves. Fictions then become pleasing or instructive falsehoods, which may mislead us or which may be enjoyable even when we know they are false, as in the case of literary fictions. Because literature entices us into a subjunctive world – what might be, should be, or might have been – it has always sparked disputes about the relations between fiction, falsehood, truth, and pleasure. This is a familiar theme. "The truest poetry is the most feigning," says Shakespeare in *As You Like*

It (3.3.17), recalling Aristotle's advice that the successful dramatist will follow Homer's art of telling lies convincingly, and will prefer plausible falsehood to an incredible truth (Aristotle, *Poetics* 133). The intent is not to deceive, but to please and to reveal through pleasure. Feigning can be an avenue to truth, even if it is not itself true, as Polonius advises in *Hamlet*:

> Your bait of falsehood takes this carp of truth;
> And thus do we of wisdom and of reach,
> With windlasses and with assays of bias,
> By indirections find directions out. (2.1.64–7)

A religious account of the interplay of fiction, falsehood, truth, and fairness would ascribe their devious partnership to human impurity or sin. Because of our fallen nature, we see through a glass darkly and must earn enlightenment through an ordeal of error and injustice. A philosophical account might locate the problem in reason itself, which can accomplish its task only by devising heuristic devices, which are strategies known to be false but useful because they offer insight. For example, social contract theories of the origin and character of society (Hobbes, Locke, Rousseau) do not require that a specific historical event occurred when the contract was devised; instead they provide an analytical model that illuminates the conditions and relations prevailing in any society. John Rawls's point of departure in *A Theory of Justice* is a modern equivalent. He posits an "original position of equality correspond[ing] to the state of nature in the traditional theory of the social contract" (Rawls 12). It is not an actual historical state of affairs, he explains, but "a purely hypothetical situation characterized so as to lead to a certain conception of justice" as fairness (12). It is an enabling fiction.

Hans Vaihinger is the modern philosopher most closely associated with the practical value of heuristic fictions. His philosophy of "as if" (first published in 1911) discerns "consciously false ideas, or rather judgments" (Vaihinger xli) at work in all systematic understanding, in all disciplines, in social life, and in the very reflexes of reasoning through analogy. All employ the "ingenious dexterity" (9) of "fictional thought" (39) in order to make the world liveable. Fictions are instruments, whose value depends on their adequacy. Because thought is *"an instrument for finding our way about more easily in this world"* (15), its success must be assessed in tactical terms – according to how well it succeeds. Unlike hypotheses, which are proposed in the belief that they may be verified, fictions are "artifices of thought"

(11) that never aspire to be true, only to be effective. They cannot be rejected as false, since they never claim to be true; they can be only satisfactory or unsatisfactory. For Vaihinger fictions operate like the necessary lies that we have noted in literature: they offer something better than truth, namely a sustaining, rewarding adaptation to reality. This is one possible definition of justice. He could be taking Aristotle's advice when he declares that "fruitful errors" are better than "barren truths" (45) and far more valuable than "harmful truths" (46): "Fiction is, after all, merely a *more conscious, more practical and more fruitful error*" (94). Vaihinger is so enthusiastic about divulging fictive thinking that he finds it pretty well everywhere. Careful inspection reveals that all the grand, metaphysical ideas (freedom, substance, the absolute) are logical monstrosities (43), because they are not only contrary to reality but contradictory in themselves. Nevertheless they are indispensable as fictions: "Without the imaginary factor neither science nor life in their highest form are [*sic*] possible. The real tragedy of life is that the most valuable ideas are, from the point of view of reality, worthless" (44).

Worth and worthiness are the prizes that Vaihinger seeks, but he ensures that they remain perilously dependent on falsehood. I am less concerned to endorse his philosophy than to situate its tragic – or, more accurately, ironic – vision of human nature in relation to nature at the opposite extreme from the one that I ascribed to *le mot juste*. In his account, humanity must adapt itself to a world for which it is ill adapted through a subterfuge that fools no one, or at least no philosopher. Because all knowledge is analogical, that is to say fictive, "it is utterly impossible to attain knowledge of the world, not because our thought is too narrowly circumscribed . . . but because knowledge is always in the form of categories and these, in the last analysis, are only analogical apperceptions" (29–30).

This defect is especially shocking when we consider essential categories of judicial judgment such as freedom and justice. Ironically, the many vices produced by human fallibility can be assessed and corrected only through ethical fictions, whose necessity is itself "a consequence of human imperfection, and, like the various aids to reflective thought, [they] are by no means an unmixed blessing" (84). Defect must correct fault. Responsibility, culpability, and liability must be calculated through fictions displaying the lineaments and powers of moral subjects who thereby can be called to account for their actions. Such fictions shape our most intimate notions of personal identity and agency. Just as Polonius' carp of truth snaps at the bait of indirection, and Marianne Moore's frog of reality appears only in an imaginary garden, so Vaihinger's ideal of justice is articulated only in "juristic fictions" (33), all based on the fundamental principle, known to be false but too valuable to reject, that individual cases can adequately be subsumed by general categories. He insists that this artifice of reasoning is not only erroneous but unjust – incapable of rendering justice to specific cases – yet without it justice is impossible.[1] Here's a pretty mess.

Like other rhetorical tropes, legal fictions are not literally true, but they permit a line of thinking that leads to a desired destination by granting the law explanatory and justifying force. Sometimes it is the explanation, sometimes the justification that requires a fictive boost. *The Oxford Dictionary of Law* explains that legal fictions provide short cuts through procedural complications by curtailing archaic procedures, offering remedies to cumbersome problems, untangling legal knots, and enlarging a court's jurisdiction (Martin 188). They are used not just in unusual or awkward cases, but pervasively and with far-reaching implications.[2] For example, the "doctrine of survival" specifies that if two people die at the same time or it is impossible to tell who died first, the older person is considered to have died first so that legal action can be taken accordingly.[3] Another strategic fiction establishes that at twenty-one years of age (or eighteen, or sixteen) a person becomes mature enough to drive a car, or vote in an election, or drink alcohol. This last fiction may conflict with another from the law of torts known as "vicarious liability," whereby an employer may be judged responsible for wrongs committed by employees while on the job, or a bar owner may be held liable for injuries to a patron who drinks to excess. One fiction confers the responsibility to drink; the other removes it for getting drunk. Surely the Mikado would approve. He would also applaud the Elizabethan "writ of *latitat*," which Bradin Cormack proclaims "one of the great moments of legal invention in English legal history" (Cormack 327). This triumph of civil jurisprudence allowed the King's Bench to have a person arrested for a crime that he did not commit in order to deliver him into another jurisdiction, the court of the Marshalsea, where he could then be accused of a crime that he did commit.

The artful interweaving of explanation and justification permitted by legal fictions appears dramatically in a 1929 landmark decision of the British Privy Council, which established that in Canada women must be considered "persons." This ruling overturned a contrary judgment by the Canadian Supreme Court (1928) and a convention in British common law (1876) that "Women are persons in matters of pains and penalties, but are not persons in matters of rights and privileges."[4] Did this legal victory, which is still celebrated in Canada, prove that the law finally recognized a natural fact (will was belatedly directed by reason), or that the law merely established personhood for women as a social fact (reason followed will)? The same puzzle emerges from another influential, late nineteenth-century legal fiction that defined a commercial corporation as a person. A business entity counted as a person before a woman did in Canada, while in the United States an unborn child still does not (Siegel 227). In *The Corporation* Joel Bakan studies the "bizarre legal alchemy" (Bakan 16) through which the corporation was declared to be a person

> with it own identity, separate from the flesh-and-blood people who were its owners and managers and empowered, like a real person, to conduct business in its own name, acquire assets, employ workers, pay taxes, and go to court to assert its rights and defend its actions. The corporate person had taken the place, at least in law, of the real people who owned corporations. Now viewed as an entity, "not imaginary or fictitious, but real, not artificial but natural," as it was described by one law professor in 1911, the corporation had been reconceived as a free and independent being. (16)

It is, of course, an additional fiction – an instance of the art of concealing art – that the corporate person should then be declared real rather than artificial. Bakan's sometimes mischievous analysis pursues this personification to reveal the corporation's psychopathic personality: "The corporation, after all, is deliberately designed to be a psychopath: purely self-interested, incapable of concern for others, amoral, and without conscience – in a word, inhuman" (134). Bakan takes seriously what Gilbert treats absurdly by accepting a figure of speech literally. Although he argues that the corporation is not really a person, and our laws justify a multitude of sins by pretending that it is, his own condemnation of its treacherous character depends on the personification that he condemns. The corporation can exhibit wicked human traits only because it has been humanized. He calls it inhuman, when really it is all too human, exhibiting the egotistical features traditionally ascribed to man in a state of nature or of natural scarcity.

As this study has shown, the role of fiction in articulating judicial thought must be matched with the role of justice in articulating the shape and authority of fiction. The fractious nexus of hopes, promises, calculations, compromises, disappointments, pardons, exonerations, and sacrifices that are assembled under the name of "justice" marks the border between art and life, both separating them and drawing them together. This is one way of interpreting Oscar Wilde's ironic quip about poetic justice in *The Importance of Being Earnest*: "the good end happily, and the bad unhappily. That is what Fiction means" (Wilde 22). Literary genres dictate rules governing their own jurisdictions, and within those limits they provide satisfaction by defining what is satisfactory for their fictional characters, and satisfying for their readers. But as we have seen, generic limits are always porous, and readers are free to contest their rules by reading against the grain, as Wilde loves to do. In the Kantian tradition, the aesthetic world is poetically just in the sense of being autonomous, at once tactile (sensual) and tactful (contemplative), disinterested yet fascinated as it surveys human life through the free play of imagination. It displays purposiveness – worldly experience – but without a purpose of its own. It does not judge, yet it sharpens judgment.

The integrity of this jurisdiction and the adequacy of its rule have continually been contested, however, especially in modernist literature which delights in transgression. On the one hand, life invades art to challenge the declared autonomy of its justice: ideological and political critics explain how aesthetic forms, which seem so pure, actually arise from and express social conditions. For example, Theodor Adorno argues that even the private, introverted form of the lyric intensifies its solitude in response to an unjust social world, which it forcefully rejects; it thereby expresses "the crisis of the individual" in an alienating society (Adorno 115). On the other hand, art invades life to expose the fallibility of its judgments: semiotic and cultural critics argue that all cultural artefacts, identities, and forms of behavior depend on the symbolic patterns and narrative dynamic exhibited in literature. For example, law is interpreted through the rituals (Winn) and narrative or dramatic models (Korobkin) by which it operates.

I have argued that in literary fiction we find a hopeful alliance of touch, tact and tactics – the sensory, sensible, and effective; the aesthetic, contemplative, and practical. Their alliance is competitive as much as cooperative, however, because the three agents stimulate the moral imagination to make justice conceivable and desirable, but also to set concept and desire at odds. Both the hopefulness and the disorderliness of their alliance – their unruly rule – are captured in Wallace Stevens's uncanny evocation of the imagination in "The Idea of Order at Key West":

> Oh! Blessed rage for order, pale Ramon,
> The maker's rage to order words of the sea,

Words of the fragrant portals, dimly-starred,
And of ourselves and of our origins,
In ghostlier demarcations, keener sounds.
(Stevens, *Palm* 98–9)

Order is motivated by a rage that it can never completely master; rage is inspired by an orderliness that it can never quite attain. Form and energy, law and its blessing, justice and the thirst for justice, all inhabit each other with an intensity that only a poetic image can express.

Notes

LE MOT JUSTE

1 Cicero, *On the Laws*, http://sow.colloquium.co.uk/~barrett/cicero.html (last accessed Apr. 22, 2006).
2 The major value of jurisdiction as an object for cultural analysis is that, as category and practice, jurisdiction identifies authority as power produced under the administrative recognition of the geographical or conceptual limits that exactly order it as authority. Jurisdiction amounts to the delimitation of a sphere – spatial (state, city, or manor; domestic, maritime, or foreign), temporal (proximate or immemorial past; regular or market days), or generic (matters spiritual or matters temporal; promise or debt) – that is the precondition for the juridical as such, for the very capacity of the law to come into effect. (Cormack 3)

For a history of legal jurisdictions see Richard T. Ford. For essays on jurisdictional places and legal authorities, see Sarat, Douglas, and Umphrey.

3 Søren Kierkegaard, *Fear and Trembling*, trans. Walter Lowrie, www.white nationalism.com/etext/fear.htm (last accessed Dec. 12, 2002).
4 Ibid.
5 Ibid.

LIFE PLUS NINETY-NINE YEARS

1 "'Mafia Cops' Get Life, and their Pensions," *New York Times*, March 6, 2009, www.nytimes.com/2009/03/07/nyregion/07about.html?ref=nyregion.
2 James Ellis comments in his introduction to Gilbert's comic poems, *The Bab Ballads*:

for the truth is that the 'Babs' are addressed to the child in each of us – to that ineradicable part of us that delights in being selfishly asocial, in having its own way at all costs, in being spiteful and vengeful, in letting chaos come again – the child we try to outgrow or at least disguise. Hovering as it does between the naive and the diabolic, it is a quality which causes some to laugh and others to wince. (James Ellis 14)

3 For O'Brien, the supreme example of the disparity between the two temperaments appears in Yum-Yum's song of smug vanity in *The Mikado* ("We really know our worth / The sun and I"), which is enchanted by Sullivan's music "into a mysteriously beautiful presence" (O'Brien 16).

4 See also Hesketh Pearson's remark that *The Bab Ballads* display "an orgy of fanciful sadism, which appeared to be of so topsy-turvy a nature, so unlike the respectable facade of the stolid mid-Victorian world, that his readers found relief in laughter over this inverted picture of their own conscious or subconscious desires" (Pearson 31).

5 Max Keith Sutton makes the same point, but reaches a different conclusion than Fischler:

> The plots are unraveled not by defying the law but by discovering a way to be technically right . . . This denouement, echoed by the ingenious reasoning at the end of *The Mikado* and *Ruddigore*, offers a verbal resolution to the clash between external restraints and personal desires. By making the resolution so artificial, Gilbert suggests the absurdity of relying upon legalism to solve human conflicts. (Sutton 20)

6 Gilbert could hardly have expected his skeptical patrons to readily accept any flawed, man-made code as a fully adequate substitute for the divine dispensation which they had held to be perfect as long as they could believe it to be real – and yet, the confession of human law now represented the only available alternative to moral anarchy. But the catharsis of laughter facilitated the acceptance of the new order: when Gilbert's characters unthinkingly or mechanically applied human law to problems it could not actually solve, the law's limitations were highlighted and the audience permitted to laugh away their discomfort about just these limitations. Purged of misgivings about the mortal imperfections of such law, these audiences would have left the theater more cheerfully inclined to obey it. (Fischler, *Modified* 53–4)

7 Fischler claims that Gilbert always gave the public exactly what it wanted: "Gilbert placed his primary emphasis on satisfying the bourgeoisie, the embodiments of the Victorian social mean" (Fischler, *Modified* 35).

8 Gilbert's magical denouement also produces the contradiction of making Ralph, who began the play as a young sailor, the same age as the Captain.

9 Gilbert wrote a play, *Eyes and No Eyes* (1875), based on "The Emperor's New Clothes" (Stedman 80).

10 Gilbert actually named a character "Mr. Satis" in his musical extravaganza of 1874, *Topsyturveydom* (Sutton 92).

11 Andrew Crowther, "Hunchbacks, Misanthropes and Outsiders: Gilbert's Self-Image," www.users.globalnet.co.uk/~ajcrowth/hunchback.htm (last accessed Nov. 17, 2000). See also Hayter 89. Crowther confirms the identification of Dick Deadeye with Gilbert by quoting a passage from his description of the opera:

> Now Dick Deadeye was generally disliked because he was so unpleasant to look at, but he was really one of the best and kindest and most sensible men on board the Pinafore, and this shows how wrong and unjust it is to judge unfavourably of a man because he is ugly and deformed. I myself am one of the plainest men I have ever met, and at the same time I don't know a more agreeable old gentleman. (Gilbert, *Story* 17)

TIME'S DESIRE

1 Hewart's dictum from 1923 is identified by Amartya Sen in "Interdependence and Global Justice," www.un.org/esa/documents/GLO-UNGA.pdf (last accessed Jan. 3, 2006).

2 Films using haunting as a means of changing or redeeming the past include *Topper* (1937), *Heaven Can Wait* (1943, 1978), *A Guy Named Joe* (1943), *The Canterville Ghost* (1944), *A Matter of Life and Death* (1946), *Angel on my Shoulder* (1946), *The Bishop's Wife* (1947), *The Ghost and Mrs. Muir* (1947), *Ghost* (1990), *Truly, Madly, Deeply* (1991), *What Dreams May Come* (1998).

3 In *Postmodern Ethics* Zygmunt Bauman discusses this moral misalliance as a postmodern perspective, but I would apply it more generally:

> The majority of moral choices are made between contradictory impulses. Most importantly, however, virtually every moral impulse, if acted upon in full, leads to immoral consequences (most characteristically, the impulse to care for the Other, when taken to its extreme, leads to the annihilation of the autonomy of the Other, to domination and oppression); yet no moral impulse can implement itself unless the moral actor earnestly strives to stretch the effort to the limit. The moral self moves, feels and acts in the context of ambivalence and is shot through with uncertainty. (Bauman 11)

4 http://archives.cnn.com/2001/LAW/06/11/mcveigh.02/index.html (last accessed June 3, 2005).

5 http://news.bbc.co.uk/2/hi/middle_east/4353449.stm (last accessed March 18, 2005).

6 Under the practical constraints of having to insure accountability and to bring justice, the law tries to make sense of the abyss or to reduce its threat (its senselessness, its unintelligible chaos) by giving it a name, by codifying it or by subsuming its reality (which is inherently nameless and unclassifiable) into the classifying logic and into the technical, procedural coherence of the trial . . . But the purpose of the literary text is, on the contrary, to show or to expose again the severance and the schism, to reveal once more the opening, the hollowness of the abyss, to wrench apart what was precisely covered over, closed or covered up by the legal trial. The literary text casts open the abyss so as to let us look, once more, into its depth, and see its bottomlessness. (Felman 95)

7 The internal quotation in this passage is taken from an earlier ruling (*Millington* v. *Southeastern Elevator Co.*) which is cited as precedent.

8 The primitive has a non-alienated dual-relation with his double. He really can trade, as we are forever forbidden to do, with his shadow (the real shadow, not a metaphor), as with some original, living thing, in order to converse, protect and conciliate this tutelary or hostile shadow . . . The primitive procedure is only aware of reciprocities: clan contra clan, death contra death (gift contra gift). We know only a system of equivalences (a death for a death) between two terms as abstract as an economic exchange . . . (Baudrillard 141, 171)

9 Jean Baudrillard, "The Spirit of Terrorism," trans. Rachel Bloul, www.egs.edu/faculty/baudrillard/baudrillard-the-spirit-of-terrorism.html (last accessed July 24, 2005).

10 Despite his enthusiasm for catastrophe, Baudrillard has called himself only an intellectual terrorist:

> If being a nihilist, is carrying, to the unbearable limit of hegemonic systems, this radical trait of derision and of violence, this challenge that the system is summoned to answer through its own death, then I am a terrorist and nihilist in theory as the others are with their weapons. Theoretical violence, not truth, is the only recourse left us. ("On Nihilism," quoted in Butterfield)

11 A photograph of one self-immolation appears at www.vietnampix.com/fire1. htm (last accessed March 5, 2004): "Passers-by stop to watch as flames envelope a young Buddhist monk, Saigon, October 5th, 1963."

12 Baudrillard, "The Spirit of Terrorism" (see n. 9 above).

13 David Attwell and Barbara Harlow illustrate the objection:

> But this project has its flaws. For one thing, it makes no provision for natural justice; forgiveness in the name of peace has been elevated above justice in the name of principle. For the good of the nation, victims have often been obliged to accept a moral and material settlement that is less than satisfactory. For another thing, by emphasizing individual acts of abuse, it has tended to obscure the systematically abusive social engineering that was apartheid. Therefore, apartheid's legacy remains evident in extensive poverty, educational deprivation, and a warped criminal justice system which, because it was developed as an instrument of political oppression, seems incapable of dealing with ordinary crime. (Attwell and Harlow 2)

The terms and conduct of the commission are available online at www.doj.gov. za/trc/legal/ct9534.htm (last accessed June 22, 2005).

14 Kimberly Wedeven Segall analyzes imagery of ghosts and haunting in *Disgrace* in "Pursuing Ghosts." Coetzee's concern with torture in South Africa appears in his essay "Into the Dark Chamber." Isadore Diala, among other critics, draws parallels between *Disgrace* and the Truth and Reconciliation Commission: "Lurie's denunciation of the demands of the committee as 'preposterous' (p. 55), and his location of those demands 'beyond the scope of the law' (p. 55), clearly allude to critiques of the 'confessional' approach of the TRC, based on its arguable equation of religious rhetoric with the legal and the conflation of catharsis with contrition" (Diala 57).

15 According to Mike Marais,

> [T]he novel offers no *definitive* interpretation of the rape and of Lucy's response to it and, in fact, relativises or discounts those interpretations which it *does* offer. *Because* Lucy and her behaviour are presented as an enigma in the text, they resist *any* interpretation and, inevitably, inscribe an irresolvable tension in the novel between that which can only ever remain unexplained and the reader's *will* to explain. (Marais 283)

ONE TOUCH OF NATURE

1 St. Thomas Aquinas, *Summa theologica*, 2.1, questions 90–5, www.sacred-texts. com/chr/aquinas/summa/sum228.htm; www.sacred-texts.com/chr/aquinas/ summa/sum195.htm (prudence) (last accessed Sept. 19, 2007).

2 Two useful websites outlining the history and key terms of natural law are plato. stanford.edu/entries/natural-law-ethics/ (last accessed July 9, 2007); and www. iep.utm.edu/n/natlaw.htm (last accessed July 9, 2007). The word "nature" has innumerable shades of meanings, sixty-six of which are documented by Lovejoy and Boas in *Primitivism and Related Ideas in Antiquity*. I will be drawing on some of these definitions in the discussion that follows.

3 For a contrary view that positive law need not rely on natural-moral sanctions, see Kramer, especially chapter 7, "On the Separability of Law and Morality": "the criteria for legal validity in any particular legal system need not include moral tests. Such tests may be present in this or that particular system, but their presence is contingent rather than a necessary feature of everything that counts as a legal regime" (Kramer 237).

4 Trilling's *Sincerity and Authenticity* still provides one of the best studies of romantic authenticity, its attractions, and its dangers.

5 See "How Widespread is the Custom of Saying 'Bless you' when Someone Sneezes?", http://answers.google.com/answers/threadview?id=557807 (last accessed Dec. 19, 2005).

6 Leibniz quotes from the *Life of Claudius*, "in libera republica crepitus atque ructus liberos esse debere," but the passage from Suetonius reads: "Dicitur etiam meditatus edictum, quo veniam daret flatum crepitumque ventris in convivio emittendi, cum periclitatum quendam prae pudore ex continentia repperisset." ("He is even said to have thought of an edict allowing the privilege of breaking wind quietly or noisily at table, having learned of a man who ran some risk by restraining himself through modesty.") See http://penelope.uchicago.edu/Thayer/L/Roman/Texts/Suetonius/12Caesars/Claudius*.html (last accessed Nov. 9, 2007).

7 Mark Twain, *Following the Equator*, http://mark-twain.classic-literature.co.uk/following-the-equator/ebook-page-92.asp (last accessed Nov. 12, 2007).

8 See http://chess.about.com/cs/reference/g/bldefjad.htm (last accessed Nov. 27, 2007).

9 The basic procedural rules governing fairness and bias are *Audi alteram partem* ("hear the other side") and *Nemo debet esse judex in propria sua causa* ("no one shall be judged in his own case"). See www.vu.edu.au/library/pdf/natural%20justice%2015%20OCT%202001.pdf (last accessed Nov. 27, 2007).

10 David F. Forte's description of natural law indicates both the gap it must negotiate, and our pleasure in overcoming that gap:

Natural law distinguishes between power and authority. Ultimately, natural law finds the freedom of the human individual as rooted in the good, and political authority as contingent upon that human freedom. Natural law not only judges what human laws ought not to be passed, but it also illuminates the benign face of the law; it looks to those laws that ought to be enacted to assist human persons in the flourishing of their free individual personalities. Natural law is not only imperative. It is aspirational. (Forte 7)

11 St. Thomas Aquinas, *Summa theologica*, 2.1, questions 90–5, www.sacred-texts.com/chr/aquinas/summa/sum228.htm; www.sacred-texts.com/chr/aquinas/summa/sum195.htm (prudence) (last accessed Sept. 19, 2007).

12 Contrast Rousseau's mistrust of prudence: "Prudence which is ever bidding us look forward into the future, a future which in many cases we shall never reach; here is the real source of all our troubles!" (Rousseau 46).

13 James Agee, John Huston, and Peter Viertel, screenplay of *The African Queen* (1951). http://www.weeklyscript.com/African%20Queen,%20The%20(1951).txt (last accessed May 16, 2007).

14 The final song is not in Agee's script, but does appear in a radio play adapted from the film: "There was a bold fisherman, set sail from off Pimlico, to catch the . . . bold figgy and the gay mack-a-rool . . ." See www.geocities.com/emruf2/otr/lux2.html (last accessed May 16, 2007).

15 The modern dominance of the constitutive view that nature is inherently rational is usually ascribed to Hugo Grotius, who writes in *The Law of War and Peace* (book 1, chapter 1, section 101):

> The law of nature, again, is unchangeable – even in the sense that it cannot be changed by God. Measureless as is the power of God, nevertheless it can be said that there are certain things over which that power does not extend; for things of which this is said are spoken only, having no sense corresponding with reality and being mutually contradictory. Just as even God, then, cannot cause that two times two should not make four, so He cannot cause that which is intrinsically evil be not evil.

See www.lonang.com/exlibris/grotius/gro-101.htm (last accessed Nov. 9, 2007).

16 Chaucer speaks of making a virtue of necessity in "Troylus and Criseyde" (4.1586), "The Knight's Tale" (line 3042), and "The Squire's Tale" (line 593).

17 Wordsworth echoes these sentiments in "The Old Cumberland Beggar":

> 'Tis Nature's law
> That none, the meanest of created things,
> Of forms created the most vile and brute,
> The dullest or most noxious, should exist
> Divorced from good – a spirit and pulse of good,
> A life and soul to every mode of being
> Inseparably link'd.   (Wordsworth 117)

THE COURSE OF A PARTICULAR

1 "Je dis: une fleur! et, hors de l'oubli où ma voix relègue aucun contour, en tant que quelque chose d'autre que les calices sus, musicalement se lève, idée même et suave, l'absente de tous bouquets." ("I say: a flower! and, out of the oblivion to which my voice consigns any contour, in as much as it is something other than known calyxes, musically arises the fragrant idea itself, the one absent from all bouquets.") (Mallarmé 368).

2 Words so ambiguous as to convey opposite meanings are known as autoant-
onyms. See www.fun-with-words.com/nym_autoantonyms.html (last accessed
Oct. 30, 2009).

3 For a detailed study of how law is used as a traumatic re-enacting of history,
see Felman's *The Juridical Unconscious*:

> Law is, in this way, an organizing force of the significance of history. But law relates to
> history through trauma. What should have been historically remembered, in effect, is
> not only the trial but the trauma that has made the trial necessary, the individual and
> social trauma that the trial was supposed to remedy, to solve, or to resolve. Yet, a trauma
> cannot simply be remembered when, in the first place, it cannot be grasped, when, as
> these trials show, it cannot even be seen. Rather than memory, it compels a traumatic
> reenactment. (Felman 84)

4 Other readings of this poem note allusions to Revelation 2:11 ("He that hath an
ear, let him hear what the Spirit saith unto the churches; He that overcometh
shall not be hurt of the second death") and to Revelation 20:6 ("Blessed and
holy is he that hath part in the first resurrection: on such the second death hath
no power, but they shall be priests of God and of Christ, and shall reign with
him a thousand years").

5 De Man's use of the word "historical" is deliberately provocative, since he is not
appealing to a historical explanation but to the rhetorical ground of historical
narratives: "One would then have to conceive of a rhetoric of history prior to
attempting a history of rhetoric or of literature or of literary criticism. Rhetoric,
however, is not in itself an historical but an epistemological discipline" (de Man,
"Epistemology" 28).

6 "In response to death it is important to feel something, and yet there is no
precedent, since every death is original, the loss of just *this* individual, just
this judging gaze. The demand to feel is addressed to me, here, now; it is not
detachable from the imperatives of my individual life and present situation"
(Scruton 15).

7 "One is one and all alone and ever more shall be so," sings the refrain of the
English folksong "Green Grow the Rushes O," which celebrates the singularity
of the divine source from which life proliferates. The song has a pagan version
(www.paganlibrary.com/music_poetry/green_grow_rushes.php; last accessed
Oct. 19, 2002) and a Christian version (www.know-britain.com/songs/green_
grow_the_rushes-o.html; last accessed Oct. 19, 2002).

8 I owe this point to Philippe Beaussant's novel *Stradella*: "c'est Anubis qui pèse
les âmes de l'autre côté de la mort et n'en trouve pas deux qui aient le même
poids" (Beaussant 259–60).

9 In his article "Does 'Ought' Imply 'Can'? And did Kant Think it does?",
www.utilitas.org.uk/pdfs/stern.pdf (last accessed May 8, 2004), Robert Stern
analyzes eleven instances where Kant expresses this principle.

10 "The ethical project, then, is to submit freedom of will to the rule of rationality
in the attempt to find criteria for human action that are universally intelligible
and valid for everyone. In this way, particular human situations are subsumed
under a general and universal order from which they receive their meaning"
(Ciaramelli 84).

11 "Consequently the judgment of taste, accompanied with the consciousness of separation from all interest, must claim validity for every man, without this universality depending on objects. That is, there must be bound up with it a title to subjective universality" (Kant, *Judgment* 46). Stephen Boos explains subjective universality as follows:

> A judgment of taste is . . . not a logical judgment but an aesthetic one, by which Kant means a judgment whose basis is subjective. On the other hand, an aesthetic judgment is not simply a matter of the agreeable, since it makes a claim to universality. When I claim that x is beautiful, I am not simply claiming that I feel that it is beautiful but making a claim that is valid for others as well . . . When we judge an object as beautiful rather than merely pleasant, one judges not only for oneself but for everyone else, that is, one judges with a universal voice, yet one does so without a concept, that is, without a category of the Understanding. To make this demand is to presuppose that the taste and feeling by which we make the judgment is common to everyone and hence implies a *sensus communis*, a "common sense." (Boos 19–20)

12 Leonard Grob explains the first moral cry as follows:

> Before the totality is rent by the manifestation of the face, there can be no will to act *immorally*, as there can be no will to act morally, in any ultimate sense of that word . . . Morality makes its first appearance when I confront the Other who is truly Other.
>
> Although the Other appears to me now, on principle, as someone I could wish to kill, he or she *in fact* summons me to respond with nonviolence: I am called to willingly renounce my power to act immorally. What I hear from the Other, Levinas claims, are the words "Thou shalt not kill." Harkening to this injunction constitutes my inaugural act as an ethical being. (Grob 8–9, Grob's emphasis)

13 "I must judge, where before I was to assume responsibilities. Here is the birth of the theoretical; here the concern for justice is born, which is the basis of the theoretical. But is it always starting out from the Face, from the responsibility for the other that justice appears, which calls for judgment and comparison, a comparison of what is in principle incomparable, for every being is unique; every other is unique" (Levinas, *Entre* 104)

14 Frye briefly extends his discussion of virginity to include men in *Words with Power*, 195.

15 An Emersonian Stevens: Bloom, *Wallace Stevens*; Nietzschean: Leggett, *Early Stevens*; Santayanian: Riddel, *The Clairvoyant Eye*; Derridean: Miller, "Stevens' Rock and Criticism as Cure."

16 Even here Riddel finds ambiguity and excess as "the imagination's forms invariably leave something out of account" (Riddel 44).

17 Levinas notes that the "oneself" lives "without metaphor, which palpitates" (Levinas, *Basic* 84).

TRUTH, JUSTICE, AND THE PATHOS OF UNDERSTANDING

1 In other essays Orwell explores the reciprocal relation between literary language and political judgment, for instance in "Inside the Whale": "Literature as we know it is an individual thing, demanding mental honesty and a minimum of censorship . . . The atmosphere of orthodoxy is always damaging to prose, and

above all it is completely ruinous to the novel, the most anarchical of all forms of literature" (Orwell 39).

2 I borrow the figure of error from Patricia Parker's study of romance *Inescapable Romance*.

3 Ondaatje does not specify which syllable, but his admiration for the Sinhalese alphabet appears more lyrically in some of the poems in *Handwriting* and in *Running in the Family*: "I still believe the most beautiful alphabet was created by the Sinhalese. The insect of ink curves into a shape that is almost sickle, spoon, eyelid. The letters are washed blunt glass which betray no jaggedness … and so a curling alphabet was derived from its Indian cousin. Moon coconut. The bones of a lover's spine" (Ondaatje, *Running* 83). These final words are grimly ironic in view of the more sinister role of bones in *Anil's Ghost*.

4 M.S. Nagarajan observes in a review of *Anil's Ghost*: "since 1963, it is reported the [*sic*] 70,000 precious lives have been lost in the large-scale campaigns of manslaughter caused by the civil war that has been plaguing the country, and from which, alas, there seems no escape" (Nagarajan). The same figure is reported in the *International Herald Tribune*, February 20, 2009, www.iht.com/articles/2009/02/20/asia/lanka.php (last accessed June 17, 2001).

5 For a study of visual and visionary imagery in Ondaatje, see Kyser.

6 Stephen Scobie notes Ondaatje's use of damaged hands in "The Reading Lesson," 102.

7 In *The Secular Scripture* Frye calls the detective story, as a form of romance, "an epiphany of law, a balancing and neutralizing activity in society, the murderer discovered at the end balancing the corpse that we normally find at the beginning" (Frye, *Secular* 137). He notes, however, that "law is not justice" (138), so the victory of law is a social rather than a moral triumph, though it may be both. Earlier, in *Anatomy of Criticism*, Frye used the phrase "an epiphany of law" somewhat differently to describe tragedy as a myth commanded by "that which is and must be" (Frye, *Anatomy* 208). I am concerned with the tragic dimension of *Anil's Ghost*, but not with fate in the classical sense. For an account of Ondaatje's use of the detective format, see Jones.

8 Readers are never told what happens to Anil, and silence can be ominous in a country where people simply disappear; but near the end we learn that "a long time later" (Ondaatje, *Anil* 285) she realized how intense was the bond between Sarath and Gamini. Evidently she survives.

9 In *Handwriting*, Ondaatje frequently associates Sri Lanka with the liminal interaction of water and rock, for instance in "Buried":

> What is eternal is brick, stone,
> a black lake where water disappears
> below mud and rises again,
> the arc of the dagoba that echoes a mountain.
> (Ondaatje, *Handwriting* 10)

10 In Goethe's poem "Der Zauberlehrling" a magician's apprentice is unable to control spirits that he raises with a spell from his master's book: "Die ich rief, die Geister / Werd ich nun nicht los" ("Spirits that I summoned / I can't get rid of them," Goethe 175). The poem inspired Paul Dukas's musical tone poem and a sequence in Walt Disney's animated film *Fantasia*.

11 Allen is the novel's harshest critic: "There is so much of this empty claptrap in *Anil's Ghost* that it stifles the novel's merits, which are not inconsiderable ... All these characters wander about in a sort of solipsistic fog, bumping against one another occasionally but all sunk too deep into their own psyches to connect on more than a primitive, nonverbal level" (Allen 63).

12 For a cogent account of the traditional political novel, see Howe.

13 For example, "While he cleverly conceals the identity of his characters in this work of fiction, there's no mistaking 'President Katugala' killed in a bomb blast" (Abeyesekera).

14 As Zygmunt Bauman explains, as soon as a "Third" joins the meeting of Self and Other, morality ends and society begins:

> The Third is also an Other, but not the Other we encountered at the "primal scene" where the moral play, not knowing of itself as a play, was staged and directed by my responsibility. The otherness of the Third is of an entirely different order. The two "others" reside in different worlds – two planets each with its own orbit which does not cross with the orbit of the other "other" – and none would survive the swapping of orbits. The two "others" do not converse with each other; if one speaks, the other one does not listen; if the other one does listen, he will not understand what he hears. Each can feel at home only if the other one steps aside, or better still stays outside. The other who is the Third can be encountered only when we leave the realm of morality proper, and enter another world, the realm of Social Order ruled by justice – not morality. (Bauman 113)

CONCLUSION

1 The psychological mechanism of their [juristic fictions'] application consists in subsuming a single case under a conceptual construct not properly intended for it, so that the apperception is, in consequence, merely an analogy. The basis of this method is as follows: since laws cannot include within their formulae all particular instances, certain special examples of an unusual nature are treated as if they belonged to them. Or else, because of some practical interest, an individual instance is brought under a general concept to which it does not really belong. Anyone conversant with the method of jurisprudence will easily understand how important this artifice is for legal practice. (Vaihinger 33)

2 For by what criterion of truth are we to test claims about social meaning of the sort law is always making? When we are discussing assertions about consent, intent, causation, property, personhood, the structure of marriage, or the scope of the private sphere, correspondence with empirical reality is not sufficient – and coherence theories of truth do not lift us out of the domain of the figural. 'Legal fiction' may itself be a figure of

speech that naturalizes the rich variety of ways that the language of the law constructs the social world we inhabit. (Siegel 228)

3 See http://en.wikipedia.org/wiki/Legal_fiction (last accessed June 21, 2008).

4 See   www.collectionscanada.gc.ca/publications/002/015002–2100-e.html   and http://canadaonline.about.com/cs/women/a/personscase.htm   (last   accessed June 21, 2008).

Bibliography

Abeyesekera, Kirthie. "Exposure of Shootings, Stabbings and Land Mines." *The Island*, Apr. 23, 2000, www.lanka.net/upali/island/2000/04/23/feature.html (last accessed June 17, 2001).

Ackroyd, Peter. *Hawksmoor*. Harmondsworth: Penguin, 1993.

Adorno, Theodor. "On Lyric Poetry and Society." *Modern Literary Theory: A Reader*, 4th edn. Ed. Philip Rice and Patricia Waugh. London: Arnold, 2001. 114–21.

Allen, Brooke. "Meditations, Good and Bad." *New Criterion* **18**.19 (May 2000): 63.

Aristotle. *The Nicomachean Ethics*. Trans. David Ross. Oxford: Oxford University Press, 1998.

The Rhetoric of Aristotle. Trans. Lane Cooper. New York: Appleton-Century-Crofts, 1932.

Aristotle's Poetics. Trans. George Whalley, ed. John Baxter and Patrick Atherton. Montreal: McGill-Queen's University Press, 1997.

Attwell, David and Barbara Harlow. "Introduction: South African Fiction after Apartheid." *Modern Fiction Studies* **46**.1 (2000): 1–9.

Austen, Jane. *Pride and Prejudice*. Oxford: Oxford University Press, 1980.

Bakan, Joel. *The Corporation: The Pathological Pursuit of Profit and Power*. New York: Free Press, 2004.

Barthes, Roland. *Camera Lucida: Reflections on Photography*. Trans. Richard Howard. New York: Hill and Wang, 1981.

Barzun, Jacques. "Introduction." In Gustave Flaubert, *The Dictionary of Accepted Ideas*. Trans. Jacques Barzun. New York: New Directions, 1954.

Baudrillard, Jean. *Symbolic Exchange and Death*. Trans. Iain Hamilton Grant. London: Sage Publications, 1993.

Bauman, Zygmunt. *Postmodern Ethics*. Oxford and Cambridge: Blackwell, 1993.

Beaussant, Philippe. *Stradella*. Paris: Gallinard, 1999.

Beddoes, Julie. "Which Side Is it On? Form, Class, and Politics in *In the Skin of a Lion*." *Essays on Canadian Writing* 53 (Spring 1999): 204–15.

Benjamin, Walter. "Critique of Violence." *Reflections: Essays, Aphorisms, Autobiographical Writings*. Trans. Edmund Jephcott. New York: Schocken Books, 1986. 277–300.

Berger, Charles. *Forms of Farewell: The Late Poetry of Wallace Stevens.* Madison: University of Wisconsin Press, 1985.

Bible. Revised Standard Version. New York: Thomas Nelson, 1953.

Bloom, Harold. *Wallace Stevens: The Poems of our Climate.* Ithaca: Cornell University Press, 1976.

The Western Canon. New York: Riverhead Books, 1995.

Bök, Christian. "Destructive Creation: The Politicization of Violence in the Work of Michael Ondaatje." *Canadian Literature* 132 (Spring 1992): 109–24.

Boos, Stephen. "Rethinking the Aesthetic: Kant, Schiller, and Hegel." *Between Ethics and Aesthetics: Crossing the Boundaries.* Ed. Dorota Blowacka and Stephen Boos. Albany: State University of New York Press, 2002. 15–27.

Bourdieu, Pierre. *Language and Symbolic Power.* Ed. John B. Thompson, trans. Gino Raymond and Matthew Adamson. Cambridge, Mass.: Harvard University Press, 1991.

Bush, Catherine. "Michael Ondaatje: An Interview." *Essays on Canadian Writing* 53 (Spring 1999): 238–49.

Butterfield, Bradley. "The Baudrillardian Symbolic, 9/11, and the War of Good and Evil." *Postmodern Culture* **13**.1 (2002). http://80-muse.jhu.edu.ezproxy.lib.ucalgary.ca:2048/journals/postmodern_culture/v013/13.1butterfield.html (last accessed Nov. 8, 2003).

Carroll, Joseph. *Wallace Stevens' Supreme Fiction: A New Romanticism.* Baton Rouge: Louisiana State University Press, 1987.

Carson, Anne. *Economy of the Unlost (Reading Simonides of Keos with Paul Celan).* Princeton: Princeton University Press, 1999.

Cellier, Francois and Cunningham Bridgeman. *Gilbert and Sullivan and their Operas.* New York: Benjamin Blom, 1914.

Chaucer, Geoffrey. *The Complete Poetry and Prose of Geoffrey Chaucer.* Ed. John H. Fisher. New York: Hold, Reinhart, and Winston, 1977.

Ciaramelli, Fabio. "Levinas's Ethical Discourse between Individuation and Universality."*Re-Reading Levinas.* Trans. Simon Critchley, ed. Robert Bernasconi and Simon Critchley. Bloomington and Indianapolis: Indiana University Press, 1991. 84–105.

Coetzee, J.M. *Disgrace.* London: Vintage, 1999.

"Into the Dark Chamber." *Doubling the Point: Essays and Interviews.* Ed. David Atwell. Cambridge, Mass.: Harvard University Press, 1992. 361–8.

Coleridge, Samuel Taylor. *Collected Letters of Samuel Taylor Coleridge.* Ed. E.L. Griggs. Oxford: Clarendon Press, 1956.

Inquiring Spirit: A New Presentation of Coleridge. Ed. Kathleen Coburn. London: Routledge and Kegan Paul, 1951.

Conrad, Joseph. *Heart of Darkness.* Ed. Paul B. Armstrong. New York: Norton, 2006.

Cooper, Pamela. "Metamorphosis and Sexuality: Reading the Strange Passions of *Disgrace.*" *Research in African Literatures* **36**.4 (2005): 22–39.

Cormack, Bradin. *A Power to Do Justice: Jurisdiction, English Literature, and the Rise of Common Law, 1509–1625.* Chicago and London: University of Chicago Press, 2007.

Cornell, Drucilla. *Beyond Accommodation: Ethical Feminism, Deconstruction, and the Law.* Lanhan, Md.: Rowman and Littlefield, 1999.

Cover, Robert M. "The Folktales of Justice: Tales of Jurisdiction." *Capital University Law Review* 14.2 (1985): 179–203.

Daiches, David. *Literary Essays.* Edinburgh and London: Oliver and Boyd, 1966.

De Man, Paul. "The Epistemology of Metaphor." *On Metaphor.* Ed. Sheldon Sacks. Chicago: University of Chicago Press, 1979. 11–28.

"Lyrical Voice in Contemporary Theory: Riffaterre and Jauss." *Lyric Poetry: Beyond New Criticism.* Ed. Chaviva Hosek and Patricia Parker. Ithaca: Cornell University Press, 1985. 55–72.

The Rhetoric of Romanticism. New York: Columbia University Press, 1984.

De Tocqueville, Alexis. *Democracy in America.* Trans. Harvey C. Mansfield and Delba Winthrop. Chicago: University of Chicago Press, 2000.

Derrida, Jacques. "Force of Law: The 'Mystical Foundation of Authority.'" *Deconstruction and the Possibility of Justice.* Ed. Drucilla Cornell, Michel Rosenfeld, and David Gray Carlson. New York: Routledge, 1992. 3–67.

The Gift of Death. Trans. David Wills. Chicago and London: University of Chicago Press, 1995.

Specters of Marx: The State of the Debt, the Work of Mourning, and the New International. Trans. Peggy Kamuf. New York and London: Routledge, 1994.

"White Mythology." Trans. F.C.T. Moore. *New Literary History* 6 (Autumn 1974): 5–74.

Diala, Isidore. "Nadine Gordimer, J.M. Coetzee, and Andre Brink: "Guilt, Expiation, and the Reconciliation Process in Post-Apartheid South Africa." *Journal of Modern Literature* 25.2 (2001–2): 50–68.

Dick, Oliver Lawson. "The Life and Times of John Aubrey." *Aubrey's Brief Lives.* Ed. Oliver Lawson Dick. Harmondsworth: Penguin, 1962. 17–162.

Dickinson, Emily. *The Complete Poems of Emily Dickinson.* Ed. Thomas H. Johnson. Boston: Little, Brown, 1961.

Dimock, Wai Chee. *Residues of Justice: Literature, Law, Philosophy.* Berkeley: University of California Press, 1997.

Eliot, T.S. *Collected Poems 1909–1962.* London: Faber and Faber, 1963.

Murder in the Cathedral. London: Faber and Faber, 1965.

Selected Prose of T.S. Eliot. Ed. Frank Kermode. London: Faber and Faber, 1975.

Ellis, James, "Introduction." In W.S. Gilbert, *The Bab Ballads.* Cambridge, Mass.: Belknap–Harvard University Press, 1970. 3–30.

Ellis, Susan. "Trade and Power, Money and War: Rethinking Masculinity in Michael Ondaatje's *The English Patient.*" *Studies in Canadian Literature / Études en literature canadienne* 21.2 (1996): 1–21.

Emerson, Ralph Waldo. *Selections from Ralph Waldo Emerson.* Ed. Stephen E. Whicher. Boston: Houghton Mifflin, 1957.

Felman, Shoshana. *The Juridical Unconscious: Trials and Traumas in the Twentieth Century*. Cambridge, Mass.: Harvard University Press, 2002.

Fischler, Alan. "From Weydon-Priors to Tower Green: The Sources of *The Yeomen of the Guard*." *ELH* **63**.1 (1996): 203–25.

Modified Rapture: Comedy in W.S. Gilbert's Savoy Operas. Charlottesville and London: University Press of Virginia, 1991.

Fish, Stanley. *The Trouble with Principle*. Cambridge, Mass.: Harvard University Press, 1999.

Fitzgerald, F. Scott. *The Great Gatsby*. New York: Scribner's, 1953.

Flaubert, Gustave. *The Dictionary of Accepted Ideas*. Trans. Jacques Barzun. New York: New Directions, 1954.

The Letters of Gustave Flaubert, vol. 1: *1830–1857*, vol. 2: *1857–1889*. Ed. and trans. Francis Steegmuller. Cambridge, Mass.: Harvard University Press, 1980, 1982.

Ford, Ford Madox. *Joseph Conrad: A Personal Reminiscence*. 1924; repr. New York: Octagon Books, 1965.

Thus to Revisit: Some Reminiscences. 1921; repr. New York: Octagon Books, 1966.

Ford, Richard T. "Law's Territory (A History of Jurisdiction)." *Michigan Law Review* **97**.4 (Feb. 1999): 843–930.

Forte, David F. "The Natural Law Movement." *Natural Law and Contemporary Public Policy*. Ed. David F. Forte. Washington, DC: Georgetown University Press, 1998. 3–9.

Foucault, Michel. *Discipline and Punish: The Birth of the Prison*. Trans. Alan Sheridan. New York: Vintage, 1995.

Language, Counter-Memory, Practice: Selected Essays and Interviews. Ed. and trans. Donald F. Bouchard and Sherry Simon. Ithaca: Cornell University Press, 1977.

Fraser, Antonia. *Cromwell: Our Chief of Men*. London: Weidenfeld and Nicolson, 1973.

Frye, Northrop. *Anatomy of Criticism*. New York: Atheneum, 1957.

The Secular Scripture: A Study of the Structure of Romance. Cambridge, Mass.: Harvard University Press, 1976.

Words with Power: Being a Second Study of the Bible and Literature. Toronto: Penguin, 1990.

Gewirtz, Paul. "Victims and Voyeurs: Two Narrative Problems at the Criminal Trial." *Law's Stories: Narrative and Rhetoric in the Law*. Ed. Peter Brooks and Paul D. Gewirtz. New Haven: Yale University Press, 1996. 135–61.

Gilbert, W.S. *The Complete Plays of Gilbert and Sullivan*. New York: Norton, 1976.

The Story of H.M.S. Pinafore. London: G. Bell and Sons, 1913.

Goethe, J.W. *Goethe: Selected Verse*. Trans. David Luke. Harmondsworth: Penguin, 1964.

Greisch, Jean. "The Face and Reading: Immediacy and Mediation." *Re-Reading Levinas*. Trans. Simon Critchley, ed. Robert Bernasconi and Simon Critchley. Bloomington and Indianapolis: Indiana University Press, 1991. 67–82.

Grob, Leonard. "Emmanuel Levinas and the Primacy of Ethics in Post-Holocaust Philosophy." *Ethics after the Holocaust: Perspectives, Critiques, and Reponses.* Ed. John K. Roth. St. Paul, Minn.: Paragon House, 1999. 1–14.

Hall, Terry. "Legislation." *Natural Law and Contemporary Public Policy.* Ed. David F. Forte. Washington, DC: Georgetown University Press, 1998. 135–56.

Hardy, Florence Emily. *The Life of Thomas Hardy 1840–1928.* London: Macmillan, 1965.

Hardy, Thomas. *The Mayor of Casterbridge.* New York: Norton, 1977.

Hart, H.L.A. *The Concept of Law,* 2nd edn. Oxford: Oxford University Press, 1994.

Hayter, Charles. *Gilbert and Sullivan.* London: Macmillan, 1987.

Heble, Ajay. "Michael Ondaatje and the Problem of History." *Clio* **19**.2 (Winter 1990): 97–110.

"'Rumours of Topography': The Cultural Politics of Michael Ondaatje's *Running in the Family.*" *Essays on Canadian Writing* **53** (Spring 1999): 186–203.

Hegel, G.W.F. *Philosophy of Right.* Trans. S.W. Dyde. Amherst, NY: Prometheus Books, 1996.

Heidegger, Martin. *What Is Called Thinking?* Trans. Fred. D. Wieck and J. Glenn Gray. New York: Harper & Row, 1968.

Hobbes, Thomas. *Leviathan.* Harmondsworth: Penguin, 1968.

Howe, Irving. *Politics and the Novel.* New York: Horizon Press, 1957.

Hulme, T.E. *Further Speculations.* Ed. Sam Hynes. Minneapolis: University of Minnesota Press, 1955.

Speculations: Essays on Humanism and the Philosophy of Art. Ed. Herbert Read. London: Routledge and Kegan Paul, 1924.

Hume, David. *An Enquiry Concerning the Principles of Morals: A Critical Edition.* Ed. Tom L. Beauchamp. Oxford: Clarendon Press, 1998.

Hyde, Alan. *Bodies of Law.* Princeton: Princeton University Press, 1997.

Jarraway, David R. *Wallace Stevens and the Question of Belief: Metaphysician in the Dark.* Baton Rouge: Louisiana State University Press, 1993.

Johnson, Samuel. *Rasselas, Poems and Selected Prose.* Ed. Bertrand H. Bronson. New York: Hold, Rinehart, Winston, 1958.

Jones, Manina. "'So Many Varieties of Murders': Detection and Biography in *Coming through Slaughter.*" *Essays on Canadian Writing* 67 (Spring 1999): 11–26.

Kant, Immanuel. *Critique of Judgment.* Trans. J.H. Bernard. New York: Hafner Press, 1951.

Critique of Practical Reason. Trans. T.K. Abbott. Amherst, NY: Prometheus Books, 1996.

Groundwork for the Metaphysics of Morals. Ed. Lara Denis, trans. Thomas K. Abbott. Peterborough, Ont.: Broadview, 2005.

Kareda, Urjo. "An Immigrant's Song." *Saturday Night,* Dec. 1983. 44–51.

Kermode, Frank. *Wallace Stevens.* New York: Chip's Bookshop, 1960.

Klein, A.M. *Complete Poems: Part 2.* Ed. Zailig Pollock. Toronto: University of Toronto Press, 1990.

Notebooks: Selections from the A.M. Klein Papers. Ed. Zailig Pollock and Usher Caplan. Toronto: University of Toronto Press, 1994.

Knight, G. Wilson. *The Golden Labyrinth: A Study of British Drama.* London: Methuen, 1965.

Korobkin, Laura Hanft. "Narrative Battles in the Courtroom." *Field Work: Sites in Literary and Cultural Studies.* Ed. Marjorie Garber. New York: Routledge, 1996. 225–36.

Kramer, Matthew H. *Where Law and Morality Meet.* Oxford: Oxford University Press, 2004.

Kyser, Kristina. "Seeing Everything in a Different Light: Vision and Revolution in Michael Ondaatje's *The English Patient.*" *University of Toronto Quarterly*, **70**.4 (Fall 2001): 889–901.

La Rochefoucauld. *Maximes.* Paris: Larousse, 1919.

Laclau, Ernesto. "Ethics, Normativity, and the Heteronomy of the Law." *Law, Justice, and Power: Between Reason and Will.* Ed. Sinkwan Cheng. Stanford: Stanford University Press, 2004. 177–86.

Launer, John. "Anna O and the 'Talking Cure.'" *Q JM: An International Journal of Medicine* **98**.6 (2005): 465–6. http://qjmed.oxfordjournals.org/cgi/content/full/98/6/465 (last accessed May 14, 2008).

Lawrence, D.H. "Introduction to New Poems." *D.H. Lawrence: Selected Literary Criticism.* Ed. Anthony Beal. New York: Viking, 1966. 84–9.

Selected Poems. Ed. Keith Sagar. Harmondsworth: Penguin, 1972.

Leggett, B.J. *Early Stevens: The Nietzschean Intertext* (Durham, NC: Duke University Press, 1992).

Leibniz, G.W. *The Political Writings of Leibniz.* Ed. and trans. Patrick Riley. Cambridge: Cambridge University Press, 1972.

Levinas, Emmanuel. *Emmanuel Levinas: Basic Philosophical Writings.* Ed. Adriaan T. Peperzak, Simon Critchley, and Robert Bernasconi. Bloomington: Indiana University Press, 1996.

Entre nous: On Thinking-of-the-Other. Trans. Michael B. Smith and Barbara Harshav. New York: Columbia University Press, 1998.

Ethics and Infinity: Conversations with Philippe Nemo. Trans. Richard A. Cohen. Pittsburgh: Duquesne University Press, 1985.

Lovejoy, A.O. and George Boas. "Some Meanings of 'Nature.'" *Primitivism and Related Ideas in Antiquity.* New York: Octagon Books, 1973. 447–56.

Lowry, Malcolm. *Under the Volcano.* Harmondsworth: Penguin, 1963.

Lyotard, Jean-François. "Gesture and Commentary." *Between Ethics and Aesthetics: Crossing the Boundaries.* Ed. Dorota Blowacka and Stephen Boos. Albany: State University of New York Press, 2002. 73–82.

and Jean-Loup Thébaud. *Just Gaming.* Trans. Wlad Godzich. Minneapolis: University of Minnesota Press, 1985.

Maimonides, Moses. *The Guide for the Perplexed.* Trans. M. Friedlander. New York: Dover, 1956.

Mallarmé, Stéphane. *Oeuvres complètes.* Paris: Pléiade, 1945.

Marais, Mike. "Reading against Race: J.M. Coetzee's *Disgrace*, Justin Cartwright's *White Lightning* and Ivan Vladislavic's *The Restless Supermarket.*" *Journal of Literary Studies* **19**.3–4 (Dec. 2003): 271–89.

Martin, Elizabeth A. (ed.). *Oxford Dictionary of Law*, 4th edn. Oxford: Oxford University Press, 1997.

Melville, Herman. *Billy Budd and Other Tales*. New York: Signet, 1961.

Miller, J. Hillis. "Stevens' Rock and Criticism as Cure." *Georgia Review* **30**.1 (Spring 1976): 5–31; **30**.2 (Summer 1976): 330–48.

Milne, A.A. *Winnie-the-Pooh*. Toronto: McClelland and Stewart, 1994.

Milton, John. *Complete Poems and Major Prose*. Ed. Merritt Y. Hughes. New York: Odyssey, 1957.

Minow, Martha. "Stories in Law." *Law's Stories: Narrative and Rhetoric in the Law*. Ed. Peter Brooks and Paul D. Gewirtz. New Haven: Yale University Press, 1996. 24–36.

Moore, Marianne. *Collected Poems*. New York: Macmillan, 1951.

Morrison, Toni. *Beloved*. New York: Penguin/Plume, 1988.

Mukherjee, Arun. *Towards an Aesthetics of Opposition: Essays on Literature, Criticism and Cultural Imperialism*. Stratford, Ont.: Williams Wallace, 1988.

Myers, Peter C. "'Sivilization' and its Discontents: Nature and Law in *The Adventures of Huckleberry Finn*." *Legal Studies Forum* **22**.4 (1998): 557–90.

Nagarajan, M.S. "Uncovering a Traumatic Past." *Hindu Sun*, Aug. 6, 2000. www.indiaserver.com/thehindu/2000/08/06/stories/1306017i.htm (last accessed June 17, 2001).

Nietzsche, Friedrich. *The Birth of Tragedy and the Genealogy of Morals*. Trans. Francis Golffing. New York: Doubleday Anchor, 1956.

   Thus Spoke Zarathustra. Trans. R.J. Hollingdale. Harmondsworth: Penguin, 1969.

   "Truth and Falsity in an Ultramoral Sense." *Critical Theory since Plato*, 3rd edn. Ed. Hazard Adams and Leroy Searle. Boston: Thomson Wadsworth, 2005. 692–7.

   The Will to Power in Science, Nature, Society and Art. Trans. Anthony M. Ludivici. New York: Frederick Publications, 1960.

O'Brien, Geoffrey. "Stompin' at the Savoy." *New York Review of Books*, Feb. 24, 2000. 16–19.

Oakley, Francis. *Natural Law, Laws of Nature, Natural Rights: Continuity and Discontinuity in the History of Ideas*. New York and London: Continuum, 2005.

Olesha, Yuri. *Envy and Other Works*. Trans. Andrew R. MacAndrew. Garden City: Anchor Books, 1967.

Ondaatje, Michael. *Anil's Ghost*. Toronto: McClelland and Steward, 2000.

   The Collected Works of Billy the Kid. Toronto: Anansi, 1970.

   Coming through Slaughter. Toronto: Anansi, 1976.

   The English Patient. Toronto: Vintage, 1993.

Handwriting. Toronto: McClelland and Stewart, 1998.

In the Skin of a Lion. Markham, Ont.: Penguin, 1987.

Running in the Family. Toronto: McClelland and Stewart, 1983.

Oppen, George. *Of Being Numerous. George Oppen: New Collected Poems*. New York: New Directions, 2002.

Orwell, George. *Inside the Whale and Other Essays*. Harmondsworth: Penguin, 1969.

Parker, Patricia. *Inescapable Romance: Studies in the Poetics of a Mode*. Princeton: Princeton University Press, 1979.

Parsons, Marni. "Poetry." *University of Toronto Quarterly* **69**.1 (Winter 1999–2000): 42–81.

Pascal, Blaise. *Pensées et opuscules*. Paris: Larousse, 1934.

Pearson, Hesketh. *Gilbert and Sullivan: A Biography*. London: MacDonald and Jane's, 1935.

Plato. *The Republic*. Trans. Desmond Lee. London: Penguin, 1974.

Pollock, Zailig. *A.M. Klein: The Story of the Poet*. Toronto: University of Toronto Press, 1994.

Pope, Alexander. *The Poems of Alexander Pope*. Ed. John Butt. London: Methuen, 1963.

Porter, Jean. *Nature as Reason: A Thomistic Theory of the Natural Law*. Grand Rapids, Mich., and Cambridge, UK: William B. Eerdmans, 2005.

Pound, Ezra. *Literary Essays of Ezra Pound*. New York: New Directions, 1968.

Quinn, Justin. *Gathered beneath the Storm: Wallace Stevens, Nature and Community*. Dublin: University College Dublin Press, 2002.

Rawls, John. *A Theory of Justice*. Cambridge, Mass.: Harvard University Press, 1971.

Ricoeur, Paul. *The Just*. Trans. David Pellauer. Chicago, London: University of Chicago Press, 2000.

Reflections on The Just. Trans. David Pellauer. Chicago and London: University of Chicago Press, 2007.

Riddel, Joseph N. *The Clairvoyant Eye*. Baton Rouge: Louisiana State University Press, 1965.

Rousseau, Jean-Jacques. *Émile*. Trans. Barbara Foxley. London: Dent, 1974.

Rymer, Thomas. *The Tragedies of the Last Age*. London, 1692. Early English Books Online: http://eebo.chadwyck.com.ezproxy.lib.ucalgary.ca/search/fulltext? SOURCE=config.cfg&ACTION=ByID&ID=D00000126897660000& WARN=N&SIZE=160&FILE=&ECCO=undefined (last accessed October 5, 2009).

Sarat, Austin and Thomas R. Kearns. "A Journey through Forgetting: Toward a Jurisprudence of Violence." *The Fate of Law*. Ed. Austin Sarat and Thomas R. Kearns. Ann Arbor: University of Michigan Press, 1993. 209–73.

Sarat, Austin, Lawrence Douglas, and Martha Merill Umphrey (eds.). *The Place of Law*. Ann Arbor: University of Michigan Press, 2003.

Scarry, Elaine. *The Body in Pain: The Making and Unmaking of the World*. Oxford: Oxford University Press, 1985.

Schopenhauer, Arthur. *Essays and Aphorisms.* Trans. R.J. Hollingdale. Harmondsworth: Penguin, 1970.

Scobie, Stephen. "The Reading Lesson: Michael Ondaatje and the Patients of Desire." *Essays in Canadian Writing* 53 (Spring 1999): 92–106.

Scruton, Roger. *Modern Culture.* London, New York: Continuum, 1998.

Segall, Kimberly Wedeven. "Pursuing Ghosts: The Traumatic Sublime in J.M. Coetzee's *Disgrace.*" *Research in African Literatures* **36**.4 (2005): 40–54.

Shakespeare, William. *The Complete Works of Shakespeare.* Ed. David Bevington. New York: HarperCollins, 1992.

Shaw, George Bernard. *Seven Plays.* New York: Dodd, Mead, 1951.

Siebers, Tobin. *The Ethics of Criticism.* Ithaca and London: Cornell University Press, 1988.

Siegel, Riva B. "In the Eyes of the Law: Reflections on the Authority of Legal Discourse." *Law's Stories: Narrative and Rhetoric in the Law.* Ed. Peter Brooks and Paul D. Gewirtz. New Haven: Yale University Press, 1996. 225–31.

Simon, Yves R. *The Tradition of Natural Law: A Philosopher's Reflections.* Ed. Vukan Kuic. New York: Fordham University Press 1965.

Smythe, Karen E. "'Listen It': Responses to Michael Ondaatje." *Essays on Canadian Writing* **53** (Spring 1999): 1–10.

Solecki, Sam. "An Interview with Michael Ondaatje." *Spider Blues: Essays on Michael Ondaatje.* Ed. Sam Solecki. Montreal: Véhicule Press, 1985. 13–27.

Stedman, Jane W. *W.S. Gilbert: A Classic Victorian and his Theatre.* Oxford: Oxford University Press, 1996.

Stein, Gertrude. *Selected Writings of Gertrude Stein.* Ed. Carl Van Vechten. New York: Vintage Books, 1962.

Stevens, Wallace. *Letters of Wallace Stevens.* Ed. Holly Stevens. New York: Knopf, 1966.

  The Necessary Angel: Essays on Reality and the Imagination. New York: Vintage Books, 1951.

  The Palm at the End of the Mind. Ed. Holly Stevens. New York: Vintage, 1972.

Sutton, Max Keith. *W.S. Gilbert.* Boston: Twayne, 1975.

Taylor, Charles. *Modern Social Imaginaries.* Durham, NC: Duke University Press, 2004.

Thomas, Dylan. *The Poems of Dylan Thomas.* Ed. Daniel Jones. New York: New Directions, 1971.

Tolstoy, Leo. *Six Masterpieces by Tolstoy.* Trans. Margaret Wettlin. New York: Laurel, 1963.

Trilling, Lionel. *Sincerity and Authenticity.* Cambridge, Mass.: Harvard University Press, 1971.

Twain, Mark. *Adventures of Huckleberry Finn* in *The Art of Huckleberry Finn.* Ed. Hamlin Hill and Walter Blair. San Francisco: Chandler Publishing, 1962.

Vaihinger, Hans. *The Philosophy of "As If": A System of the Theoretical, Practical and Religious Fictions of Mankind.* Trans. C.K. Ogden. London: Routledge and Kegan Paul, 1952.

Volokh, Alexander. "*n* Guilty Men." *University of Pennsylvania Law Review* 173 (1997). www.law.ucla.edu/volokh/guilty.htm (last accessed May 16, 2008).

Wachtel, Eleanor. "An Interview with Michael Ondaatje." *Essays on Canadian Writing* **53** (Spring 1999): 250–61.

Walbrook, H.M. *Gilbert and Sullivan Opera: A History and a Comment*. London: F.V. White, 1922.

Walker, Margaret Urban. "Moral Repair and Its Limits." *Mapping the Ethical Turn: A Reader in Ethics, Culture, and Literary Theory*. Ed. Todd F. Davis and Kenneth Womack. Charlotte and London: University Press of Virginia, 2001. 110–27.

Wilde, Oscar. *The Importance of Being Earnest*. New York: Dover, 1990.

Williams, William Carlos. *The Great American Novel*. 1923; repr. Folcroft, Pa.: Folcroft Library Editions, 1973.

Winn, Peter A. "Legal Ritual." *Readings in Ritual Studies*. Ed. Ronald L. Grimes. Upper Saddle River, NJ: Prentice Hall, 1996. 552–65.

Wolfe, Christopher. "Judicial Review." *Natural Law and Contemporary Public Policy*. Ed. David F. Forte. Washington, DC: Georgetown University Press, 1998. 157–89.

Woolf, Virginia. *Mrs. Dalloway*. Oxford: Oxford University Press, 2000.

Wordsworth, William. *The Prelude, Selected Poems and Sonnets*. Ed. Carlos Baker. New York: Holt, Rinehart and Winston, 1965.

Yeats, W.B. *A Vision*. 1937; repr. New York: Collier, 1966.

York, Lorraine M. "Whirling Blindfolded in the House of Women: Gender Politics in the Poetry and Fiction of Michael Ondaatje." *Essays on Canadian Writing* **53** (Spring 1999): 71–91.

Index